Structure and Transformation

The Origins of Behavior

Michael Lewis and
Leonard A. Rosenblum, Editors

Volume 1
The Effect of the Infant on Its Caregiver

Michael Lewis and
Leonard A. Rosenblum, Editors

Volume 2
The Origins of Fear

Michael Lewis and
Leonard A. Rosenblum, Editors

Volume 3

Structure and Transformation:
Developmental and Historical Aspects

Klaus F. Riegel and
George C. Rosenwald, Editors

Structure and Transformation
Developmental and Historical Aspects

Edited by

Klaus F. Riegel

and

George C. Rosenwald

The University of Michigan
Ann Arbor

A Wiley-Interscience Publication

JOHN WILEY & SONS

New York • London • Sydney • Toronto

To the memory of
William R. Looft

Library of Congress Cataloging in Publication Data:

Structure and transformation.

    (The Origins of behavior; v. 3)
    "A Wiley-Interscience publication."
    Includes bibliographical references and index.
    1. Cognition (child psychology) 2. Languages—
Psychology. 3. Structuralism. I. Riegel, Klaus
F. II. Rosenwald, George C., 1932- III. Se-
ries.
BF723.C5S76   155.4'13   75-15659
ISBN 0-471-72140-9

Printed in the United States of America

10 9 8 7 6 5 4 3 2 1

Contributors

Arthur L. Blumenthal
Graduate School of Education
Harvard University
Cambridge, Massachusetts

Sheila Blumstein
Department of Linguistics
Brown University
Providence, Rhode Island

Wilbur A. Hass
Shimer College
Mount Carroll, Illinois

Michael Lewis
Educational Testing Service
Princeton, New Jersey

William R. Looft
Deceased

Willis F. Overton
Psychology Department
Temple University
Philadelphia, Pennsylvania

Susan Lee-Painter
Educational Testing Service
Princeton, New Jersey

Klaus F. Riegel
Department of Psychology
University of Michigan
Ann Arbor, Michigan

George C. Rosenwald
Department of Psychology
University of Michigan
Ann Arbor, Michigan

Cyril P. Svoboda
Institute for Child Study
University of Maryland
College Park, Maryland

Anthony Wilden
Department of Communications
Simon Fraser University
Burnaby, Canada

Robert Wozniak
Institute of Child Development
University of Minnesota
Minneapolis, Minnesota

Series Preface

*"The childhood shows the man,
as morning shows the day."*

Milton, Paradise Regained

None can doubt that the study of man begins in the study of childhood. Few would contend that the newborn lacks the challenge of his evolutionary heritage. This series addresses itself to the task of bringing together, on a continuing basis, that confluence of theory and data on ontogeny and phylogeny which will serve to illustrate *The Origins of Behavior*.

Whether our social, human, and professional concerns lie in the psychological disorders of childhood or adulthood or merely in the presumptively normal range of expression in development in different cultures, varied environments, or diverse family constellations, we can never hope to discern order and regularity from the mass of uncertain observation and groundless speculation if we fail to nurture the scientific study of development. Fortunately, the last two decades have seen an enormous burgeoning of effort toward this end, both at the human and nonhuman level. However, despite this growth of effort and interest, no single means of pooling our growing knowledge on development in children and animals and communicating that fusion of material to the broad scientific community now exists. This series seeks to fill the gap. It is our intention to have each volume deal with a specific theme that is either of social or of theoretical relevance to developmental issues. In keeping with the integrated perspective that we consider to be vital, and to provide a meaningful context within which these issues may be considered, each volume in the series will contain a broad range of material and will seek to encompass theoretical and sound empirical studies of the behavior of human infants as well as pertinent aspects of animal behavior with a particular emphasis on the primates. It is our view, furthermore, that not only is it necessary to focus our interest on both human infants and animals, but that the levels of analysis which will explicate the processes of development that are our concern must ultimately involve the study of behavior at all levels of discourse. Thus studies of developmental significance may be found in genetic, physiological, morphological, dyadic, and societal levels and an increased interdigitation of these separate disciplines is among the major goals of this series.

In light of the diversity of topics to be considered, the breadth of material to be covered, and the variety of orientations that will be included in these discourses on the origins of human behavior, we expect this series to serve the needs of the broad social science community, not merely of those interested in behavioral development alone. Just as the series itself will draw upon the knowledge and research of psychologists, ethologists, sociologists, psychiatrists, pediatricians, obstetricians, and devoted scientists and clinicians in a number of related disciplines, it is our hope that the material in this series will provide both stimulation and guidance to all among us who are concerned with man, his past, his present, and his future.

Michael Lewis
Leonard A. Rosenblum
Editors

June 1973

Preface

Near the end of the nineteenth century, the concepts of structure, transformation, and interaction entered into the terminology of behavioral and social scientists. Although introduced with sufficient distinctiveness, the use of these concepts varied widely. Their increasing application during the twentieth century did not lead to more uniform and consistent employment. Not surprisingly, therefore, the conference on which the present book is based also has been plagued by terminological and conceptual difficulties. At the outset, let us clarify some of the issues.

1. The term structure, as distinguished from function, was applied by Titchener (1898) to characterize one of two major approaches in psychology. Titchener's use of these terms reflects the distinction between anatomy and physiology in medicine. At the time of his writings structural psychology was well on its way to becoming a major branch of psychology, that is, through the work of Wundt and Titchener himself. Functional psychology, as yet, was less well developed. However the designation of their psychology as structural was appropriate only in contradistinction to the functionalism that, instead of dissecting the mind, focused on mental operations and the adaptation of the organism to the environment. Wundt's and Titchener's psychology was concerned with the anatomy of the mind and its components but lacked one of the main features of a structural approach: a dominating emphasis on organization.

The experimental psychology of the nineteenth century has often been called mental chemistry. In admiration of the advances in the natural sciences, psychology's task was considered to be the determination of the major elements of the mind which, in the language of Wundt, were called sensations, images, and simple feelings. However, it would be simplistic to identify the task of chemistry exclusively with such analytical goals and with the delineation of a set of basic elements. To the contrary, the exploration of complex radicals (as well as subatomic particles) at higher levels of analysis and without a reduction to basic elements necessitates explanations of their autonomous operations. Most important, the major knowledge about units at any level consists of detailed information about their tendency to enter into compounds with other units, the force necessary or the energy released by such compounding, and the conditions of possible arrangements. Thus, much of the success in this field of the natural sciences consisted of descriptions of structural organization and transformation rather than of mere analytical dissections.

Although it is true that Wundt and his co-workers were concerned with the combinatory qualities of simple feelings and other such elements, this merely represented the reverse of their dominant analytic procedure and not what we refer to as organization—a term having a stronger significance than the reconstitution of what previously has been dissected.

During the twentieth century, especially in the United States, schools of psychology that explored the laws of compounding received considerable acclaim, that is, behaviorism and the psychology of learning. However, almost without exception, they failed to give attention to structural components and organizations. Even if these offsprings of early functionalism had been wedded to the analytical elementarism of the earlier psychology, such a consolidation would still have fallen short of a comprehensive synthesis. They would still lack emphasis upon structural organization and structural changes. This failure has been due to the consistent lack of interest in developmental and historical issues.

Titchener (1898), already quite modern in his conception, argued that the antagonism between structure and function could be overcome with genetic psychological interpretations. He refrained, however, from undertaking such a synthesis. The first psychologist to promote this was Felix Krüger, Wundt's successor in Leipzig (1915), but it was not until much later that such a synthesis received widespread recognition in cognitive developmental psychology. Led most imaginatively by Piaget, cognitive developmental psychology emphasizes structure and transformation, both the components and organization of the operations.

Considerable attention is given to this movement here. William Looft and Cyril Svoboda discuss different viewpoints in the history of thought which led to the structuralism of cognitive developmental psychology. Anthony Wilden criticizes this movement for its lack of concern with sociohistorical issues. Willis Overton extends this discussion to the developmental interpretations of Heinz Werner who regards sociohistorical conditions as an important basis for the study of development. Primarily, Overton relates Piaget's psychology to general systems theory as extended to developmental issues by L. von Bertalanffy. Finally, Michael Lewis and Susan Lee-Painter try to establish the important linkage to observational and experimental methodologies in the study of the child and of development. That is, they translate the conceptual models discussed in the earlier chapters into operational terms of research strategies.

2. The antagonism between general systematic interpretations (characteristic

of both experimental psychology and the study of individual differences) and developmental-historical interpretation was most clearly brought into focus through discussions in linguistics by Saussure (1916).

Saussure drew on the distinction between synchronic linguistics (the description of a particular "state" of a language at some "point" in time) and diachronic linguistics (the description of its historical development "through time"). By deemphasizing the latter and focusing on the former, he moved linguistics into a new, ahistorical, systematic direction. As we have argued elsewhere (Riegel, 1975), Saussure's distinction is extremely problematic. Nevertheless, it continues to be used uncritically not only in linguistics but also in most other branches of the behavioral and social sciences. The unexplored problems implied in Saussure's distinction can be demonstrated in a discussion of developmental research designs.

In line with accepted research practice, developmental psychologists are content with making cross-sectional comparisons among groups of subjects of different ages, that is, subjects born at different historical times. In doing so, these researchers confound differences due to chronological age (in which they are primarily interested) with differences due to historical period or generation ("vintage"). Longitudinal studies do not circumvent this difficulty successfully. Here only one historical group or cohort is being investigated through repeated testing. Thus historical differences between cohorts or generations do not affect selectively the age comparisons as in cross-sectional analyses but, as the cohort of individuals grows up and ages, the sociocultural conditions change concurrently. Thus, the longitudinal design does not allow one to separate individual from societal changes either.

As limited as the results of these two types of developmental investigations are, the linguistic analyses promoted by Saussure, that is, synchronic and diachronic linguistics, are still much more restricted.

Synchronic linguistics disregards changes both in the individual and in society. Thus, the object of study is not the language-using individual (who is, of course, continuously changing within changing sociocultural conditions) but an abstract being removed from or fixated upon a particular point in individual and historical time. Diachronic linguistics is supposed to describe "historical development through time," but all that linguists accomplish here is to study language at different historical periods. A design of this type, a time-lag design, compares different generations or cohorts with one another. Thus it merely explores historical differences but not as claimed "historical development through time." To study such changes, the investigation would have to be combined with longitudinal methodology (Baltes, 1968; and Schaie, 1965). Subsequently the individual would have to be reintroduced into the analysis, the individual who through his own changes with and within his cohort or generation has made historical development possible at all. However, introducing the individual into the analysis would be contrary to Saussure's primary goal: to establish the autonomy of linguistics by eliminating psychology. Unfortunately, by liberating linguistics from psychology, Saussure also eliminated the most important object of study, the language-using individual.

In elaborating some of these issues, a second major section of the present volume is devoted to the concepts of structure and transformation in psychological linguistics. The four articles included in this section follow traditional distinctions. Arthur Blumenthal provides a historical introduction. Sheila Blumstein discusses syntactic aspects. Klaus Riegel compares semantic organizations with stages in the history of monetary systems and, thereby, emphasizes activities and processes rather than linguistic content as the basis for language acquisition. Similarly, Wilbur Hass calls attention to pragmatic structures, an underdeveloped topic in psychology and linguistics.

3. Synchronic linguistics separates the historical individual from the language by which he relates to the world. It also disregards both individual-developmental and societal-historical changes. Diachronic linguistics, too, bypasses the individual and individual changes. It takes slices out of the historical trajectory and thus yields successive differences instead of integrative changes. A full synthesis is possible only if the individual is reintroduced as a concrete being rather than as an idealized abstraction that is neither affected by developmental nor by historical changes.

If this kind of synthesis is attempted, the topics of structure and transformation become interpretable in a consistent manner. As an individual exhibits structural organization (for instance, by creating a sentence), he influences and changes the social environment with which he interacts. The changing outer conditions, for instance, the utterances produced by the parents of a child, in turn change the individual, and so on. Thus through continuous interactions, both the inner and outer structures are transformed in a dialectic manner.

In general, developmental scientists are less interested in short-term interactions, such as those occurring in dialogues, than in long-term transformations, such as the ones that have been most comprehensively investigated and interpreted by Piaget. Piaget's theory qualitatively describes different organizations that represent stages in the child's development. These structures are transformationally related to one another. Since they vary greatly in complexity and since they are widely separated along the age dimension, it might seem that Piaget's efforts consist mainly in delineating different structures but not in describing transitions and their transformations. Most recently, however (in a book with the paradoxical title *Structuralism*), Piaget (1970) has drawn special attention to the topic of structural changes. Indeed, he even has proposed that transformations might be conceived of as independent of the objects or structures to which they are applied. Transformations, representing activities or processes in the individual or social group, might be logically prior to structures. They define structures through their application. Structures are the properties that appear invariant under transformation.

In summary, structures are relational organizations found both within and outside of the organism. They are the properties that remain partially stable under transformations. The continuous interactions among inner and outer structures but, especially, between inner and outer structures lead to changes. Changes represent transformations of structures. Transformations can be short-termed, as in interactive dialogues, or long-termed, as in the progression of the child through different forms of grammars or logics.

Neither a pure structuralist's approach (which would be comparable to an inspection of the separate frames of a film strip) nor a pure transformationalist's approach (which would analyze the flow of movements in the film without any separate inspections of the frames) can lead to satisfactory interpretation of the individual, of society, and their changes. What we should aim to study are structural transformations or transforming structures. These processes are brought about through interactions of inner and outer conditions. Interactions are thus the most general concept; but they are also the emptiest of the three. Structure and transformation denote more specific conditions.

The proposed synthesis of structure and transformation proceeds on a developmental-historical basis. Such an approach characterizes dialectic psychology and philosophy. The historical roots of this movement are discussed in Chapter 1. Robert Wozniak (in Chapter 2) explores the foundations of the dialectic and structural psychology in the Soviet Union. Both chapters provide historical introductions and, besides psychology, touch on various neighboring disciplines: philosophy, sociology, linguistics, and mathematics.

4. Throughout the entire sequence of chapters, there is relatively little emphasis on cultural anthropology, that is, on that discipline in which the conceptualization and methodology of structuralism have been most vigorously discussed. In part, this disregard must be attributed to the special interest and background of the participants at the Ann Arbor conferences. Most of them have been affiliated with psychology, and a few with philosophy and literature. However, this

disregard was somewhat intentional and was motivated by the desire to apply structuralist and transformationalist conceptualizations to areas in which they had not been intensively discussed (except by Piaget). Yet we are not unaware of structuralism's lusty expansiveness. Beyond the scope of this book, authors lay claim to widely scattered fields in which the method will bear fruit. Among these disciplines, forever vexing and tempting, is the one that deals with man's relationship to the social world. Here the priority of structure or relations over elements takes on a grave, even sinister, meaning. We might have ignored this in the present volume, which is limited to cognition and linguistics, if our view of knowledge and language had not been emphatically interactionist—socially and historically. We, therefore, consider some cautions in the epilogue.

In October, 1971 we held our first workshop in Ann Arbor. In November, 1971 a larger group assembled for two days, including several out-of-town visitors. Both meetings helped to prepare for the main conference held in the Inglis House at the University of Michigan from August 28 to 30, 1972. Prior to that time, the contributions were written, and many of them were circulated among the participants of the meeting. This volume is based on these contributions, although all of the manuscripts have been revised since their presentation and subsequent discussion.

The contributors are grateful for the stimulating comments and aid provided by the 20 to 30 participants of the 1972 conference. Special thanks are given to Frithjof Bergmann, Clinton Fink, John Gyr, Adrienne Harris, Oliver Holmes, Lynn Liben, J. C. Mathes, Hayne Reese, Ruth Riegel, Silvia Thrupp, Larry Wilder, and Peter Wolff.

The conference was supported by a grant from the President's Fund of the University of Michigan made available by Vice-President Allan F. Smith. A loan was generously granted by Thomas Karger of Basel, Switzerland. The organizers are grateful for this support, and also to the University of Michigan for making Inglis House available for the meeting. The editors express their gratitude to Frithjof Bergmann, Oliver Holmes, Ruth Riegel, and Gay Rosenwald who participated in the planning and execution of the meetings.

When the editorial work on this volume was almost completed, we learned of the sudden and early death of William R. Looft. To many of us, Bill Looft was a close friend for years. To others he became a friend during the meeting that prompted the publication of this volume. Although it may not have been evident on first acquaintance, Bill was always provocative, stimulating, and rebellious, and yet he was insightful and supportive to others. He always tried hard—often too hard! All of the contributors will miss him, and so will many, many others. We dedicate this book to the memory of Bill Looft.

Klaus F. Riegel
George C. Rosenwald

Ann Arbor, Michigan
March 1975

Contents

Contents

PART ONE

Philosophical

CHAPTER 1

Structure and Transformation in Modern Intellectual History

KLAUS F. RIEGEL

This introductory essay considers structuralism from several different points of view. In the first section the concept of *structure* (and in extension those of schema, pattern, gestalt, etc.) is contrasted with that of *function* (and in extension those of activity, interaction, transformation, etc). Such a comparison not only reconfirms the old dichotomy that was introduced into psychology by James and Titchener but emphasizes the mutual dependency of structure and function. In our discussion we rely on Piaget's interpretations and, thus, emphasize genetic aspects. Reference is also given to recent trends in linguistics, especially to Chomsky's transformational grammar.

In the second section, we trace the origin of these ideas to some reformulations in mathematics as they were proposed during the second half of the nineteenth century by Dedekind, Frege, Russell, and others. That new emphasis stressed the analysis of relational orders and classes and thus contributed to the foundation for structural interpretations.

Further steps in this direction were taken in Carnap's early work, which we discuss in the third section. Carnap provides explicit descriptions of structural interpretations by relying on some positivists of the late ninteenth century, especially Mach, Poincaré, and Avenarius, whose contributions—unfortunately—have frequently been viewed in clear antithesis to structural descriptions. Carnap's interpretations come closest to those held by Avenarius; Mach relates to the psychologism of Wundt, and Poincaré to the early positivism of Comte. Poincaré, in turn, influences the school of French sociology with Durkheim, Mauss, Blondel, Halbwachs, and Lévy-Bruhl, which finally leads to the structural anthropology of Lévi-Strauss and to the genetic structuralism of Piaget.

In the fourth section we question, in alliance with modern sociologists and anthropologists, the role of the psychic self as a primary base of knowledge and of psychology as an independent science. Piaget has been criticized for viewing development as emerging, essentially, from within the individual and for failing to give equally strong emphasis to the interactive changes of the sociohistorical conditions. Rubinstejn's theory, with which we conclude our presentation, proposed such a dialectic interpretation of a changing organism in a changing world.

PSYCHOLOGY AND LINGUISTICS

Early Structuralism

The distinction between structure and function gained its directive influence on psychology through Titchener. Although it was previously discussed by James (1890) (see also Ruckmick, 1911), Titchener (1898) elaborated this distinction in detail and thereby, paradoxically, helped his adversaries in founding functionalism in America (Boring, 1957, p. 555). Titchener, by drawing an analogy from biology, proposed a threefold distinction.

"We may enquire into the structure of an organism, without regard to function—by analysis determining its component parts, and by synthesis exhibiting the mode of its formation from the parts. Or we may enquire into the function of the various structures which our analysis has revealed, and into the manner of their interrelation as functional organs. Or, again, we may enquire into the changes of form and function that accompany the persistence of the organism in time, the phenomena of growth and of decay. Biology, the science of living things, comprises the three mutually interdependent sciences of morphology, physiology, and ontogeny [1898, p. 449]."

Titchener delineates this distinction not only in regard to the individual organism but also in regard to the species, the "collective life." He continues:

"Corresponding to morphology, we have taxonomy or systematic zoology, the science of classification. The whole world of living things is here the organism, and species and sub-species and races are its parts. Corresponding to physiology, we have that department of biology—it has been termed 'oecology'—which deals with questions of geographical distribution, of the function of species in the general economy of nature. Corresponding to ontogeny we have the science of phylogeny: the biology of evolution, with its problems of descent and of transmission [1898, p. 449]."

Titchener's contrastive description of structuralism and functionalism (under exclusion of the third major possibility for scientific psychology, geneticism) has had a formative influence on the development of American psychology or, at least, on its historical description (especially through Boring's work, 1957). Nevertheless, his view of structure, being atomistic and mechanistic, was an exceptionally unfortunate choice. More appropriately, his approach ought to be called the "psychology of content," a denotation commonly reserved for Wundt in distinction to the "psychology of act" by Brentano. Titchener's structuralism emphasizes the analytic identification of psychic constituents (sensations, ideas, and emotions). Organizational aspects enter into the discussion only secondarily.

Gestalt Psychology

Structural considerations were firmly introduced into psychology by the Gestalt movement of Wertheimer, Köhler, and Koffka. Here, organized patterns become the foundation of scientific inquiries as well as of the phenomenal experience of subjects. The identification of constituent elements attains only negligible importance if any. As for Titchener, genetic aspects remain neglected. Gestalt psychologists analyze psychic conditions from an "ahistorical" point of view. They are concerned, however, with functional aspects that, as introduced by the forerunner of Gestalt psychology, von Ehrenfels (1890), are implied in the so-called "second law of Gestalt."

As commonly expressed, the "first law" states that a Gestalt is more than the sum of its parts, that is, organizational, structural properties are implied. The "second law" concerns transpositions or transformations through which all parts may lose their absolute positions, although the structural properties are retained, that is, are kept invariant. Convincing cases of the "second law" are the transpositions of a melody into different keys, or in a more general sense (i.e., keeping fewer properties invariant), the variations on a musical theme. In regard to spatio-visual conditions, the perception of a simple object, for example, a suspended triangle, is subject to ceaseless transformations. Not only does the location, illumination, and color of the object change relative to the observer, but also the sensory organs of the observer himself undergo ceaseless transformations produced by their gross and fine movements. Thus the scientific exploration of perceived patterns is as much an abstraction from the ongoing physical and psychic activities as was the abstraction of constituent elements from these patterns by the pre-Gestalt psychologists. What underlies both these abstractions, and therefore ought to be of major interest to the psychologist, are ceaseless sequences of transformations.

Gestalt psychologists recognized this issue, especially through their investigation of the phi-phenomenon. The phi-phenomenon is produced by switching two light sources on and off. Dependent on the rate of switching, among other things, the lights are either perceived as alternating discrete stimuli, as two continuously lighted stimuli, or as a connecting lighted line. These investigations have primarily been used to refute earlier atomistic viewpoints; they question the identifiability of discrete sensory elements. They could be used equally well to criticize the preponderance of fixed stimulus patterns. The investigations of the phi-phenomenon clearly support a transformational or transactional interpretation, that is, an interpretation that characterizes psychic operations, such as perception, by sets of invariant transformations both within and outside the organism rather than on the basis of fixed inner and outer properties. The opposite dominated, however, through Köhler's (1920) analysis of the isomorphism between external physical and internal neurophysiological patterns with its implied priority of the former in the tradition of philosophical realism. A convincing argument for transposition as the key principle was published by Witte (1960). More recently, Henle (1972) thoroughly reviewed Wolfgang Köhler's contributions to this discussion.

Cognitive Developmental Psychology

Among present-day psychologists, only Piaget (1970) has drawn a conclusion similar to transformationism, and has, thereby, reversed the order of the laws of Gestalt psychology. The "law of transposition," now, gains priority over the "law of the Gestalt." As an organism engages physiologically and psychologically in ceaseless transformations, he attains patterns during his internal transitions and attends to patterns as transitional external conditions. These patterns represent momentarily objectified states of equilibrium; the organism moves forward through a stream of transformations. In his considerations, Piaget is willing to conclude that "transformations may be disengaged from the objects subject to such transformation and the group defined solely in terms of the set of transformations [Piaget, 1970, pp. 23–24]."

Piaget is, of course, best known for his "stage theory" in which he proposes a fixed sequence of synchronic structures for the characterization of developmental progression. If we take the above quotation seriously, however, development should be characterized by groups of permissible transformations rather than by fixed forms or schemata. The notion of the "group" implies that the freedom of transformation is never unlimited. In regard to mathematical systems, for example measurement scales, it implies that basic properties must be kept "invariant," for example, in metric systems the relative distances between points. In Piaget's theory of cognitive development, conditions of invariance are represented as temporary states of equilibrium from which the individual will constantly divert, but to which he will always return.

With this emphasis on transformational processes, Piaget also inverts the meaning of structure and function as it was originally conceived by Titchener. Now structures emerge through continuous transformational activities; they are, in other words, determined by functions. Moreover, structures emerge from within, whereas for Gestalt psychologists they originate from the outside. In further contrast to these and to most other structuralists, Piaget relates both the concepts of structure and function to genetic interpretations. Structures not only emerge through quick transformations but are subjected to slow, continuous changes. The individual's development is characterized by shifts in structures brought about by transformational activities. Thus Piaget relates all three aspects of Titchener's outline to one another; his theory is structural, functional, and genetic. Development is no longer characterized as a sequence of synchronic schemata, but, instead, by diachronic clusters of transformations.

Linguistics

Piaget's emphasis on the connection between structures and transformations directs our attention to recent developments in linguistics. Two major schools in linguistics have been called "structuralists" and "transformationists," respectively. The structuralists adopted the methodology of the behaviorists to determine the major form classes and their arrangements in the natural language. Apart from their emphasis on methodological rigor, they share with the behaviorists a disrespect for underlying organizations, forces or meanings. Their inquiries depart from and focus on the surface of the linguistic corpus. Quite paradoxically, of course, the designation of these linguists as "structuralists" must not be transferred to their allies, the "behaviorists," who, from Titchener's point of view, were regarded as "functionalists." Titchener reserved the label of "structuralism" for his own school of introspective elementarism.

Structuralism, as proposed by Bloomfield (1933), dominated American linguistics for many decades. Although objections were expressed repeatedly—for instance, Jesperson (1937) claimed that the purpose of a linguistic analysis is "to denote all the most important interrelations of words and parts of words in connected speech. . . . Forms as such have no place in the system [1937, pp. 13 and 104]"—a major revision was not undertaken until the appearance of Chomsky's transformational grammar.

Much like Piaget, Chomsky's (1957, 1959) publications reveal some major changes in his thinking. Chomsky began by describing alternative models of syntactic structures (1957) and by polemicizing against behavioristic interpretations (1959). He then elaborated his syntactic theory (Chomsky, 1965, 1968), which is of primary interest for our present discussion. His most recent interpretations, nevertheless, are not as radical as those by Piaget (1970). In contrast to Piaget's transformationism, Chomsky argues at two distinct levels: for grammars of the surface structures of the natural languages and for that of an underlying universal deep structure. Most of his efforts are directed toward the delineation of the latter. As that description is achieved, attention can shift toward the specification of transformation rules by which surface structures are derived from deep structure. Transformations are thus performed on given structures and do not attain the priority that Piaget is willing to assign to them. Instead of considering these transformations as the universal basis, they merely operate on the deep structure to which such a priority is assigned. Not surprisingly, therefore, some of his followers (Lenneberg, 1967; McNeill, 1968, 1970) have identified these universal forms of the deep structure with innate schemata of the organisms, and thus have revitalized the nativism of nineteenth-century psychology. What needs to be done is to relate the transformations to intrinsic activities of the organism instead of to their forms.

The modern linguists' concept of "transformation" creates as many difficulties as did Titchener's concept of "structure." Transformations have their well-defined place in the logic and mathematics of numerical systems. As they were first elaborated by Hölder (1901) and were discussed in many different treatises in the behavioral and social sciences (see Stevens, 1951; Coombs, 1964), measurements can be based on numerical systems of varying complexity, that is, on cardinal, ordinal, rational systems, and the like. As the complexity of the numerical systems increases (and with it the number of operative prerequisites that must be fulfilled), the complexity of the transformations that can be imposed on these systems decreases. Thus cardinal numbers can be subjected to a wide range of transformations while rational numbers can only be subjected to a few. In other words, with increasing complexity, larger sets of properties must be kept invariant so that the structure of the whole system is not jeopardized.

Whereas the structure of these numerical systems and their sets of permissible transformations can be specified with precision, the use of the latter term in linguistics is rather ambiguous. Linguistic transformations not only change the order of items within strings but also alter basic features of expressions—for example, they change declarative statements into negatives, questions into passives, and vice versa. Since the dimensions of linguistic expressions are difficult to determine and vary from investigation to investigation, linguistic transformations also lack descriptive rigor. In particular, the invariant properties are not spelled out. Indeed, mathematicians tend to emphasize the invariances; linguists point to the modifications brought about by transformations.

MATHEMATICS

Theories of Numbers

In the discussion of reformulations in mathematical thinking that have contributed to the development of modern structuralism, we consider the work of Cassirer (1910). As is implied in the German title of his book, *The Concepts of Substance and Functions*, early philosophizing relied heavily on the concept of smallest, substantive elements. With the objective basis of these particles taken for granted, the task of philosophy and sciences was to analyze the systematic connections between them. In opposition to such conceptualizations, Cassirer argues for the priority of functional relations or operations, a switch in thinking that characterizes structural interpretations. This shift in conceptualization also occurred in mathematics.

During the early historical periods, at least to Descartes, mathematics was viewed as a reflection of or an ideal abstraction from the real world with its substantive particle properties. A major reformulation was brought about by Leibniz for whom the basis of knowledge did not lie in the reflection and abstraction of ideas themselves but in the relationship between ideas. As a general example of this change in thinking, consider the notion of geometrical points and lines. Traditionally, points were taken for granted and, thereafter, notions about their shortest connections, that is, through straight lines, were derived. Thus, the solution was achieved through operations performed on these points. Similarly in algebra, the natural numbers, as experienced by counting real objects, were taken for granted. Whenever problems arose, for example, when a larger number was to be subtracted from a smaller one, extensions of the system were introduced, in this case, an extension into the domain of negative numbers. In many other cases, new numbers were interspersed between the natural numbers, such as fractional, irrational, and imaginary numbers. Thereby, the notions of the infinity in extension and in partition of the domain of numbers emerged. However, it also became even more apparent that the prerequisites, which made these developments possible, lie in our full use of operative capabilities instead of in better and better approximations of the range of real objects. In other words, mathematics began to be viewed as a system of operations rather than as a reflection of substantive conglomerates. Since the full range of these operations had been hardly explored, many new forms of mathematics could emerge. Developments since the second half of the nineteenth century have confirmed this possibility, leading to non-Euclidean geometries and to some of the number systems mentioned above, for example, irrational and imaginary numbers.

Related to these developments are changes in the concepts of time and space (Cohen & Riegel 1972; Riegel, 1972c). Traditionally, *time* had been regarded as finite and discrete; thus, the concept of time was similar to the concept of substance. As the natural number system was extended and as the slots between numbers were filled to a greater and greater extent, the notion of infinity was introduced through induction. Now, instead of emphasizing the periodicity of time, its beginning and its end, an abstract continuum was derived. To Cassirer, however, the question of whether time is discrete or continuous, finite or infinite, relative or absolute depends solely on the operations selected by the observer and not on external, nonintellectual criteria.

Cassirer relates our conception of time to the theories of numbers and algebra. Geometry, on the other hand, he relates to the simultaneity and coexistence of several such number systems. Subsequently, also our concept of *space* can be continuous or discrete, absolute or relative, Euclidean or non-Euclidean. Originally, according to Cassirer, the concept of space was discrete and bound by the three dimensionality of our experience. Through inductive generalizations the notion of a continuous space was derived, and attempts were made to shift from the three dimensions of the experienced space to non-Euclidean interpretations. Although this has been intellectually achieved, Cassirer insists that our conception of space ought not to be regarded as a generalization from objective, substantive conditions of the real world but, instead, viewed as a fuller elaboration of our intellectual operations which enable us to generate these notions as well as many others not yet proposed.

Dedekind, Frege, and Russell

Cassirer's views, which occasionally have been called "logical idealism," are shared by the mathematician Dedekind (1893) who argues that our concept of numbers, being a representation of pure laws of thinking, is independent of our conceptions of space and time. Quite to the contrary, only through the logical derivation of a theory of numbers and the attainment of a monotone domain of numbers have we become able to explicate our conceptions of space and time. If, in the pursuit of these explorations, we try "to determine what we are doing when counting a class or a number of things, we are bound to recognize the capability of the mind to relate things to things, to compare one thing with another, or to map one thing upon another; without this capability thought would not be possible at all [Dedekind, 1893, pp. III-IV, author's translation]."

According to Dedekind, our basic conception of numbers is relational. Through implicit mental comparisons we derive ordinal numbers. By explication we become able to categorize numbers or items. For example, we might, within a given range, group all those items that are below a certain value a into a class. Items above the value are assigned to a different class. Following this procedure (the well-known Dedekind "cut"), the criterion itself, a, cannot belong to either of the two classes that it defines. Therefore, we need to elaborate other operations that will lead to a new numerical system and include the criterion a, that is, the system of irrational numbers. By applying these deductive procedures step by step and thereby extending the domain of numbers encompassed, Dedekind and the following generation of mathematicians succeeded in deriving the whole field of mathematics from such a deductive basis.

Dedekind's procedure is based on ordinal judgments. For the derivation of cardinal numbers and categorizations in general—it has been argued by Frege (1903) and Russel (1903)—judgments of equivalence are more fundamental. Contrary to the traditional conception, in which numbers are considered as given and, subsequently, judged as equivalent or not, it is the goal of their approach to determine an operation of equivalence first, and then to derive sets of equivalent and nonequivalent numbers on the basis of such an operation. As Frege states, "It is our intention to form the content of an operation which can be expressed in an equation in such a way that there is a number on each side of it. . . . Thus, by means of the familiar concept of equivalence we are to obtain what we have to consider as equal [1903, p. 27]."

In comparing the approach by Dedekind and Cassirer with that by Frege and Russell, their similarities and dialectic interdependencies need to be emphasized. First, both camps rely on relations—the former on asymmetric relations of different kinds, the latter on the symmetric relation of equivalence. Second, both emphasize operative, constructive aspects through which complex structures are derived. They neither regard these structures nor the equivalences and relations as given in the external world, but as founded in the operations of the organism. Thus their interpretations are closely attuned to and anticipate Piaget's cognitive developmental theory. They are at variance, however, with sociocultural theories which assign, at least in part, these operative, constructive, or transformational activities to society which, in turn, will determine, at least in part, the activities of the individual. Before we discuss these modern trends, we give a brief overview of recent philosophical developments that parallel those in mathematical theory. In particular, we refer to Carnap's (1928) early work.

PHILOSOPHY

Positivism and Conventionalism

The philosophical roots of modern structuralism lie in rather unusual grounds.

At first, we might not at all appreciate the connection. This is due to some common misconceptions about certain schools of thought, especially those of French and German positivism and, to a lesser extent, phenomenology.

The German positivism of the late nineteenth century became instrumental and supportive for a scientific psychology of which Titchener was one of the late representatives. Contrary to frequent statements, especially expressed by American writers, positivism of this type did not at all support a blind search for "facts" but argued against the notion of "facts" as a form of evidence independent of the observer and solely determined by external conditions of "nature." To Mach (1886), for example, there were only sensory impressions; all knowledge had to be derived from them and, thus, was in the mind. He strongly supported the "psychologism" of the late nineteenth century—which epistemologically subordinated all other sciences to psychology—and emphasized, although timidly, the constructive aspects of scientific efforts in maintaining that "facts" are merely theories to which we have become sufficiently accustomed.

Quite similar in orientation, although with much stronger emphasis on the sociocultural basis of knowledge, Poincaré's conventionalism leads us far back in the history of philosophy, at least, to Locke's critical realism. The notion of sociolinguistic conventions was introduced to account for the agreement between different observers in regard to secondary qualities, that is, those qualities that do not directly reflect properties of nature (primary qualities) but depend on the observers' interpretations, such as his impressions of warmth, redness, brightness, and the like. Poincaré carried this interpretation to its conclusion by considering all our impressions (not only those representing secondary qualities) as dependent on sociolinguistic conventions. According to him, each individual has his subjective experiences; in order to make general knowledge possible, certain agreements must be reached on how to talk about these impressions. Consequently, knowledge is not only dependent on the sensory impressions and observations but on the constructive efforts by the observers to state their experience in communicable terms.

The last issue received concentrated attention in the work of Avenarius (1894/5) who, for the first time, emphasized logical and syntactic organizations as a necessary prerequisite for the acquisition of knowledge. Although previously the agreement on communicable concepts was stressed, Avenarius pointed to the need for consensus about logical and linguistic structures. To Avenarius these structures were arbitrarily selected in about the same way in which the rules of a game, such as chess, are set up. There is neither intrinsic nor extrinsic validity in these systems; their value is dependent on criteria such as internal consistency, simplicity, and comprehensiveness. What these views have in common with contemporary positivism is the exaltation of the knower over what is to be known—the acquisition of positive truth in disregard of the power and weight of the object world.

Constructivism

Avenarius' interpretations failed to have a major effect on the philosophy and the execution of the behavioral and social sciences. His ideas gained considerable importance, however, through the extensions by the early Carnap (1928). Accepting the shift from substantive to functional conceptualization (Cassirer, 1910), Carnap elaborated structural interpretations with a strong nominalistic and constructivistic emphasis. He traced his interpretations to Russell's (1903) theory of relations and to the "reduction of 'reality' to the 'given' [1928, p. 7]" as successfully performed by Avenarius, Mach, Poincaré, Külpe, Ziehen, and Driesch. The "givens" must be sought in the unmediated, phenomenal experience. Rather than halting at such a contemplative state, Carnap asks that constructive steps be taken out of these experiences. Knowledge does not so much consist in introspective apprehension but in active construction. At the beginning, he would agree with Cassirer (1910), is not the sensory impression but the sentence ("Satz" as related to "setzen," "proposing") which alone generates knowledge by making it communicable, social, and human.

There are two basic components on which individual and scientific knowledge is based: property description and relation description.

"A *property description* indicates the properties which the individual objects of a given domain have, while a *relation description* indicates the relations which hold between these objects, but does not make any assertion about the objects as individuals. Thus, a property description makes individual or, in a sense, absolute, assertions while a relation description makes relative assertions [Carnap, 1967, p. 19]."

Although I would take exception to the notion that property descriptions are nonrelational (see Chapter VIII), Carnap's main attention, anyhow, centers around the relation descriptions. Construction of knowledge consists in transforming relation descriptions (which ultimately might have been generated from property descriptions) according to *construction rules* or *constructional definitions*.

".... to *construct* a out of b (and) c means to produce a general rule that indicates for each individual case how a statement about a must be transformed in order to yield a statement about b, c [Carnap, 1967, p. 6]."

The development of constructivism has been prepared by Poincaré's emphasis that knowledge cannot be based on the "givens" alone, for example, sensations, but that "only relations between the sensations have an objective value [Poincaré, 1902, p. 198]" For Carnap, this move, although in the right direction, does not go far enough. Scientific knowledge becomes possible only through the systematic explication of the interrelation of relations, that is, through the study of structures. Ultimately, all knowledge is structural and is removed and separated from its base, the property descriptions or, in Poincaré's sense, the relations with objective value.

Within a system of structural description, Carnap distinguishes two kinds of definitions: *Ostensive definitions* and *definite descriptions*. The former resemble property descriptions but are stated in relational terms.

"Here, . . . the object which is meant is brought within the range of perception and is then indicated by an appropriate gesture, e.g., 'That is Mont Blanc' . . . definite descriptions . . . list . . . essential characteristics, but only as many . . . as are required to recognize unequivocally the object which is meant within the object domain under discussion, e.g., 'Mont Blanc indicates the highest mountain in the Alps,' or . . . 'the mountain so many kilometers east of Geneva' [Carnap, 1928, p. 24]."

Although empirical sciences must incorporate ostensive statements to relate to their specialized fields of observations, science will, ultimately, remove itself from this basis through purely formal, structural descriptions. Scientific disciplines differ in the degree to which these transformations have been accomplished. Physics, in certain areas, can be removed from its ostensive basis. Psychology has not reached such an advanced status. According to Carnap, such "de-subjectivization" will always result in formal structural descriptions. "Each scientific statement can in principle be so transformed that it is nothing but a structural statement [Carnap, 1928, p. 29]."

An Example of Structural Description

Carnap provides a simple demonstration of structural descriptions, the example of a railroad schedule. From such a record sufficient specifications can be deduced in regard to any point (in this instance, station) without going outside of the system. Our own analysis of language and meaning—we believe—represents an equally strong demonstration (see Riegel, 1970).

Contrary to common as well as to scientific conceptions, meaning is a relation (or rather a set of relations); concrete experience consists of such relations; elements and words are abstractions. Early in life and in unfamiliar situations, meaning is introduced through ostensive or, more generally, extralingual relations, that is, by pointing toward labeled objects and qualities, or by directing or performing requested actions. These extralingual relations represent, however, exceptional circumstances for depicting the meaning of objects, events, or qualities. Regularly, such information will be substituted by intralingual relations. We will, for example, explicate the meaning of ZEBRA by saying that it "is an ANIMAL, has STRIPES, is found in AFRICA, is like a HORSE, etc." rather than by pointing at one.

These explications presuppose that the listener has already acquired a repertoire of relational expressions so that he may insert the new information into the network available to him. This is achieved, for instance, by both relating and differentiating ZEBRA from other ANIMALS, by grouping ZEBRA into its spatial location, by recognizing criterial attributes of ZEBRA, and so on. Undoubtedly, the meaning of ZEBRA, as explicated through these relational statements, is incomplete (e.g., for zoological purposes) and subjective both in regard to the speaker and the listener. There is no assurance but, in principle, doubt that both will imply precisely the same understanding of the term. ZEBRA for one might denote a dangerous beast, and for the other, a handsome creature.

In spite of these idiosyncratic interpretations, communication is possible as long as, within a limited group of speakers, major sections of such a relational structure are being shared. Individuals will communicate within the boundaries of those networks by attending to subsections, like those included in our example above. Under still more limited conditions (e.g., if only the information "ANIMAL with STRIPES" is transmitted leading in turn to multiple interpretations, such as ZEBRA, TIGER, or HYENA), the need may arise to extend the subset within the relational network by including references to specific locations, that is, AFRICA or INDIA, to types, that is, HORSE or CAT, and so on. In other words, the domain of the relational structure will vary along numerous dimensions, such as individuals (abilities, age), groups (language, sex, occupation), and situations (school, job site, cocktail party). Theoretically, the structure can always be extended to make a disambiguation possible. The repertoire of linguistic expressions is rich enough or can always be enriched to make identifications possible.

Our last remarks call attention to the fluctuating and shifting state of relational structures. Such conditions are characteristic, in particular, of languages. The example used by Carnap (1928, pp. 25–27), that is, of a railroad network, is less convincing in this regard, because it seems unreasonable to consider this structure, the system of railroad tracks, as anything but fixed. Moreover, to depict this structure by activities, that is, by the moving trains, would be unusual. Language, however, might well be regarded as a system of activities. Its underlying neuroanatomical organization is known only in its grossest features, and any particular nervous impulse may reach a cortical destination simultaneously along many alternative tracks. Moreover, neither the source nor the destination are clearly given. Thus neither the tracks (relations) nor the intersections (elements) are firmly fixed. In most psychological and sociological interpretations, however, the notion of fixed structures has been given preference. Traditionally language, too, has been regarded as a system of elements (words) and connections (associations), but rarely as a system of transformed relations. Language has always been regarded as an objectified product but not as transformational labor. With our example, we are thus led, once more, to our previous contrastive comparison between the major trend in Gestalt psychology and Piaget, the former emphasizing the priority of organized structure, and the latter the priority of transformational activity.

SOCIOLOGY AND ANTHROPOLOGY

French Sociology

The contributions of the three positivists of the late nineteenth century have supplemented one another. Mach, in his analysis of sensory impressions, explored the foundation of the experimental psychology of Helmholtz, Wundt, Külpe, and Titchener. His French counterpart, Poincaré, in following the tradition initiated by the founder of positivism, Auguste Comte, emphasized the conventional and communicative basis of knowledge and thus placed emphasis on sociology and linguistics. Finally, Avenarius explored the logical structure of knowledge and thereby synthesized the trends explored by Mach and Poincaré. In this section, we elaborate further on the contributions by French sociologists and anthropologists.

Because psychic processes could become an object of scientific explorations only if the objective conditions were observed that cause their occurrence and progression, Comte, in his classification of the sciences, did not assign a separate place to psychology. The requested observations would either have to focus on the anatomical and physiological basis of the organism or on the conditions and development of the social milieu. During his later years Comte paid increasing attention to these sociological aspects. This tradition was continued by Poincaré and led to the foundation of the French school of sociology.

In contrast to their British counterparts who, like Tylor and Frazer, would insist on the universal permanence of human traits, French sociologists, led by

Durkheim (1912), regarded psychic functions as a product of social conditions and, therefore, as variable. Perhaps even more important than the sociologization of psychology, was that sociology became psychologized. This trend is most clearly expressed in Durkheim's concept of "collective images" and "collective mind," both of which are psychological terms generalized to sociology. Everything social consists of images or is the product of images. Although these images cannot be reduced to physical conditions, man exists, at the same time, as a physical being. Thus Durkheim supports a distinct dualism: man is both an individual physical and a communal social being. If one were to approach a study of psychology at all, it would have to consist either of psychophysiology or of psychosociology. The object for sociology, on the other hand, the collective mind, is independent of the individual and his consciousness.

Durkheim, together with Mauss (1903), applied this conceptualization to the study of intellectual functions. Logical categories were viewed as originating from social relations. The concept of space, for example, was derived from the notion of social territory and forces. Similarly, Halbwachs (1925, 1950) analyzed the social conditions of memory by explaining that in recall we reconstruct past events by connecting them with conditions of the social life. Blondel (1928), finally, combines interpretations of the collective mind with Bergson's idea of an individualistic *élan vital*. In his analyses of psychological constructs such as volition, affects, and perceptions, he transcends Durkheim's formulation. Instead of eliminating psychology in favor of biological and, especially, sociological interpretations, he proposes individual psychology as a third approach. For example, the study of perception must be concerned with collective aspects insofar as it deals with general concepts, such as "book," "table," and so on. On the other hand, it must be concerned with neurophysiological and anatomical conditions, which are equally general and common to all human beings. But, finally, the study of perception also must be concerned with experiences that are unique for an individual. It is on this last issue that Blondel deviates from Durkheim's dualistic conception and reintroduces psychology as a third mode of exploration.

Blondel's deviation from Durkheim was criticized by Halbwachs (1929) for failing to recognize sufficiently the formative role of social customs, habits, and concepts. An individual outside of society, Halbwachs maintains, would not be able to function generatively. The discrepancy between these two ways of thinking becomes most apparent in Blondel's analysis of volition. On the one hand, volition originates from biological reflexes; on the other, it represents an act that is distinctly social in nature. Although genetic connection does not exist between these two forms of volition, there exists, in between, an individual will that is psychological in nature and free. Of course, most people do not develop this tendency; they are solely directed by collective volition to which they subject themselves "obediently," and by their biological drives to which they submit themselves in an equally "obedient" manner. Only the intellectual "elite" is capable of developing individual volition.

Blondel's interpretations share basic features with the cultural anthropology of Lévy-Bruhl (1922) and, although nongenetic, they are similar to the cognitive developmental psychology of the early Piaget (1928). Lévy-Bruhl adopts from Durkheim the concept of the "collective images." But while Durkheim postulates a "collective subject" as the carrier of these images, Lévy-Bruhl rejects such a metaphysical construct. For Lévy-Bruhl "collective images," although they are determined by the society, are conceptions of and located in the individual. Closely in line with Blondel's distinction, Lévy-Bruhl investigates different levels of the "collective mind." He is known for his study of the "primitive mind," which he contrasts sharply with that of modern man without emphasizing—as Durkheim did—the continuity in the development of the human race and human consciousness.

As Leach (1970) convincingly shows, these different trends represented by Lévy-Bruhl, on the one hand, and Durkheim, on the other, converge in anthropology on the functionalism of Malinowski (1926) and the structuralism of Lévi-Strauss (1958). It is also at this juncture that one of Piaget's (1928) early contributions attains significance. Piaget tries to resolve the conflict between Durkheim's emphasis of the continuity in the development of man and Lévy-Bruhl's emphasis on qualitative differences by elaborating his famous distinction between functions and schemata. Functions remain the same throughout the stages of human evolution and individual development; schemata change, like organs in the evolution of species, or forms of logical operations in the development of the individual. In both instances, functions and schemata complement one another; functions do not exist without schemata and schemata do not exist without functions.

In his early writings, Piaget (especially 1923, 1924) reveals the influence of the social psychology of Blondel and the anthropology of Lévy-Bruhl. Indeed, he succeeded in fusing the sharp dichotomy created by Durkheim between the inner biological and the outer social nature of man. These were also the years in which he contributed his interpretations of the development of language functions in terms of egocentric and socialized speech, which were rebutted by Vygotsky (1962). In his later writings, Piaget abandoned his emphasis on the impact of social conditions, however, and increasingly focused his attention on *psychic* structures and functions. Thus the opposition to the viewpoints emerging from the followers of Vygotsky grew stronger. The latter came to represent the new interpretations of Soviet psychologists.

Dialectic Anthropology

Recent thinking in the Soviet Union about the philosophical foundation of the behavioral and social sciences seems to follow the viewpoints expressed by French sociologists. In regarding psychic activities as the joint outcome of inner biological and outer sociocultural conditions, they too reject a central and independent role for psychology. In contrast to the reductionism of French sociologists, they do not merely split these conditions apart but emphasize interactive processes through which psychic activity and consciousness emerge. Moreover, they consider these interactions in their temporal dependencies and thus provide dialectic interpretations. Similar to Piaget, changes in psychic activities may produce changes in inner biological conditions and these, in turn, may change psychic activities. In contrast to Piaget, there exist also active interventions from the outer sociocultural to the psychic conditions and vice versa.

Soviet psychology has its roots in two separate movements: the reflexology of Sechenov, Bekhterev, and Pavlov, and the dialectic materialism of Marx, Engels, and Lenin. The first foundation is sufficiently known and need not concern us in detail. It should be emphasized, however, that in contrast to the behaviorists, who mechanistically split the reflex arc into its superficial external components, that is, the stimulus and the response, Pavlov regarded the reflex as a functional unit. Only an extended conditioning history will enable the organism to separate out the stimulus from the response. In the Soviet conception, at this stage, the response becomes a *reaction* to the stimulus but, at the same time, the response *reflects* on the stimulus. This antimechanistic notion became a fundamental ingredient of the Soviet interpretations and is referred to by Rubinstejn as "constitutive relationism." Interestingly enough, the same viewpoints were expressed in one of the founding articles of American functionalism, that is, in John Dewey's (1896) treatise on the reflex arc which, often misunderstood, was soon discarded from consideration by American psychologists.

The first foundation of Soviet psychology relates psychic activities to their inner biological material basis. The second foundation relates them to their outer cultural-historical material basis. This conceptualization builds on the historical and dialectical materialism of Marx and Engels that was injected into Soviet psychology through the posthumous publication of Lenin's (1929) philosophical notebook. The discussions emerging after this event elaborated, in particular, two notions, the dialectic interpenetration of opposites and dialectic leaps.

By emphasizing the interaction between psychic and cultural-historical activities, Soviet psychologists recognized the social dependency of the former. As psychic activities emerge (and their emergence is, of course, codetermined by their interaction with biological activities), the social conditions are being changed as well. Through his own labor—as Marx stated—man transforms the conditions around him which, in turn, will change him (or, at least, the generations that follow him). Thus man creates himself through his own labor. For instance, by inventing a tool, by generating new conceptual or linguistic expressions, man produces a lasting effect that "backfires" on him and the following generations of individuals, who thus will emerge under changed conditions. At least in regard to its psychosocial implication, the notion of dialectic interpenetration explains the superficiality of the thesis that ontogeny recapitulates phylogeny. Both sequences are bound to coincide because both are the product of interactive human efforts.

The principle of progression by qualitative leaps is closely related to that of dialectic interpenetration. It resembles Piaget's description of cognitive development, although it emphasizes the interaction between psychic activity and outer, material cultural-historical conditions rather than intrapsychic shifts captured by Piaget's dialectic contrast of assimilation and accommodation. As our previous examples imply, dialectic leaps are brought about by human activity. Thus the invention of tools, of linguistic expressions, or of language in general, changes dramatically the sociocultural conditions under which human beings grow up. Conversely, as these sociocultural conditions have come into existence during the history of mankind, they will have induced stepwise changes in the organism, each reflecting basic reorganizations of the operations that the individual will be able to perform, for example, to speak, to write, and to formalize.

Our last statements indicate, once more, the intimate connections between functional changes produced by human activities and the structural shifts representing the products of these activities. Thus our discussion returns to the interpretations advanced by Piaget. The interactive process of shifts is not restricted to the activities of the individual, however, but embraces all other individuals in his social world, indeed, all individuals who through their ceaseless efforts over generations have created the cultural-historical conditions under which any present-day descendent grows up and lives.

During the most recent period in the short history of Soviet psychology, a double interaction theory has been proposed by S. L. Rubinstejn (1958, 1963; for English discussions see Payne, 1968; Riegel, 1972a,b; Wozniak, 1972). Rubinstejn's dialectic interpretation deviates from the dichotomizing attempts of French sociologists. He agrees with them, however, in assigning to psychology a secondary role. Both biology and sociology, because of the material foundations emphasized by Soviet psychologists, rest on more fundamental bases. Psychology is a construct and could not exist without the former.

Of course, these evaluations also indicate an intrinsic strength of psychology. Psychology, more than biology and sociology, is or ought to be concerned with activities rather than with products. This conclusion, once more, redirects our attention to the comparison of function and structure. Rubinstejn agrees with Piaget by emphasizing the mutual dependence of both; he disagrees with him (at least, with Piaget's writings during the forties and fifties) by emphasizing that the function-structure relationship ought not to be limited to the activities of the separate individual but ought to be extended to the interactions within his cultural-historical world. He disagrees, furthermore, with Piaget by trying to trace the two interactions to their material foundations.

THE DIALECTIC RELATION OF STRUCTURE AND TRANSFORMATION

In the previous section, Piaget's developmental structuralism was submerged within Rubinstejn's double interaction theory. Such an interpretation seems to handle all those issues that have been proposed in opposition to the traditional mechanistic viewpoints of American psychology, that is, issues that focus on the active organism in an active environment. However, in contradiction to their dialectic foundation, Soviet psychologists consistently emphasize the material bases of psychic processes. Thus they emphasize the products rather than the activities that generate them. In concluding our discussion, we consider alternative interpretations and review, once more, the trends and options of structural-transformational psychology.

Western psychology has one of its most authentic representations in William Stern's (1935) *Psychology on a Personalistic Basis* which, appropriately, has been criticized by Vygotsky (1962) as individualistic and intellectualistic. Stern exemplifies a trend that derives from the British philosophy of Locke, Hume, and Berkeley (especially the latter) and continues to dominate Western thinking in the behavioral and social sciences. In extension this emphasis has led, as we have indicated, to the positivism of Mach, to the psychologism of Wundt, Helmholtz, and Külpe and to the phenomenologism of Husserl. In spite of their wide differences, all of these scholars built their interpretations on the sensory, perceptual basis of knowledge. The world around us came to be regarded as a mere outward projection of the mind. Psychology became the most fundamental of all sciences.

While for this group of scholars knowledge was to be gained through sensory experience and contemplations based on them, a second school of thought, associated with the advances in the natural sciences, began to emphasize the constructive aspects of knowledge. According to Russel and Carnap, physics and astronomy, for example, represent prototypes of constructive sciences whose founding components, unlike psychological sensations, are not directly accessible to us but are intellectually generated. From this point of view, knowledge is founded on the "sentence," in its German sense of "Satz" and "setzen." Knowledge is gained by proposing sentences rather than by receiving sensory information in a passive state.

Although related viewpoints were expressed early in psychology—for example in Brentano's Act-Psychology (1874)—they never attained an appreciation comparable to those based on a sensory basis of knowledge. However, philosophers have paid increasing attention to this issue, an emphasis revealed in the work of Russell and Carnap as well as in such antiscientific movements as existentialism. More recently, Holzkamp (1972) has interpreted sciences in general, and psychology in particular, as an activity and, therefore, as a movement concerned with and dependent on social conditions and historical relevance. Most influential, however, is Piaget's (1950) notion of the individual's intellectual development and of the growth of knowledge in society, of genetic epistemology, based on the premise that progress can only occur through spontaneous, generative activities of the organism.

Aside from its sensory-perceptual and its operative-constructive bases, science and knowledge represent forms of organization and structure. Again, these organizations may either be viewed as existing outside the individual, recognizable through sensory experience, or as generatively produced by the individual and imposed on the outside world through his interpretations. Regardless of this choice, organizational aspects have received increasing attention through the work of Avenarius, Russell, Carnap, Piaget and, finally, Rubinstejn. Because of the complexity of the structures, these theories have shown a strong tendency toward formalism, at least, among the Western scholars. This trend is clearly exemplified in the progression of Piaget's research and theory. He advanced—in terms of his own theory—from an operative to a figurative psychology. His early studies of early developmental periods consist of rich but ambiguous interpretations of children's operations. Next he produced equally rich displays of imaginative, although less than fully standardized, experiments that were coupled with formal descriptions of the children's logic. In discussing the highest stage of development, he provides little more than an abstract model of intellectual operations, essentially a theory of what these operations, logically, ought to be. Supportive evidence is not supplied and, apparently, is not intended to be supplied. All that such evidence would provide are some superficial demonstrations that are neither sufficient to confirm the consistency of the theory nor to suggest important extensions.

Piaget's theory ties structuralism to the perceptionism of the earlier psychologists. Structures are confirmed by observations; structures organize experience. Soviet psychologists go beyond such a perceptionism and consider their evidence as originating from the material world outside of the observer. In contrast to earlier materialistic interpretations, they insist, however, that these conditions are not independent of the human organism; they are as much the product of human labor as they are forces impinging on the human being. Although Soviet psychologists opt for constructive theories, they abandon these theories all too soon by emphasizing the objectified material products rather than the activities by which these products are generated. Piaget, on the other hand, while emphasizing activities rather than material products, restricts himself to the developing individual under exclusion of the cultural-historical activities within which the individual grows.

A synthesizing extension would have to emphasize perception, action, and organization both in the individual and in the society. By emphasizing the products, this theory would be structural; by emphasizing the activities, it would be transformational. This theory would relate psychic activities both to their inner biological and their outer sociocultural foundations without exclusive emphasis on their material nature. These foundations become material if the products and structures are emphasized; they remain psychological if the activities and transformations are emphasized. Development proceeds through dialectic interactions between psychic activities and their inner biological and outer sociocultural foundations. Again, if we look at the objectified conditions, development represents, both for the individual and for the society, a sequence of temporarily stable schemata; if we look at the activities, development represents a constant flux of transformations.

Summary

In this chapter we traced the concepts of structure and transformation to their historical origins in psychology, that is, to Wundt, Titchener, and Gestalt psychology. Piaget, through his developmental interpretations, brought about a synthesizing conception of structure and function. Such a synthesis is still lacking in modern linguistics, which remains dichotomized with respect to its approaches (synchronic versus diachronic) and its theorizing (competence versus performance). Linguistics has not yet reached an advanced integration on the basis of developmental-historical thinking. Issues of cognitive and linguistic theories are discussed in detail in the two major parts of the present volume.

In this historical chapter we have related these intellectual movements in psychology and linguistics to basic reformulations in mathematical theory, most notably by Dedekind, Frege, and Russell. According to these scientists, mathematical theories are founded on constructive operations of the mind that are relational in character, instead of on representative reflections of objective, substantive properties of the universe. The idea of constructive operation was systematically extended by Cassirer and Carnap and led to explicit structural interpretations.

In philosophy some of the roots of structuralism must be sought among the positivists of the late nineteenth century. Among these, Mach relates to the psychologism of Wundt, Titchener, and Külpe; Poincaré relates to the biosociologism of Comte and Durkheim. Avenarius, finally, is most closely akin to the logical constructivism of Cassirer and Carnap.

The further development of structuralism in France emphasized sociology and anthropology at the expense of psychological considerations. The early Piaget tried to reconcile the growing conflict in his genetic interpretations. But, ultimately, he retreated and began to deemphasize the sociohistorical conditions as determinants of individual development.

The needed emphasis of structures, as emerging in dialectic interaction both from within and without the individual, has been stressed—as it is distinguished from the static dualism of French sociology—in recent Soviet writings, especially in those by S. L. Rubinstejn. The next chapter is devoted to a detailed exploration of these theories and approaches.

CHAPTER 2

Dialecticism and Structuralism: The Philosophical Foundation of Soviet Psychology and Piagetian Cognitive Developmental Theory[1]

R. H. WOZNIAK

Anyone who endeavors to explicate, even partially, the conceptual relationships between the structuralist movement in the human sciences and other contemporary methods must, of course, seek to answer the prior question: "What is structuralism as a method?" The problems that this question presents are surprisingly great. In part, this results from the diversity of disciplinary applications that the structuralist method has had and from the local peculiarities of treatment it has received within each discipline. In part, it is because in many of the works purported to be "structuralist," "structuralism the method" is rarely to be distinguished from "structuralism the theory," and those who claim to employ the method in common may, and often do, possess opposing theoretical points of view even on issues often considered to be focal to the structuralist program (e.g., Piaget & Inhelder, 1969, versus Foucault, 1966; Barthes, 1967; Derrida, 1970; etc. on the relationship of logic to language).

Moreover two further problems add to the confusion. The first is an almost characteristically imprecise use of language in the description of the enterprise itself, in the description of the properties of the structuralist method (often despite careful formalization in the description of the products of the method, that is, particular structures). The second is variation between theorists in the use of terms common to the entire movement. Thus, for example, critical terms such as "structure," "schema," "organization," "pattern," "form," "system," "stage," "organic," "group," "operation," "representation," "transformation," "interaction," and "opposition" often appear to the student of structur-

[1] I gratefully acknowledge the contribution made to the development of ideas expressed in this chapter by Jan Smedslund, Jacobus Lempers, and Richard Aslin with whom I shared several months of discussion of the nature and role of stage theories in developmental psychology, and by Carl Johnson for his participation in the above and for his critical reading of an earlier version of the manuscript.

alism to spring full-blown from the head of the author, undefined, or worse, formally defined in one context and loosely used in another.

This, admittedly, places rather severe restrictions on the degree to which it can be deemed possible to interrelate the method of structuralism with that of materialist dialectics as it is embodied in the prevailing philosophy and psychology of the Soviet Union. The only alternative, in fact, seems to be to seize on some weak definition of structuralism to which all parties might be willing to assent as presenting a necessary if not sufficient characterization of the approach. From such a beginning, it might be possible to proceed to a discussion of, at least, the general ties that bind structuralism and dialecticism and to note occasionally, where possible, interesting divergences or correspondences between materialist dialectics and various individual structuralist conceptions like those of Piaget (1952), Lévi-Strauss (1963), Chomsky (1965), systems theorists such as Weiss (1971), and cyberneticists such as Ashby (1952).

If a common, although weak, definition of structuralism can be formulated, it might, after Martinet (1970), be "an approach to the understanding of objects and phenomena in which these are analyzed in terms of the manner of their internal construction" (i.e., in terms of a structure). Implied in even this weak definition are three basic methodological characteristics. The first is that analysis must proceed by seeking that which is latent in the phenomenon or object of study. Understanding cannot be based solely on a knowledge of surface characteristics, of that which is directly sensible. This, however, immediately confronts us with a problem, a problem none too well defined by the structuralists themselves. Is "structure" a reality? Is structure something that actually exists in the object of study and that, therefore, must be modeled with greater and greater precision? In addition, an affirmative answer to this query immediately raises the corollary Cartesian (Descartes, 1890) problem of the guarantee of an identity between scientific discourse and reality. If structure is real, what then is the relationship between real structure and the structural model, the formalization proposed to account for the structure?

One response to this difficulty is to view the question of what exists in the object as, epistemologically at least, irrelevant. If positing structure assists the scientist in achieving a deeper understanding of the object (by whatever criterion understanding is understood to be judged by), then structure should by all means be posited. This position, however, is disputed by those whom we might term "structural realists" such as Martinet (1970) on the grounds that:

"it remains to be proven that a structure of the latter type (i.e., posited by the scholar to allow a better understanding of the facts without regard to the ontological question) might reach its goal, namely account for the facts, if it did not tally with the data afforded by the object itself . . . and thus (the) relations of structure to object may never be considered as unimportant [p. 1].''

The view taken by Piaget must certainly also be characterized as implying a form of ''structural realism.''[2] At the lowest levels of sensorimotor intelligence, the hereditary reflexes and their initial intercoordinations constitute real psychological structures from which assimilatory action schemes and, with the interiorization of action, operational structures will be constructed. The attribution of these structures to human intelligence, for Piaget, is no more a simple heuristic device than is the attribution of intelligence to human behavior. Behavior is intelligent and, for Piaget, that requires that it be ''structured.''

The answer Piaget appears to give to the problem of the correspondence between the structural descriptions that he proposes and the structures that he seeks to describe suggests the structural realism of his view. For Piaget, the fundamental characteristic of the nature of fully developed human thought is that it is essentially logical and mathematical. Consequently, the use of logico-mathematical formalizations to describe the structure of formal operations, far from constituting an arbitrary model which might or might not correspond to the actual structure of thought, guarantees a certain identity between the structural model and the structural reality.

A middle ground view is held by those who might be referred to as the ''competence theorists of North America.'' As Pylyshyn (1972) discusses, competence theories suggest ''that those aspects of the universe that are ultimately comprehensible to the human mind are comprehensible precisely because one can see in them a structure that is essentially mathematical. . . . A competence theory is . . . committed to the belief that underlying observed behavior is a more perfect mathematical structure. Indeed, its concern is not with behavior per se but rather with how information about the world is represented in a person's mind which makes it possible for him to perform the way he does or the way he could perform under a variety of conceivable circumstances [p. 547–8].'' Formalization of such representational structures attempts to set boundary conditions that those structures must satisfy, that is, to describe the distinctions and relations that are necessary if a particular performance is to be displayed in some conceivable situation. For this purpose, the competence theory chosen is, on the grounds of parsimony, the least complex formulation consistent with the structural characteristics of the representation it describes. The implication of this point of view is that, since any given competence theory is only one among an unlimited number of such descriptions and, in general, one chosen on the basis of parsimony (which nature may or may not respect), its symbols and operations do not necessarily have any psychological reality. On the other hand, however, the requirement that a competence theory be consistent with the structural characteristics of the object that it models appears to suggest that competence theories, although perhaps needing to make no claim regarding the ontological status of their own symbols and operations, must at least assert the existence of some real structural elements underlying the phenomena they purport to explain. The competence theorist, then, must necessarily assume the reality of some structure; although, *as* a competence theorist, he need not ask, or at the very least, he need not stress the question of correspondence between his formalization and that reality, whatever it might be. Questions of the adequacy of formalization are decided on formal grounds.

The second methodological characteristic of structuralism is that analysis must proceed by seeking, in particular, those latent properties of the object or phenomenon that are organizational in nature. This is implied in the notion that it is the manner of construction of the thing or phenomenon that is the object of analysis. Construction is the placement of elements into interrelationship in the organization of an object; and analysis must seek to specify the form of this interrelationship. It is, in fact, the totality of the organization, the system of interrelationships, that defines the structure supposed to be latent in the object or phenomenon. Once again, however, we are confronted with an immediate problem. When a "system" of interrelationships is spoken of, what is meant by a "system?" There are network communications systems. There are biological systems. There are linguistic systems. There are mathematical systems; and although all have certain properties in common, they are clearly not identical. Yet each is used as the dominant explanatory metaphor by a different group of scientists, and each such group might well be given title to the appellation "structuralist." Rather than attempt a definition of system that would lack generality, therefore, it might be well simply to allow "structural analysis" in this context to refer to the identification of elements and interrelationships between elements, regardless of the particular properties of those interrelationships (although as we shall show this is partly belied by the next point).

The last methodological characteristic of structuralism to be discussed is implied in the term "manner" of construction. This suggests that analysis must proceed by recognizing that in the phenomenal world both momentary stability and constant change must be sought within as well as, or instead of, from without the object or phenomenon of study. Once again there is great disagreement on the type and source of activity and stability and on the definition of structural models to account for this activity and stability. Sometimes activity is considered as developmental; sometimes as mere dynamics without any reference to development. Sometimes this notion is captured in the self-regulating system of transformations known as a mathematical group (Piaget, 1970). Sometimes it is a procedural description, a set of rules dictating which actions on which primitive terms will lead to the construction of instances of the concept (or sentence) whose structure the description purports to model (Pylyshyn, 1972). Sometimes it is implied in an inversion of a relationship between polar opposites (Lévi-Strauss, 1963)—the point is that in whatever form structure takes, the structuralist method is one of analysis of stability in the midst of change. It is an attempt to make something sensible out of previously inexplicable phenomenal variation.

In summary, a structural analysis in this simple and, I hope, somewhat general sense represents an attempt to discover latent organization within the objects and phenomena of study to explain both the momentary stability and the constant change that takes place in those objects and phenomena.

MATERIALIST DIALECTICS AS A STRUCTURAL APPROACH

Materialist dialectics is a method of cognizing reality and an instrument of the revolutionary remaking of the world (cf., Afanasyev, 1968). Although, here, we typically emphasize the first of these attributes at the expense of the second, since the epistemological aspects of Marxist-Leninist dialectics are of particular interest, this emphasis should be recognized as the abstraction that it is because these two aspects of materialist dialects cannot, in fact, be separated. Cognition of the world in Marxism is a process involved with and in the service of the socialist revolution, and the socialist revolution must look to correct knowledge and understanding of reality as a guide to its progressive realization. Cognition and revolution, in other words, are a unity. Nonetheless, as long as this is kept in mind, it is possible to concentrate on only one aspect of this unity, on dialectics as a cognitive method.

The essence of the dialectical method, as proposed by Marx, is captured in a quotation from the Afterword to the second German edition of the first volume of *Capital* in which he says of "inquiry" that it "has to appropriate the material in detail, to analyse its different forms of development, to trace out their inner connection. Only after this work is done, can the actual movement be adequately described [Marx, 1912, pp. 24–5]." Already, in this statement, the outline of the structuralist approach can be discerned. Marx suggests tracing out "inner connection" in order to adequately describe "actual movement." The principal methodological characteristic of structuralism—search for that which is latent, organizing, and stable through change appears as present from the outset in Marxist thought.

In addition to this immediate link to structuralism, there is another, somewhat more mediated similarity that is also of interest. For Marx-Leninism, method is determined by the nature and intrinsic laws of the phenomena to be analyzed. Thus, for example, each scientific and technical discipline develops its own particular methods. What is distinctive about the method of materialist dialectics, however, is that it is the method of the science of philosophy and, as such, is viewed as furnishing "a key to understanding not only separate spheres of reality, but literally all fields of nature, society and thought; it is the key to the cognition of the world as a whole [Afanasyev, 1968, p. 14]." This claim of integrative transcendence of the specific methods of the various subdisciplines which Marx-Leninism makes for dialectics bears, in my opinion, more than a little resemblance to certain statements made on the behalf of "structuralism" by some of its enthusiasts. Thus, for example, Piaget (1968), in an article entitled "The problem of common mechanisms in the human sciences," notes:

"From our inter-disciplinary point of view, it is extremely interesting to observe that this trend [structuralism], which is becoming more and more evident within the human sciences, in fact has an even wider application, for it is manifesting itself with equal clarity in both mathematics and biology [p. 171]."

MATERIALIST DIALECTICS AS A METHOD

In the previous quotation from *Capital,* Marx describes the dialectical method in terms of four critical terms. Not in their order of occurrence, these were "material," "actual movement," "development," and "inner connection." If we try to clarify the implications of each of these terms, the significance of the materialist dialectical method becomes apparent.

Material

The use of the word "material" to refer to the object or phenomenon of study, whether Marx intended it or not, has the convenient double effect of specifying both its immediate referent, namely the objects or phenomena for study, and simultaneously labeling their mode of existence. For Marxism, as is well known, the material is all that which exists outside of human consciousness and independently of it, in other words, objectively. Materialist dialectics begins by making the realist assumption that the world exists independently of any knower and the concomitant epistemological assumption that this objective world is knowable. Thus Lenin writes in *Materialism and Empirio-criticism* (1927):

"Matter is a philosophic category which refers to the objective reality given to man in his sensations—a reality which is copied, photographed, and reflected by our sensations, but which exists independently of them [pp. 101–2]."

Motion

The "actual movement" of objects and phenomena of which Marx speaks in his description of materialist dialectics refers to the methodological premise that matter exists only in motion and manifests itself through motion, and must be analyzed as such. In other words, all concrete objects and processes in reality are conceived to be mere manifestations of forms of the motion of matter, where motion is conceived of as any change, change in general, including all process from mechanical displacement to human thought. As Engels (1958) stated regarding materialist dialectics:

"Nothing is absolute. It reveals the transitory character of everything and in everything; nothing can endure before it except the uninterrupted process of becoming and of passing away, of endless ascendancy from the lower to the higher [p. 363]."

This characteristic of the materialist dialectical method brands it as inherently focused on change and on the explanation of stability in the midst of change.

This is a characteristic it shares with structuralism, since the positing of structural models is also an attempt to make some sense out of phenomenal variability, to achieve some stability in the midst of change. Thus, for example, Paul Weiss (1971) in discussing his essentially structural view of the biological system makes stability in the midst of change a definitional characteristic of "organization." "The salient feature of the 'organized' state," he writes, "is that the overall features of this pattern [of relations] are essentially invariant, whereas the behavior of the components varies greatly in detail from case to case and from moment to moment [p. 33]."

Development

An important distinction must be drawn between motion as change, as variability of component units, and motion as development. Development implies not only the systems property that relative stability and identity be maintained over some period of time in the midst of component variability but that, in addition, a modification, a conversion of identity must occur. Identity must, in fact, be transformed into other identity (that which is both the same and not the same as that which was), and this transformation must occur as a conversion of the form of the motion of matter from one form into another. This alteration in the form of the motion of matter is what Marx referred to as "development."

The forms of the motion of matter are considered to be interconnected and insep-arable. One form can be transformed into another. The lower forms of motion are necessarily contained in the higher forms; but higher forms are not reducible to lower, since higher forms are characterized by their own systems of laws, determining their own particular qualitative features.

These qualitative features in the motion of matter are what give rise to what we recognize as sensible objects and phenomena. Thus in the continuous pro-cess of material change, in the midst of constant motion, there is identity, achieved as moments of relative equilibrium or rest. This equilibrium is relative because it exists only among specific objects and phenomena in relation to other objects and phenomena in a certain group, at a given level of reality while, in fact, all matter always remains in motion. Motion is absolute; rest is relative. "An object arises in motion, while rest fixes, as it were, the result of motion, in consequence of which this object is preserved for a certain time and remains what it is [Afanasyev, 1968, p. 62]."

This concept is much the same as that found in the genetic structuralism of Piaget (1952, 1971). For example, Piaget employs the term "reflective abstrac-tion" to denote the process in which an operation that organizes one level of application is rediscovered at a second more general level and, in organizing this new level, enriches and integrates the previous level by combining it with new elements. Thus a continuity and coherence are maintained in development while simultaneously allowing for the production of novelty.

Furthermore, such structures define only relative periods of constancy and identity in the child's psychological functioning, tending toward a state of equi-librium. A "structure d'ensemble," for example, is a period of relative and not absolute stability, that is, it represents stable structures only when viewed at the macro level as a totality. When taken in terms of its constituent substructures which exist at lower levels, macro-stability is no longer evident. The young child's intelligence never stops developing; but certain structures at certain lev-els at certain points in time achieve relative stability.

Inner connection

Inner connection in Materialist Dialectics refers to what is often considered the heart of the method: the analysis of the general laws and categories of motion and development of nature, human society, and thought as a process of the re-solution of internal contradictions inherent in all objects and phenomena. This analysis consists in the search for that which conforms to the three laws of ma-terialist dialectics, namely, the unity and struggle of opposites, the transforma-tion of quantity into quality, and the negation of the negation. These laws are, in turn, based on the application of a number of basic philosophical categories.

LAWS AND CATEGORIES OF MATERIALIST DIALECTICS

Law I: the Unity and Struggle of Opposites

Opposites are "the internal aspects, tendencies, forces of an object, which are mutually exclusive but at the same time presuppose each other [Afanasyev, 1968, p. 94]." Typical Marxist examples of this opposition are the wave-particle nature of light, the positive-negative nature of the atom, and the associative-dissociative nature of the chemical bond. It is the inseverable interconnection of these aspects that makes up the unity of opposites.

This is the cardinal principle of dialectics and it is easily found in at least one of the contemporary structuralists. For Piaget (1952), intelligence is organization and adaptation in mutual contradiction. Functional adaptation can only occur through and be guided by organizational structures in intelligence; structure, on the other hand, is formed and altered by the exercise, the functioning of intelligence. Within adaptation, Piaget discloses another dialectical contradiction. Adaptation is regarded as the unity of two other mutually contradictory functions: assimilation, which is the conservation of the organism's structures at the expense of the alteration of the environment, and accommodation, which is the alteration of the organism's structures in conformity with the requirements of the environment. In actuality, any adaptive act of intelligence is both accommodative and assimilative and any form of intelligence is both organized and adaptive.

Law II: The Transformation of Quantitative into Qualitative Change

Quality is that which makes an object what it is. It is whatever allows us to distinguish it from other objects. It is, in other words, some invariant system of features that is made manifest through a number of properties (e.g., size, density, malleability, etc). Although properties of this kind characterize the object *from one aspect only*, quality, as a system underlying a set of properties, carries the general idea of the object as a whole.

Quantity reflects the degree of development or intensity of each of the individual properties that characterize an object. With quality, quantity forms a unity—a representation of two aspects of the same object. The second law of dialectics addresses itself to the nature of this unity. When quantity is altered within certain limits, no transformation in the object as object is wrought; however, if quantitative change is of sufficient magnitude, then such change can pass into a change in quality, that is, the object may be effectively changed into another, into a new object. It acquires new characteristics and becomes subject to new laws to which it formerly did not conform. Such qualitative changes do not come about gradually but occur suddenly with a definite leap. The prime and oft-quoted example of such change is the state transition in physics, that which occurs, for example, with the conversion of water into ice or steam through sudden leaps at specific points in a purely quantitative continuum, that is, temperature.

One aspect of the materialist dialectical definition of quality and, hence, of qualitative change which should be emphasized is that, although its specification of quality in terms of properties seems to suggest an almost empiricist view of qualitative change as occurring in the interrelationship of observerable facts (namely, properties), at the level of those facts, quality in the Marxist view is definitely not a conglomeration of properties but is, instead, something that underlies and is made manifest through those properties. This, it may be argued, is a structural concept. It is structure that underlies properties, that makes the object what it is, and that changes when qualitative changes occur.

Once again in the work of Piaget (1952), in his dialectical treatment of sensorimotor development, we find the conception of quantitative change passing over into qualitative change in alterations of a purely quantitative sort in the equilibrium relations between assimilation and accommodation leading, with full equilibration at a given level, to a sudden transition from the current to the next higher stage of functioning and to a new higher state of disequilibrium, which must then itself be reequilibrated.

Law III: The Negation of the Negation

This third law of dialectics prescribes that the dialectic analyst seek change in the replacement of the old by the new (negation), and the re-replacement of the new by the newer still (negation of the negation), which would reinstate aspects of the old but at a higher level than they existed in the old. Since objects and phenomena are internally contradictory by their nature, they carry within themselves the conditions for their own destruction and transformation into a higher form. This transformation, or negation, retains something of the old, assimilates it, and raises it to a higher level in creating the new. In its turn, the new is then itself negated (a negation of negation); and, in this process, there is a certain return to the old, but at a higher level. Thus development proceeds in a spiral with stages being repeated, but on ever higher planes.

A prototypical example of negation of negation in Piaget (1952) is the equilibration (i.e., negation) of a state of disequilibrium during the period of a given stage, followed, at the point of final equilibration, by a new higher disequilibration (negation of the negation) at a new higher stage. Examples of the use of this developmental analytic technique are not common, however, in Piaget nor, apparently, among any of the structuralists.

One of the implications of the principle of the negation of the negation is that development never ceases. It is a continuous process. This is not a view to be found among structuralists as a rule. For Lévi-Strauss (1968), for example, whose emphasis on language as "the source and content of human thought has dictated an emphasis on the completed systems of thought, which have developed over the ages, are shared by all members of a culture, and can be simply transmitted to the young (Gardner, 1970, p. 357)," the genesis of structures, the continuing development of human thought, is relatively unimportant. For Piaget the stage of formal operations appears to be the pinnacle of human thought, a state of final equilibrium from which further development is unnecessary. He bases this position on the fact that formal operational thought is characterized by the logical manipulation of propositions according to operations that conform structurally to "both a full and complete lattice and a full and complete group [Flavell, 1963, p. 212]" integrated within one completed structure. Presumably, once this level has been achieved, the individual's cognitive capabilities are structurally complete. Although he may continue to integrate new content into his cognitive repertoire, the form in which this knowledge is assimilated, the forms of thought, will not be further altered. For all practical purposes, cognitive development (as distinct from learning) ceases at this point.

For dialectical materialism with its emphasis on the unceasing nature of development, this characteristic of Piagetian structuralism is somewhat problematic. It appears to lose sight of the most fundamental characteristic of human thought just at the precise moment when it becomes most important, that is, thought *is* dialectic. Soviet psychologists and epistemologists refer to thought as the "subjective dialectic." In their view,

"If the subjective dialectic is a reflection of the objective dialectic [the real world, matter in motion] and this latter is in eternal, contradictory movement and change . . . then the subjective dialectic must reflect . . . [this] eternal, contradictory movement and change [Blakeley, 1964, p. 58]."

However, since

"The essence of the objective dialectic lies in the fact that the objects of the real world are not rigidly isolated from one another, that a thing can pass over into another thing—even into its 'opposite' or 'contradictory,' . . . the forms of thought—concept, judgement, and reasoning [as reflections of objects in the real world] must [also] pass over into one another in harmony with the movement and change of the objects they reflect [Blakeley, 1964, p. 58]."

This continuing, contradictory, alteration and development of the forms of thought is referred to by Marxist scholars[3] as "dialectical logic"; and they view it as encompassing, enriching, and integrating formal logic much the way Piaget views formal operations to encompass, enrich, and integrate concrete operations (see Riegel, 1973b).

Categories of Materialist Dialectics

In addition to the general laws, materialist dialectics encompasses a number of philosophical categories. These are concepts that it employs to supplement the laws of development in the analysis of objects and phenomena. Like all concepts, the philosophic categories are forms "of thought in which are reflected the most general, essential and necessary properties, characteristics, and qualities of real things and phenomena [Andreev, in Blakeley, 1964, p. 55]." Furthermore, their development is viewed as the end product of the history of human experience, labor, and knowledge in which man, through his practical activity, cognized reality, discovered its essential properties, and perpetuated his knowledge by incorporating it into the shared sociocultural-conceptual heritage.

For our purposes, the categories of importance (although there are others) are "essence," "phenomenon," "reflection," "refraction," "practice," "socioculture," and "language."

Essence and Phenomenon ● "Essence" is the principal, internal, relatively stable feature of the totality of aspects and relations that constitutes a phenomenon. The nature of the phenomenon is determined by its essence from which all of its other characteristics follow. "Phenomenon is the outward, direct expression of essence, the form in which it is manifested [Afanasyev, 1968, p. 141]." These two concepts stand for realities that are in dialectical opposition to one another. Essence can only be made manifest phenomenally; phenomenon requires essence for its existence as it is. Phenomenon is the surface level of real-

---

[3]It is very important to note that the nature and role of "dialectical logic" vis-à-vis formal logic has been a subject of continuing debate in philosophical circles in the Soviet Union. At the time of Blakeley's (1964) writing, a substantial contingent of Soviet thinkers accepted only the notion that the content of a concept could reflect the objective dialectic. According to them, "the logical forms of thought are the stable framework of every mental process. . . . To maintain that the forms of thought reflect the real contradictions of the objective dialectic would mean to abandon any possibility of distinguishing logical validity from inconsequence [Blakeley, 1964, p. 59]." One might suggest that an appropriate synthesis of these extremes ought to take the distinction between transformation within a system of change (but not development) and development as the alteration of the system *as a system* more seriously. Formal logico-mathematical structures may not only be adequate but necessary for the description of closed systems of such transformations; and the mature human mind most certainly can and does, operate on logical propositions. The critical question is whether or not such activity alone can form the basis for the development of man's thought, which continues throughout his lifetime (see Riegel, 1973).

ity, the empirical sense data level, the individual properties and aspects of objects. Essence is the same phenomenon, the identical numerous properties, aspects, relationships, and so on but in their most stable, internal, general form.

In summarizing the nature of these categories, Afanasyev (1968) notes:

"Essence is necessarily revealed in each phenomenon, but not fully, only a certain small part of it. Phenomenon does not exhaust essence, but presents it from one aspect only. . . . Essence is not seen on the surface, it is hidden and cannot be directly observed. It can be disclosed only in the course of the prolonged, comprehensive study of an object [p. 142]."

Thus Marx (1968) wrote:

"If the form of manifestation and the essence of things coincided directly, every science would be superfluous. It is the task of science to reveal the essence, the internal, deep and underlying processes behind the multitude of phenomena, outward aspects and features of reality [p. 352]."

It is hard to imagine a clearer, more concise statement of the structuralist undertaking, the simultaneous analysis of several levels of reality in order to arrive at an explanation for the constellation of phenomena. Marxism is, as Goddard (1970) has pointed out, "a progressive stripping away of the outer forms of the real . . . in order to reveal and progressively verify the skeleton, the immanent structure of the real [p. 370]"; and it is this search for underlying essence that characterizes both Marxism and the structuralist platform. This is evident, for example, in the position taken by Lévi-Strauss in his criticism of Radcliffe-Brown's (1924) analysis of kinship systems. For Radcliffe-Brown (1952), explanation lies only in ordering empirical facts, in the analysis of data that are immediately observable. This is the denial of any "essence" in the Marxist sense, of any reality beneath the level of the phenomenal real. For Lévi-Strauss, on the other hand, "the realities investigated through the structural models are structural realities [Goddard, 1970, p. 377]." Lévi-Strauss (1953) distinguishes between them as follows.

"Reality and concrete reality . . . In my mind, models are reality and I would even say that they are the only reality. They are certainly not abstractions . . . [as Radcliffe-Brown had referred to them] but they do not correspond to the concrete reality of observation. It is necessary, in order to *reach* the model which is the true reality to *transcend* this concrete appearing reality [p. 115]."

Here Lévi-Strauss uses the term "concrete reality" as materialist dialectics uses "phenomenon" and "reality" as materialist dialectics uses "essence." The approach is much the same, although Lévi-Strauss' interpretation is distinctly non-Marxist in its identification of models with reality.

Reflection, Refraction, and Practice ● The primary source for the elaboration in materialist dialectics of the concepts of "reflection," "refraction," and "practice" is Lenin's (1909) *Materialism and Empirio-criticism.* This work is a critique of the writings of a number of Russian Marxists who, following Avenarius (1888) and Mach (1905), had adopted the main tenets of empirio-criticism. Their contention was that man has direct and immediate knowledge of only his sense impressions. Objects and phenomena that appear to him as independently existing are merely mental symbols of complexes of those sense impressions in states of relative equilibrium. Lenin criticized this positivistic view from the standpoint of materialism and insisted on the reality of the material world in independence of a knower. Sensation, Lenin argued, is a "reflection" of the external world:

"Our sensation, our consciousness is only a representation of the outer world ... [and] it is obvious that although a representation cannot exist without someone for whom it is a representation, the represented thing exists independently of the one for whom it is a representation [p. 47]."

* * *

"Sense perception is not the reality existing outside of us, it is only the image of that reality [p. 87]."

This position of materialist dialectics suggests that for psychology, the content of thought, as the reflection of material reality, has a form of objectivity that lends itself to scientific investigation. If the source and basis of thought is objectively existent reality, then thought can be studied as a reflection of that reality without resort to subjective methods.

Since representations, for Marx-Leninism, are reflections of an objective, independently existent reality, knowledge of reality, of the thing-in-itself, is possible. Thus Engels (1878) and Lenin (1909) accept "absolute knowledge," and "absolute truth" which exists independent of man. Such absolute knowledge is not expressed by any given individual but lies rather in the cultural, historical development of man in general. Human knowledge progresses toward the absolute; while, at any given time, knowledge is relative. Reflection of reality, although accurate in many ways, is not a complete reflection but is continually developing, continually being corrected and refined. Human conception which gives expression to absolute truth does not express it in its entirety, at one time, unconditionally and absolutely, but only approximately, relatively. This is the dialectical nature of man's knowledge. Knowledge is both absolute in its possibility, in the collective end point of development, and is relative in its particular expression in time. "Our knowledge," Lenin (1909) asserts, is not "ready made and unchangeable, but . . . from ignorance, knowledge is gradually built up and . . . incomplete, inexact knowledge becomes more complete and more exact [p. 77]." "For Engels," Lenin notes, "absolute truth is made up of relative truths [p. 106]."

As far as dialectical materialism is concerned, therefore, "there does not exist a fixed immutable boundary between relative and absolute truth [Lenin, 1909, p. 107]." Knowlege is a process of continuous change. Cognition is "the transformation of the thing-in-itself into the thing-for-us [Lenin, 1909, p. 93]." Thus, "for the materialist, the world is richer, livelier, more varied than it actually seems, for with each scientific step taken in advance, new parts of it are discovered [Lenin, 1909, p. 101]." This process of discovery, the process whereby we *approximate* to the cognition of the objective is, however, historically conditioned, despite the fact that the existence of the truth toward which we progress is not at all conditioned. Materialist dialectics, in other words, "recognizes the relativity of all our knowledge, not in the sense of the denial of objective truth, but in the sense of the historical conditions which determine the degrees of our knowledge as it approaches this truth [Lenin, 1909, p. 108]." The implications of this view for a materialist dialectic psychology are obvious. Psychology must study human thought in its genesis, in its formation, and this investigation must recognize that development occurs within a set of concrete socio-historical conditions and within an objectively existent physical world.

We have already implied in this discussion of reflection, that is, in the notion that reflection is never complete but continually develops through a process of correction and refinement, the dialectical contradiction of reflection, namely "refraction." This notion, implied in Lenin (1909) and developed by S. L. Rubinstejn (1959) in the principle that he termed "dialectical-materialist determinism [Rubinstejn, 1959, p. 7]," is "a general theory, applicable to all parts of the material world . . . [which] . . . is formulated as follows: the outer cause works through and is refracted by the inner conditions of the object on which it acts [Payne, 1968, p. 75]." The implications of this principle for psychology are quite clear. Human thought must be conceived as the product of the interaction of the individual with the outer world. Exogenous forces can work only through endogenous factors. "The effect of the agent is modified, refracted by the inner characteristics of the thing on which it acts, so that the end effect is to be explained by the combined action of the agent and the thing acted upon [Payne, p. 105]." Reflection and refraction are two sides of the same process. On the one hand, the form and content of thought is determined by the external world; on the other hand, the effect of the external world is determined by the inner characteristics of the form and content of thought.

Once the notion is accepted of a progressive historical approximation (both by the culture in history and the individual in ontogenesis) to an accurate reflection of reality refracted through the inner characteristics of the knower, the question immediately arises as to the criterion by which the truth of reflection is to be judged. This criterion, for dialectical materialism, is "practice." Thus Lenin (1909) quotes Engels to the effect that "the success of our actions proves the correspondence of our perception with the objective nature of the object perceived [p. 109]." "From the standpoint of life," Lenin continues, "practice ought to be the first and fundamental criterion of the theory of knowledge . . . (though we must not forget that the criterion of practice, in the nature of things, neither confirms nor refutes completely any human presentation) [p. 113]." The implication of this view is that knowledge and human activity are mutually interdependent. Knowledge acts to guide and direct the activity by which man alters his surroundings. Activity in the surround acts to correct and develop man's knowledge.

For a dialectical psychology, this implies that thought, already shown to be susceptible to objective study as the reflection of an objective reality, is also open to investigation as it is expressed and formed in the practical activity of man. By an objective analysis of man's activity, science can arrive at an understanding of human thought. Correlative to this view is the further principle that for psychology the study of activity in its relationship to developing intelligence is not only useful as a means of achieving an understanding of that intelligence but is essential in and of itself. An introspective psychology of thought alone, in other words, is as incomplete as is a behavioristic psychology of action.

Anyone reading the above who is also familiar with the Piagetian perspective must, I think, be rather struck with the numerous parallels that exist between the materialist dialectic point of view and that espoused by Piaget. Both are fundamentally interactionist, conceiving of cognitive development as determined by the interpenetration of activity (practice, assimilation) guided by the internal characteristics of the individual (refractive principles, assimilatory schemes) with a reality guided modification of those characteristics under the influence of the environment (reflection, accommodation). Both approaches accept the reality of an external world; and, for both, knowledge of that external reality becomes progressively more adequate with development.

Despite these similarities, there are subtle but fundamental differences in emphasis between the two positions that have had a number of very important consequences for the further elaboration and differentiation of their respective views. First we briefly consider one important source of this difference in emphasis; and then we explore certain of its implications.

When two opposites such as the external environment and internal organization interpenetrate in a dialectical unity, they presuppose one another in a mutual interdependence. Nonetheless, one or the other term of the interaction may be given relatively greater emphasis or primacy without doing violence to the basic notion that is implied in "interdependence." This tendency to regard one of the two terms as primary appears to be the case with both materialist dialectics and Piagetian theory; but the terms which receive that relative emphasis in the two respective views are not the same. For materialist dialectics, even though intelligence is a unity of reflection and refraction, it is the environment (exogenous factors), through reflection, that is given the leading role. This epistemological primacy of the external, objective dialectic, the movement from object to subject, parallels the materialist-realist ontology in dialectical materialism which accords the primacy of being to objects in existence independent of human thought.

Piaget, on the other hand, although also asserting a mutual interpenetration of assimilation and accommodation in the adaptational process, has accorded the leading role in his theory to assimilatory structures. Thus he views the origin of both experience and reason in the coordination of the subject's actions, in movement from subject to object, and this in turn depends on underlying biological coordinations given in the genotype—on endogenous conditions.

It is important to reemphasize that both positions are interactionist. Materialist dialectics is no more pure empiricism than Piagetian theory is pure maturationism, but their respective emphases on one or the other of the terms in the interaction are different, and this colors the relation that they bear to one another in a number of important respects. For example, for materialist dialectics, the progressively deeper and more adequate correspondence between subjective knowledge and the objective known is based on the nature of the relationship that human thought bears to that reality, namely, that thought, in relation to reality, is reflection. As such, it has its roots firmly implanted in the external world. This is manifest in three sets of relations that constitute thought as the reflection of reality.

At the phylogenetic level, human thought is the evolutionary end product of a long process of the development of reflection as a property common in different forms to all matter. Thought is the highest realization of this reflective property. Thus thought has its revolutionary roots in the objective dialectic; and, consequently, it must reflect that dialectic and reflect it more adequately than do lower forms of reflection, for example, sensation in lower animals.

At the ontogenetic level, alteration in both the content and forms of thought is dependent on the reflection of the content and forms of reality. This reflection occurs through the concepts, judgments, and rational processes which allow the subject to penetrate beneath the variability that exists at the level of the phenomenal real to the underlying essential qualities that structure the temporary stabilities we know as objects. Thought, in other words, although its reflection of the objective dialectic is never perfect, depends on that dialectic for the development of the very forms of thought that permit a deeper, more adequate cognition of reality.

The third tie between human thought and external reality is apparent in the fact that thought, although subjective, is itself a real phenomenon depending on underlying material-neural activity for its existence. As such, it must obey the general laws of all material processes, namely, the laws of the dialectic; and this also guarantees it a certain correspondence to the form of the objective dialectic.

For Piaget, however, emphasis in understanding the increasing adequacy of the cognitive constructions of the subject with respect to the characteristics of the world to which he must adapt has thus far been placed primarily (though in no sense entirely) on the relationship that human thought bears to its biological heritage. All living systems, in Piaget's view, are characterized by the property of self-regulation; and logico-mathematical thought represents the fullest realization of that property. It is by means of increasingly more complex and integrated structures—generalized, reversible operations—that man becomes able to systematically manipulate reality internally, varying certain properties and holding others constant *in thought,* in order to penetrate below the level of phenomenal variability to the essential structures of reality.

The key to comprehending the nature of the progressive deepening of knowledge for Piaget, however, does not primarily lie, as it does for materialist dialectics, in the connections that thought bears to the external world; but rather in the nature of thought as logical and mathematical and in the relation that thought bears to its biological origins. Biological inheritance provides both the initial structures and the driving force for the interconnection of these structures in feedback corrected regulation and, eventually, in the internalized, anticipatory operations that characterize mature thought. This emphasis can be observed in the character of the four factors that Piaget (1969) lists as central to mental development: (1) "organic growth and especially the maturation of the nervous system and the endocrine systems [p. 154]"; (2) experience in the form of "(a) physical experience, which consists of acting upon objects in order to abstract their properties (for example, comparing two weights independently of volume); and

(b) logico-mathematical experience, which consists of acting upon objects with a view to learning the results of the coordination of the actions (for example, discovering empirically that the sum of a group of objects is independent of their spatial disposition or the order in which they are counted) [p. 155]''; (3) "social interaction and transmission [p. 156]''; and (4) the "internal mechanism . . . of self-regulation; that is, a series of active compensations on the part of the subject in response to external disturbances and an adjustment that is both retroactive (loop systems or feedbacks) and anticipatory, constituting a permanent system of compensations [p. 157]."

The biologically based subject-to-object emphasis of the first and the fourth of these factors is obvious. What is crucial to distinguishing Piagetian theory from the materialist dialectic point of view, however, is to realize that even the second and third factors—experience with objects and experience with people—although certainly interactionist, are given a subject-to-object cast by Piaget. With respect to experience with objects, Piaget (1969) says, "physical experience is by no means a simple recording of phenomena but constitutes an active structuration, since it always involves an *assimilation* to logico-mathematical structures . . . [p. 155]." Logico mathematical experience derives knowledge . . . "from action (which organizes or combines) rather than from the objects; experience in this case is simply the practical and quasi-motor phase of what will later be operatory deduction, which is not to be equated with experience in the sense of action of the external milieu; on the contrary, it is a question of constructive action performed by the subject upon external objects [p. 155]." Similarly, concerning social experience, Piaget notes that "socialization is a structuration to which the individual contributes as much as he receives from it . . . [156]." The action of others, "such as school teaching, . . . is ineffective without an active assimilation by the child, which presupposes adequate operatory structures [p. 156]."

Socioculture andLanguage● The emphasis that Piagetian theory and materialist dialectics place on internal processes and external factors, respectively, leads to another major difference in their approach to understanding cognitive development. This involves the importance of social interaction and, particularly, language as one form of that interaction for the development of cognitive structure. Piaget's emphasis on the biological origins of intelligence leads him to discuss cognitive growth in terms of logical operations whose form (although not, of course, content or ultimate level of development) is relatively unamenable to sociocultural influences. As we have discussed, social interaction, for Piaget (1969), is effective only through predeveloped and already adequate operatory structures. It is, in other words, merely the occasion for learning, for acquiring knowledge content in experience, instead of for the development of cognitive forms.

Language, in Piaget's view (1969), has much the same limitations on its psychological effects as do other social interactions. Although it is part of the general semiotic function as a whole and, consequently, is capable of increasing the "powers of thought in range and rapidity . . . [p. 87]," its essential characteristic is that it . . . "contains a [socially elaborated] notation for an entire system of cognitive instruments (relationships, classifications, etc.) for use in the service of thought [p. 87]." This implies, for Piaget, that "language not only does not constitute the source of logic but it is, on the contrary, structured by it. The roots of logic are to be sought in the general coordination of actions . . . [which] . . . continues thereafter to develop and to structure thought, even verbal thought, in terms of the progress of actions, until the formation of the logico-mathematical operations [p. 90]."

Materialistic dialectics, on the other hand, although certainly as interactionist in its point of view as Piagetian theory, places its relative emphasis on the real, external origins of intelligence. This leads Soviet psychology to view the forms as well as the content and efficiency of thought as subject to the influence of social interaction, particularly social interaction of a linguistic nature (since language is viewed in materialist dialectics as embodying the shared sociocultural experience of man).

This is most clearly perceived in the work of L. S. Vygotsky (1929) who noted the importance of what he termed "cultural mediators" (of which language is the most important) which are employed in social intercourse as socially developed aids in relating to reality and as a primary means by which the child comes to regulate his own higher mental functions. Words and other social mediators (e.g., gestures) possess the unique characteristic, in Vygotsky's view, that they are always a "sign," a reflection of something. By employing such signs, man becomes capable of easily introducing changes into external reality which, in turn, reflect back on and develop his consciousness. By altering his environment, man is able to regulate his own behavior and control his own psychic functioning. He is no longer dependent on the reality of the external situation.

In discussing the ontogenesis of this regulatory process, Vygotsky (1962) as-

[4]Vygotsky's point of view, that all specifically mediated human mental processes arise in the course of social interaction, has been criticized by contemporary Soviet psychologists (Leontiev & Luria, 1968) for counterposing "too sharply the various forms of conscious activity of social origin with 'naturally formed' mental processes [p. 342]."

serted that all[4] specifically mediated human mental processes arise only in the course of social activity, in the process of cooperation and social intercourse. Psychological functions at first shared between two people, in particular between a child and an adult, become the internalized psychological processes of one person (in particular, though not exclusively, the child). Thus the *structure* of mental processes may at first be present in man's external social activity and only later become internalized as the *structure* of his inner mental functions. The paradigm example of this process involves language. Language arises and is structured in the process of adult-child communication. From this communicative function, an egocentric, speech-for-itself, function differentiates and is restructured. This is then eventually internalized as the structure of inner speech or verbal thought.

Conclusion

The Soviet view of the importance of social interaction and language for cognitive development is, as is shown, diametrically opposed to that of Piaget (1969). The source of this difference, as I point out, lies in the relative emphases given to the two different terms of the subject-object interaction by Soviet psychology and Piaget, respectively. These differences are theoretical. They are statements that reflect the two schools' differing hypotheses concerning the primacy of real psychologically important relationships. As such, they are, to some extent, falsifiable (cf. Piaget, 1969, for discussion of empirical data that bears on his claim that logic is prior to language).

Differences of this kind should be sharply distinguished, however, from much of what is common to Piaget and the materialist dialectic approach underlying Soviet psychology. These similarities—such as the notion that cognition is structured, that development conforms to the laws of the dialectic, that change is absolute and rest relative, that the development of intelligence is an interpenetration of assimilation and accommodation, refraction and reflection, that structural changes occur as stepwise reorganization, and that knowledge becomes progressively more adequate—are meta-theoretical. As such, they are not falsifiable. They exist as products of a conceptual method that both Piaget and materialist dialectics share in common with a number of other theorists who are working in other domains (Lévi-Strauss, 1963; Chomsky, 1965; Weiss, 1971; Jakobson, 1968; Foucault, 1966; and Ashby, 1952). This is the method of structuralism—a method that, although in existence since at least the time of Marx, has only recently become one of the most generally employed and important conceptual tools of the human sciences.

PART TWO

Cognitive

CHAPTER 3

Structuralism in Cognitive Developmental Psychology: Past, Contemporary and Future Perspectives

WILLIAM R. LOOFT AND CYRIL P. SVOBODA

Structuralism has been viewed by some as a fad (Boileau, 1970; Gardner, 1972). However, we believe that it is more than the posture Lévi-Strauss assumes in his disputation with Jean-Paul Sartre. It is also more than a scientific paradigm (Kuhn, 1962). Structuralism is a broader perspective. Its analyses apply to several disciplines, including anthropology, linguistics, epistemology, psychology, and mathematics, and to a new field that Bateson (1972) has designated the "ecology of mind." To indicate the durability and scope of this point of view, we prefer to speak of structuralism as a *mentality*.

A mentality provides an interpretative point of departure and emphasis from which new explanatory models of experience follow. Furthermore, a mentality does not come from one source only, nor does it pertain to only one part of experience. Structuralism, therefore, represents not the development of a single insight but the integration of several insights. To complete our explanation we list some principles that are synthesized in a mentality, that is, ones that are employed but not yet fully comprehended.

A first principle is that any "whole" has a greater capability than the sum of its parts. Structuralism is a holistic mentality which emphasizes that the power of any entity resides in the *integration* of its parts, not merely in their temporal or spatial contiguity. An example of this principle might be seen in our explanation of the structuralist mentality. One who employs such a perspective interprets experience in determined ways, but not to any one of the component insights but to all of them as integrated in this particular *Weltanschauung*. Cassirer (1944) has shown that language is not just a cognitive activity but the amalgamation of conceptual, emotional, logical, scientific, and poetic activities. Man is not a mind entombed in a body, but a synthesis of material, mental, social, and environmental forces (Svoboda, 1971).

A second principle of structuralism emphasizes that the parts of any "whole" are structurally integrated, that is, in a definite pattern of organization. Physicists have come to view the atom as an organization of electrons and protons orbiting around a central nucleus rather than as an aggregate of electrons in a magnetic sphere (Andrade, 1957). Sociologists describe society as a macrosystem composed of interdependent functional and structural subsystems (Johnson, 1960). Anthropologists consider culture as a "whole" which synthesizes the political, artistic, religious, scientific, and humanistic behavior of any community (Varene, 1970). From a structuralist perspective a scientist either observes or infers that his subject of investigation is composed of distinguishable parts which are interrelated in a union.

A third principle posits that reality is dynamic, not static. Previously the Eleatic view regarded the universe as filled which unchanging entities. Any observed change was considered to be accidental or a matter of opinion, not substantial or essential. The modern scientific mentality focused on operational patterns and movements, but its accompanying metaphysical persuasion produced no change in the view of static essences of the various objects observed. Such is not the picture of reality projected by modern structuralism. (However, we shall describe later how contemporary forms of structuralist analyses assume two forms—the static, ahistorical approach, and the dynamic, developmental approach.) Although no structuralist cosmology has yet been developed, it could be expected to emphasize the dynamic nature of this cosmos.

A fourth principle maintains that change is a patterned process from an initial stage of simplicity through intermediate stages of increasing complexity. Just as the structuralist does not explain the intricate constitution and replication of any species as a chance event, so he does not explain growth and development or any process of change as a mere happenstance. Although structuralists do not advocate identical processes of development for each member of any species, they do insist on a definite order of stages or phases through which growth proceeds. Teilhard de Chardin (1959) speculated that all life forms develop toward goals of "centro-complexity" and the whole of creation is itself developing toward a Point Omega. Piaget (1950) and Kohlberg (1969) restrict themselves to cognitive and moral development, but both project a similar process through stages of progressive complexity or sophistication.

A fifth principle states that the source of any dynamism is not single but multiple. An individual entity is viewed as an integrated composite of distinguishable parts, and the mature behavior of any individual entity is attributed not to one force but to the interplay of several forces. Human behavior is the conjunction of material, mental, environmental, and social forces. Likewise, structuralists view dynamic behavior as a reciprocal union of a developing response to a developing need; as an organism responds to a need, it develops a capability to respond more subtly to a more demanding need. As the response develops, the need increases in demand—from objects at hand to objects no longer present to objects in no sensorily observable form. Structuralists regard behavior as a series of developing responses to a set of needs influenced by the confluence of several forces.

The Origins of Structuralism ● To understand the implications of structuralism for the study of cognition, we attempted to reach behind their second-order plane and infer the first-order rationale underlying the research (cf. Peters, 1965). Although we run the risk of oversimplification, we consider structuralism as the third mentality to provide an interpretative framework within which cognition can be studied. All three mentalities have produced a different concept of cognitive activity.

The earliest mentality was developed in ancient Greece. This culture revealed an order and permanence in a world that appeared both confusing and changing. Both order and permanence were thought to reside in the unchanging forms (the Platonic view). The distinguishing features of any existent collected together form its essence. This inner core remained substantially the same in the midst of the accidental changes of the existent. By attending only to the distinguishing features of objects, man was able to construct classification schemes with which he could group some things as similar and others as dissimilar. This *essentialist mentality* created an image of a world filled with unchanging essences that one could categorize and arrange into a logical hierarchy.

The concept of cognition associated with the essentialist mentality introduced a dualistic split between subject and object. In the act of knowledge both the knowing-subject and the known-object are obviously distinct. But if these two were separated, knowledge healed the breach by building a link between subject and object. The unchanging essential forms of the world introduced themselves into a mind where they were apprehended: for Plato through remembrance of former perfect forms, for Aristotle through a more complicated process. Corresponding to the hylomorphic constitution of the world (matter/form), Aristotle proposed that the mind is twofold: active, illuminating intelligible forms of things encountered, and recipient, apprehending illuminated forms. The locus of impulse of knowledge was largely external to the mind, residing in a blooming, buzzing world that clamored for apprehension. Although the mind could make judgments, they were always about things that it had first experienced. And the judgments were mostly analytical and deductive.

Aristotelian thought eventually degenerated into a closed system in the schools. In reaction the Renaissance unleashed many new insights that eventually were woven into a new mentality. Descartes absolutized the chasm between matter and spirit. Scientists could study the material world liberated from theological inhibitions. Francis Bacon reacted against the speculative methods of deduction by advocating empirical methods of induction. The object of the new studies was not the world of unchanging essences, but the world as it operated according to its own set of laws. The resulting mentality still reflected order and permanence. All things fit together as if in a perfect machine, obeying a constant set of laws. Whereas in the essentialist mentality the world is classified, in the *operationalist mentality* the world is regulated.[1] In both views the world is composed of eternal forms and is obedient to rigid laws.

Against this background, we now outline a concept of cognition in which the activity of the mind is emphasized. Descartes diverted attention away from intelligible forms, which act on the mind, to the clear and distinct ideas that arise in the mind. Kant argued that we cannot know things as they are in themselves but as they appear to us under forms and categories that are logical prerequisites of knowledge. Both of these men preserved the dualistic split between the subject and object, but with Leibniz the locus for cognitive activity was firmly placed inside the subject. And thus the stage was set for a new, synthesizing mentality to appear. For the essentialists cognition emphasized the contribution of the object: through intelligible forms. For the operationalists cognition emphasized the contribution of the subject: through its own forms and categories. There was need for a mentality that would emphasize union. The promise of dualism had been exhausted, and man had now to solve all the dichotomies he had posed for himself. Neither the essentialist nor the activist mentality could help man with these; both perspectives were rooted in analysis and separation.

The new mentality of structuralism also returns to reality as experienced, where a source of unity is found in consciousness that presents data indiscriminately from within and from without. Philosophies of vitalism, existentialism, and common sense signaled a recovery of life, not as it is conceptualized, but as it is lived. The most prominent feature of life is unity, both internal and external. Individual objects encountered are complex units of several parts. All the units perceived exhibit a unity with one another. The focus of this mentality emphasizes relations both within individuals and between individuals. The world is an integrated system, composed of a number of subsystems, which themselves are syntheses of systems.

Cognition deals with neither the intelligible constitution of the object nor the

---

[1] As to be explained further below, the term operationalism is used in a broader sense than originally introduced by Bridgman (1928).

rational operation of the subject. Rather, it takes reality as presented in consciousness. In this return to experience the dualistic breach between subject and object is repaired. Brentano, Husserl, and Merleau-Ponty advocated their phenomenological method as the means to comprehend the world as experienced. Earlier philosophers reasoned that because man can assume the stance of a detached observer, he must be separate from the world—perhaps even superior to it. Phenomenology brings attention to consciousness, uncovering it as a process within which the many data are assimilated into its complex structure and by means of which one person realizes his relatedness to others.

We have presented a progression of three mentalities. All of them are perspectives on the same world, although each emphasizes or ignores facets different from the others. Subsequently, there are different sets of questions legitimate and proper to each perspective. *Essentialism* and its hylomorphic concept of cognition address the questions of natures and ranks; they produce various classification schemes and a hierarchical "chain of being." *Operationalism* and its intellectualistic concept of cognition properly respond to questions concerning parameters of functions; man has discovered the "laws of nature" and has developed reliable research methodologies. *Structuralism* and its phenomenological concept of cognition deals with relationships; they uncover interrelated systems extant in this world.

Philosophers of science typically argue that questions legitimate for one mentality are not proper for another (Kuhn, 1962; Overton & Reese, 1972); however, there are also those who insist that because of historical progression, the kinds of questions posed by structuralist analyses are more advanced than those inherent in the previous mentalities (cf. Riegel's introductory chapter in this volume). The three mentalities we have portrayed represent three different planes of conceptualization. Each speaks its own language and constructs its own reality. In one respect, structuralism differs from the two former mentalities. They produced an either/or view of the world: A thing was either this or that; an event obeyed either this or that set of laws. Structuralism represents a shift in perspective from either/or to both/and. The structuralist focuses on the bonds that unite parts to one another. The phenomenon of light is both corpuscular and undulatory. Man is mental and material, physical and social. Human development is the conjunction of both individual and historical forces. These are *not* statements about essences or operations, but about relationships. They cannot resolve essentialist paradoxes and operationalist anomalies. The mentality of structuralism and the phenomenological concept of cognition are the theoretical foundations for contemporary cognitive developmental psychology.

STRUCTURALISM IN CONTEMPORARY COGNITIVE DEVELOPMENTAL PSYCHOLOGY

Piaget's Constructivism ● In Piaget's theory (1970b), the form or the structure of thought, not its content, is what is of consequence. Of the two basic epistemological alternatives within structuralistic thinking, Piaget has unequivocally cast his lot with the constructivistic orientation, as opposed to the other form, which emphasizes ahistorical, static organization. In his own words: "To call on essences to furnish the virtual with its underpinnings is to beg the question [1970b, p. 67]." *"There is no structure apart from construction,* either abstract or genetic [1970b, p. 140]." For the constructivist, reality is not an aggregate of preformed structures; rather, its nature is one of a continual reconstruction of itself. Primary concern is for the etiology and genesis of structures, or the nature of the passage from one structure to another.

Also human knowledge is fundamentally active: To know an object is to act upon it. The roots of logical thought are not to be found in external organizations such as language but in the coordination of actions—the basis of "reflective abstractions." In Piaget's analysis, structure and genesis are necessarily interdependent. A structure is a system of transformations with operational roots that becomes progressively more adequate in the course of ontogeny.

The first of the three general properties of the structure, according to Piaget, is totality. A system is governed by laws that apply to the total system and, therefore, it cannot be reduced to cumulative elements or aggregates. As an example, there are laws that apply to the system of numbers, for example, associativity, commutativity, and transitivity. The second property of a structure is a set of laws for transformation. There are laws pertaining to the combination of elements, and these structural ties are dynamic, not static. Continuing our example, numbers can be transformed by adding another number to it. The third general property is self-regulation. It is unnecessary to go outside the system to find some external element to carry out the transformation. Moreover, once the transformation has been applied, the product remains within the system. When a number is added to another, one does not have to go outside the series of numbers to find the sum; the result remains within the structure.

The starting point in Piaget's analysis of the development of logical thought is the "coordination of actions" in infancy. As logical structures become constructed—and reconstructed, there occurs an interplay of reflective abstraction, which provides increasingly complex materials for construction, and of self-regulation mechanisms. Some of the structural elements in this process are order relations (e.g., order of movements in the habitual act or in matching the means to the end), subordination schemes (e.g., the subordination of the relatively more simple schema of grasping to the more complex schema of pulling), and correspondences (such as those involved in "generalizing assimilation").

Piaget's theory allows for two distinct but interdependent aspects of thought. The figurative aspect pertains to processes in their static and momentary forms. Figurative functions include overt imitation, perception, and mental (interiorized) imitation. The operative aspect deals with transformations from one state to another. Intellectual operations are essentially systems of transformations; actions are taken to transform objects or states. Operative aspects are capable of becoming "internalized"; that is, they can be carried out through mental representation and thus no longer have to be acted out overtly. The figurative aspect of thinking is always subordinate to the operative aspect. A state is meaningful only after certain transformations have been carried out or as a point of departure for other transformations (Piaget, 1970a).

The construction of logical structures requires about 12 years and proceeds through four major stages of intellectual functioning. The typical actions or operations within a given stage are not merely superimposed on each other in an additive fashion, but they are organically interrelated by linkages of reciprocal dependence that unite and group them into total, harmonious structures (structures d'ensemble). The final articulation of these structures is not complete until the end of each of the corresponding developmental stages. Flavell (1971, 1972) has provided detailed analyses of the stage-properties and stage sequence properties.

Problems in Piaget's System ● Piaget (1970b) has sharply criticized the archeology of the human sciences proposed by Foucault (1970) for its "negation of the subject to an unprecedented degree." But his own theory has evolved over the past five decades to higher and higher levels of abstraction; the person has dropped out and has been replaced by logico-mathematical structures. Piaget dismisses the notion that his constructivism has brought about the death of the "subject" (as he chooses to call the person). Instead, his concern is for the "epistemic subject"—the cognitive nucleus that is common to all subjects at the same stage after other such elements as the "me" and "individual experience" have been centrifuged out. One is then left with the subject's operations—that which he draws out from the general coordinations of his actions by reflective abstraction.

What, then, is a structure? If structures do not exist in the consciousness of subjects, but rather in their coordinated operational behaviors, a problem seems to arise. How are we to understand the necessary and continual nature of these laws of coordination if the subject does the coordinating, and does so at his own choosing? Piaget replies that, indeed, the subject is the artificer of structures; he makes and conserves them, and thus he is the dynamic aspect of the entire constructive process. This process, however, also includes the process of restoring equilibrium, which immediately imposes a constraint on the subject: His activities or operations must be combined in such a way that they are reversible; any given operation must potentially be accompanied by the inverse operation, which thereby can cancel it. The process of equilibrium inexorably leads to states of equilibrium (i.e., structures) (cf. Chelstowski, 1971). Structures are inseparable from performance, or functions in the biological sense of the word. Thus, if it is to be insisted that cognitive structures can be attributed to a "subject," then it is sufficient for Piaget's analysis to define the subject as the center for functional activity. The riddle of Piaget's structure would be resolved by the dynamization of its own concept.

What Piaget calls formal operational thought begins to emerge during late childhood and early adolescence. The subject can now begin to undertake in combinatorial operations; that is, he can classify his classifications, thus raising his operations to the second power. This yields classes of subclasses and Boolean networks, and there appears what is called the quaternary INRC group, which coordinates the inversions proper and necessary for the reversibility of semigroups of relations. The subject now has the capacity to reason hypothetically and to deduce the consequences which the hypotheses necessarily entail. This form of thinking enables the individual to understand that the actual is only one subset in the total realm of the possible. He can now construct theories and proceed experimentally to find solutions.

Surprisingly, Piaget chooses to end his analysis at this rather early juncture of the life cycle. Of course, it is certainly possible that the human being's final and persisting form of thought appears in adolescence, but this position seems inconsistent with Piaget's constructivistic stance. Piaget himself makes the point: "If it be true that all structures are generated, it is just as true that generation is always a passing from a simpler to a more complex structure, this process, according to the present state of our knowledge, being endless [Piaget, 1970b, p. 62]."

In response to the recurring question, just what developments, if any, occur after mid-adolescence?, Piaget (1972) has recently offered an opinion. Most normal subjects reach the stage of formal operations between 11 and 15 years, but these structures are not applied in the same way by all adults, because of their differing aptitudes and occupational specializations. Piaget further admitted that the various tests of formal operational thought used at Geneva are all of a physical and logical-mathematical nature, and thus they probably are not very general and applicable to persons in other kinds of environment and with other educational histories.

In a recent seminar Piaget[2] commented that he is not averse to studying people beyond the ages of 12 to 15 years, but he believes that this kind of research becomes increasingly difficult to do. "for our purposes," he claimed "studies of adults are completely worthless," for adults do not give spontaneous responses to questions as do children. Furthermore, "if one wishes to continue the study of stages beyond adolescence, the only method would be to use history, for example the history of scientific thought, however, history is always very incomplete." Despite these methodological problems, Piaget has expressed a sensitivity about the significance of post-adolescent development:

"Unfortunately the study of young adults is much more difficult than the study of the young child as they are less creative, and already part of an organized society that not only limits them and slows them down but sometimes even rouses them to revolt [Piaget, 1972, pp. 11–12]."

Formulators of organismic models, including Piaget, have drawn heavily on biological concepts of development. However, these theorists have turned to embryology instead of life-span zoology in their construction of theories of psychological epigenesis (Looft, 1973; Roberton, 1972). Piaget is quick to acknowledge his biological heritage, as indicated by statements such as: "The order of succession of these (mental) stages has been shown to be extremely regular and comparable to the stages of embryogenesis [Piaget, 1972, p. 2]."

The life-span orientation poses challenging problems to the Piagetian theoretician. (Of course, one strategy is to ignore or dismiss this orientation altogether, as many have chosen to do; cf. Flavell, 1970.) Such a theory must be internally consistent for psychological events throughout the entire life span, not just for the first quarter of it. The conceptual delineations handed down from the previous age-segmented psychologies must be reconsidered and a comprehensive interpretation of "maturity" must be provided.

Existing cognitive developmental theories—and especially Piaget's theory—cannot account for the kinds of research findings that are now beginning to appear. Admittedly, to date there is a paucity of data from adults on Piagetian forms of intellectual tasks. The few studies available report results that should not have been obtained according to the strictures of the present theory. [See Hooper, Fitzgerald, & Papalia (1971), Looft (1972), and Riegel (1973) for reviews of this research.] New conceptualization about structural changes in adulthood and aging seems imperative.

The traditional understanding of the concept of development is one of progression, increasing complexity, and expansion. Piaget's theory fits this description well, as do most other organismic theories (with the possible exception of Werner) (Looft, 1973). Claims that certain behaviors are indications of developmental regression or of some form other than that predicted by theory can be dismissed by Piagetians on the grounds that these behaviors are not manifestations of true structural changes; indeed, Flavell (1970) has taken exactly this position. Perhaps the boldest statement to be put forth by a Piagetian would be that there is no ''true'' regression from formal operational structures, and that only temporary regressions could occur, indicative of momentary instability of the equilibrium state. This argument calls on the competence/performance distinction; that is, what we observe are only performance changes, but the underlying competence remains unchanged (cf. Flavell & Wohlwill, 1969; Riegel, 1972b).

If future researchers choose to accept the idea that cognitive capacities might deteriorate in late life, several cautions must be taken. Consistent with Piaget's constructivism, it must *not* be assumed that the individual returns to earlier, childhood forms of logic. The individual's world has changed as he himself has changed. Regression is always a change to another stage as it exists presently in the individual's hierarchy of structures, not to a stage as it existed previously. When ''higher'' structures become dysfunctional, inappropriate, or perhaps even deteriorate, the movement is toward the next most appropriate, functional structures available (Langer, 1969; Looft, 1972). Researchers investigating the qualitative aspects of adult thought must furthermore accept that the operations generating the subject's response are of primary importance; one must not be distracted by the content (as Kohlberg, 1973, now admits was his problem in his earlier interpretation of young-adult ''regressions'' in moral judgment). In the words of Turiel (1969), ''. . . the conditions causing regressive change may not be the same as those causing progressive change [p. 113].''

In conclusion, we emphasize that the growth of mental structures parallels the growth of the individual's social world and biological structures. In later life, with the nearly inevitable loss of social supports and with bodily deterioration, perhaps there occur accompanying cognitive structural changes. The greater the variety of situations to which the child must accommodate his operational structures, the more differentiated and mobile these structures become; the concurrent processes of social disengagement and physical decline in late life may accordingly spell less differentiated and less mobile cognitive structures.

PERSPECTIVE FOR THE FUTURE

Undoubtedly, Piaget will long influence the thinking of theorists and researchers in cognitive developmental psychology. His adoption of the constructivistic approach permits a far more powerful analysis than the static, ahistorical methodologies. Nevertheless, we retain a sufficient amount of skepticism, which is expressed in the following summary.

First, Piaget's system seems all too sheltered and oblivious to many other factors that influence mental development. In drawing parallels between Piaget and Freud, El'konin (1972) has suggested that Freud's orientation was almost exclusively "child-society," while Piaget's orientation has been "child-object." Consequently, a dualism has evolved, with those persons who have been influenced by Freud pursuing developments within the need-motivational sphere, and those influenced by Piaget preoccupied with cognitive, intellectual developments. Freudians study the mechanism (such as substitution and displacement) for the child's adaptation to a "world of people," while Piagetians concern themselves with the intellect as an adaptive mechanism to a "world of things." This duality in developmental theorization is at least partly responsible for the isolation of the two major institutionalized processes of socialization that adults impose upon children—education (for intellectual growth) and child-care (for affective growth) (cf. Looft, 1971; Riegel, 1972).

Second, Piaget's restriction to the study of cognition and to the periods of childhood and adolescence stunts a fully developed, structuralist system. If the dynamism that structuralists attribute to reality is a permanent property, it does not inexplicably wither at some arbitrary time. If it is short-lived property, its temporality demands some explanation. The ignoring of cognitive structures fashioned after a certain period in life is a human decision, not a logical conclusion. Structuralist change is a process that resides in the vitality of life itself. As long as there is life, there is change in forms that develop from past forms.

---

[3]The argument can be made that what appears to be intellectual regression in old age is not regression at all; it is a new stage of thought, indeed, a progression. The constant effort of making fine cognitive differentiations diminishes in importance, and the individual once again can merge his ego with nature. This is exactly the position offered by Hall (1922) and by Eastern philosophers (cf. Feagan, 1972).

Third, a structuralist should not ignore the contribution of many influences in generating developmental dynamism. Piaget limits himself only to the study of cognition. But he seems to consider that activity solely as the processing of logico-mathematical principles in more sophisticated forms or structures. The contributions of social, environmental, biological, or personal factors are largely ignored. An essentialist or operationalist might identify and isolate these factors as separate from one another; a structuralist mentality demands that a place be given to all simultaneously. Cognitive activity can be conceptualized as a function separate from affective or social activity, but it is not experienced as separate.

CHAPTER 4

General Systems, Structure and Development

WILLIS F. OVERTON

Originally, my aim in this essay was to describe and explore the major features of general system theory and to relate them to current structuralist and developmental considerations in the field of human behavior. However, while analyzing both the literature of structuralism and that of general system theory, I became impressed, and at first a bit dismayed, with the diverse interpretations applied to each of these concepts by various authors. In fact, at times it appeared that the only unity within each concept was that provided by the label itself. An example of this problem is particularly evident in two recently edited works on general systems (Buckley, 1968; Klir, 1972). These volumes illustrate a gamut of approaches from Bertalanffy's organismic view through cybernetics and information processing theories to various mathematical treatments and, ultimately, to a behavioristic account of perception and language by Osgood.

To the cynical observer this might imply that general systems and structuralism have attained the popularity of catch phrases and have also either achieved or are at the precipice of the ultimate mark of all catch phrases—vacuousness. But such a judgment is both too harsh and too simple, for on a deeper reading it is possible to discern in this literature several recurrent themes which suggest that the diverse interpretations are the products of implicitly held basic and incompatible positions concerning the very nature of the explanatory process.

The various accounts thus reflect both underlying unities and schisms, and the nature of them go beyond specific content to the philosophical prerequisites for the understanding and explanation of object and events. In very specific, if sometimes implicit ways the concepts of "structuralism" and "general system theory" have been formulated within the determining context of general world views, such as the organismic and mechanistic world views (see Overton and Reese, 1973; Reese and Overton, 1970) and, as such, the concepts themselves have come to reflect the struggles over assumptions of holism versus elementarism; emergence versus reductionism; organized versus simple complexity; and other corollaries of these basic metaphysical and epistemological positions.

If this analysis of the literature is correct, then attempts to understand the nature of a general system theory approach or a structuralist approach, as well as any attempts to establish relationships between them, require a prior understanding of the specific paradigms, models, or world views within which each is constructed. Meaningful relationships between concepts can occur only to the extent that each is generated from within the same general model. For the mixing of models leads to ambiguities and the vacuousness of catch phrases mentioned previously.

The following discussion relates structuralism and general system theory by exploring their paradigmatic origins. As a first step, we examine structuralism and raise the question as to why one would choose to embrace such a view. Various answers to this question will illustrate paradigm differences concerning the nature of structuralism. We give similar consideration to the notion of general system theory and compare the latter with structuralism. Along with the examination of each of these views, the emphasis or lack of emphasis placed on the change or developmental dimensions is explored.

STRUCTURALISM

At a minimum, structuralism is a general approach or method employed in the understanding and explanation of various phenomena. It has been explicitly applied across disciplinary boundaries as diverse as anthropology, linguistics, mathematics, and psychology and, as an essentially content-free method, it may have, in fact, been less self-consciously employed in virtually every field of human understanding. The hallmark of the approach is a commitment to going beyond an observational level and constructing models to represent the assumed underlying organization of the objects and events under study. Thus, in terms of acknowledged structuralists, Piaget, as a psychologist, has constructed logical models termed ''groupings'' to represent the classificatory and relational behaviors of children at approximately ages 6 to 11. Lévi-Strauss, in anthropology, has constructed models of social structure to represent various ways in which individuals interact. As Lévi-Strauss stated:

''The term 'social structure' has nothing to do with empirical reality but with models which are built up after it . . . social relations consist of the raw materials out of which the models making up the social structure are built . . . [1973, p. 271]''.

The *organization, form, or pattern of the phenomenon under study constitutes its structure* and, hence, the structuralist attempts to represent this feature. The particular content is irrelevant for the study to be a structuralist enterprise. Content may range from the structure of the atom, or a molecule such as DNA, to the structure of behavior, society, or the cosmos (e.g., Whyte, Wilson & Wilson, 1969). Thus, as J. J. Thompson proposed that the structure of an atom be thought of as not unlike plums in a pudding and Rutherford later eclipsed that view by constructing an atomic structural model analogous to the orbits of the planets about the sun (Guillemin, 1968) and, as Copernicus and Tycho vied over a view of the organization of the solar system as heliocentric or geocentric (Gingerich, 1973), each was employing a structuralist approach in his particular discipline.

It is exactly at this point, however, that the meaning of structuralism teeters on the brink of vacuousness. For if structuralism merely involves a commitment to representing the abstract regularities of objects and events, then it is not a very unique orientation, but rather one that is virtually universal in the sciences as well as in other forms of knowledge-building activities. Viewed in this way it is simply an "inferred entities" analysis (Wartofsky, 1971) which, if we use psychology as an example, is undertaken in some manner by most theorists in their attempt to understand and explain behavior and its development. Individuals who differ as widely in their views as cognitive theorists like Piaget ("scheme," "operation"), George Kelly ("personal constructs"), social learning theorists like Bandura ("internal representational processes") and W. Mischel ("self-regulating systems and plans"), and learning theorists like Kendler and Kendler ("mediating response") and Osgood ("mediating response") all propose some types of inferred entities in their systems. In fact, even those who take instrumental-conditioning approaches (e.g., Gewirtz, 1971) recognize the inferred entities of other approaches but view them as mere conventions, more relevant to the pre- or extrascientific "context of discovery" than to the "essential" scientific activity of verification (Reichenbach, 1938; 1951).

If "structuralism" is to have any distinct meaning, it cannot merely be in the sense of method, for in this sense, depending on the tenor of the times, everyone could well claim to be a structuralist. A situation of universal structuralism might be acceptable or not, depending on one's perspective, but if a concept means everything it also means nothing and, as such, it is not worth the trouble to explore. Rather than consigning "structuralism" to this fate, I suggest that the concept does have a distinct meaning or distinct meanings but that these meanings have to do with the *assumed* or *postulated* status or nature of "structures" rather than whether or not they are introduced in the scientific enterprise.

Structure as Primitive or Derived

Stated most simply, the particular distinctive meaning of "structuralism" is a function of whether "structure" enters the theoretical system as a primitive or derived construct. To the extent "structure" is introduced as a primitive construct that plays a *necessary* role in the explanation and understanding of objects and events, a structuralism develops that is defined in terms of a deep commitment to critical-idealist philosophical traditions. These include commitments to function or activity as primary over substance; to emergent holism; to dialectic causation and change; and to various constructivist epistemologies. These various commitments, among others, constitute a basic metaphysical system or world view, and it is within its framework that the structuralisms of Chomsky, Piaget, and Lévi-Strauss have been elaborated.

On the other hand, to the extent that "structure" is asserted as a derived concept that, in principle at least, could ultimately be reduced to more basic concepts and, hence, plays either a temporary role or no role in explanation, a structuralism develops that has deep commitments to realistic, empiricistic philosophical traditions. Commitments to this perspective include the acceptance of substance over activity as primary; an atomistic elementarism; simple one-way causation and linear change; and "copy" theories of knowledge.

Holistic versus Elementaristic Structuralism

Examples of "structure" abound that yield what might best be termed *holistic structuralism* as against *elementaristic structuralism*. Piaget's theory of cognitive development is a particularly straightforward illustration of holistic structuralism, although many critiques and competing views have been presented from an elementaristic structuralist point of view.

To understand Piaget's theory as an example of holistic structuralism it is necessary to work backward from the assumptions of the theory to its philosophical metatheoretical base. This yields the prerequisites for any holistic structuralism, and these prerequisites constitute the form for which Piaget's specific theory is one content. In addition, this permits the elaboration of issues that ultimately answer to the question of why one might choose to assert a structuralism.

The most basic assumptive commitment of Piaget's theory is to the primacy of activity. This is reflected in the theory itself through concepts such as "assimilation," "accommodation," and "equilibration" among others. It is also most succinctly captured in the assertion that "the being of structures consists in their coming to be, that is, their being 'under construction' . . . *There is no structure apart from construction* [activity] (Piaget 1970a, p. 140).'' This statement, in turn, is a rather faithful reflection at the theoretical level, of the relationship between Being and Becoming—an issue that underlies any theory as a philosophical foundation. That is, at the level of metaphysics, which constitutes the framework within which theoretical statements are constructed, there exists and has continued to exist throughout the history of human understanding, the issue of whether the nature of the universe, including man, is best understood or *represented* as basically static or active (Heisenberg, 1958). The choice of one or another of these basic categories has a contextual or formative influence on how all other subsidiary categories are constructed. Thus, for example, the choice of "static" resulted in the formation of the Newtonian mechanical world view, which *represented* all bodies as ultimately static and inert. The choice of "activity," on the other hand, is more compatible with some forms of modern physics which assert that, "since mass and energy are, according to the theory of relativity, essentially the same concepts, we may say that all elementary particles consist of energy. This could be interpreted as defining energy as the primary substance of the world. . . . Energy is in fact that which moves . . . [Heisenberg, 1958, p. 70–71].'' (See Overton, 1973 and especially Overton, 1974 for an elaboration of this view.)

The choice of static leads directly to the "analytic ideal" of science. That is, once the object is taken as primary, understanding proceeds by breaking the object down into its ultimate constituent simple elements. The simple elements are then related in unidirectional and linear causal sequences. But understanding proceeds quite differently if activity is chosen as basic. In this situation the choice is to find being in becoming, constancy in change, stability in instability. Here, as Lovejoy stated, "objects of sense and even of empirical scientific knowledge are unstable, contingent, forever breaking down logically into mere relations to other things which when scrutinized prove equally relative and elusive [1936, p. 25].'' To understand a universe thus represented has been the task of dynamic philosophers from Leibnitz to Hegel to Cassirer, Whitehead, and Merleau-Ponty. To understand more limited spheres of phenomena thus represented has been the task of holistic structuralism in the various fields of human understanding. The task itself generates a program of logically related requirements, which we now describe.

The first requirement of a holistic structuralist program is the specification or definition of the activity (functions) of the phenomena under study. The second requirement entails the rational discovery (i.e., representation) of the organization of the activity. That is, the problem is to impose order and organization on the activity and thus establish a workable stability, or momentary constancy in the face of change. This does not in any way deny the basic dialectic nature of the universe, but rather it asserts the necessity of conceptualizing organization for complete understanding.

The significance of the recognition of an organization or system should be immediately apparent, for form or organization is the "structure" to which structuralism makes reference. Furthermore, it is at this point that we can demonstrate the necessary relationship between holism and structuralism understood in this way (see Lane, 1970). The process of understanding does not cease with the imposition of a structure on the phenomena, instead, it proceeds with an examination of the relations between the general system and various subsystems or structures similarly defined. But since the parts or subsystems are themselves understood only in the context of the posited general organization, it is quite useless or meaningless to attempt to introduce, within this framework, the previously mentioned analytic ideal. The whole or organization is here necessarily, not contingently, prior to the parts. This is not a question of whether one *might* decompose the whole or organization or structure into independent elements and their relations but, rather, a metatheoretical postulate that one will not proceed in such a fashion. To assert that someday in some way someone will find an appropriate method for applying the analytic ideal to all organizations is quite simply an assertion that derives from a very different category system. It is much like attacking ideas of Euclidean space from a non-Euclidean perspective.

The ideas of holistic structuralism then are based on the views of the universe as activity. From this perspective the organization or structure of the phenomena is not reducible to something else but, instead, it is a representation of the flux of everyday particulars. Structure is a *primitive construct* in the sense that it is given as a basic explanatory construct. Thus, the introduction of the category "structure" or "form" (Merleau-Ponty, 1963) also reflects what Lovejoy (1936) called the attitude of "other worldliness" and Hayek (1969) and Weimer (1973) referred to as "the primacy of abstract categories." That is:

"Particular 'facts' can only be known as instances of abstract, theory-determined, thing kinds. What we are 'presented' with by the construction of experience is neither concrete nor particular. Particulars depend for their very existence on the primacy of abstract categories [Weimer, 1973, p. 21]."

Structures or forms then are not properties of a physical reality, at least not in holistic structuralism. "In the final analysis form cannot be defined in terms of reality but in terms of knowledge, not as a thing of the physical world . . . [Merleau-Ponty, 1963, p. 143]." To assert that structures are properties of a physical reality is to maintain that the static object is basic and that structure is nothing other than elements of the object and their relations. From such a stance, structure then would be a derived construct which would not be employed to explain but would itself be explained by other constructs. This is the position of *elementaristic structuralism*.

The Program of Holistic Structuralism

To return directly to the understanding of phenomena from a holistic structuralist perspective, the first requirement of the program is to specify the activity or function of the phenomena; the second is to introduce structure or organization or system and analyze subsystems in the context of more general systems. The problem of the analysis of subsystems or substructures, however, also leads to the question of how structures are to be best represented and this ultimately results in the question of the role of a formalism in holistic structuralism. Structures can be represented either in conceptual or logico-mathematical terms. Piaget's theory gives examples of both. In his earlier work, he placed emphasis on verbal conceptual descriptions of structures through concepts such as "egocentrism," "syncretism," and "pre-causality." His later emphasis, however, was displaced to logico-mathematical descriptions involving concepts of "operations," "groups," and the like (Flavell, 1963).

Any movement from conceptual representations to logico-mathematical representations is a movement toward the introduction of a formalism into the structuralist method. The advantages of a formalism consist in greater explicitness and precision. However, there are also disadvantages. One such disadvantage is that the interest in formalism itself may come to obscure the basic function (activity)—structure problems. In examining the field of structural linguistics, Blumstein has analyzed this issue:

"The formal machinery developed has to a large extent become the major theoretical question . . . The formal machinery has become more and more complex, all in the name of simplicity. Moreover, it is not clear whether this formal apparatus reflects the actual structure of the system or the formal apparatus itself . . . Although formalization of underlying structures may be essential to understanding the actual system to be described, formalism is *not* the major objective of a structural analysis. Rather it is the insight to the structure of the system which a formal approach may give [Blumstein]."

A second disadvantage is that a formalism may sometimes inadvertently, sometimes intentionally, reintroduce an elementarism into a holistically understood system (see Brainerd, 1973 and Van den Daele, 1974, as examples). This

is accomplished by the acceptance of the mathematical system as the best representation of structures. A mathematical system is composed "of a set of elements (e.g., numbers, points, vectors, matrices, etc.) and the precisely specified
relations among them [Rapoport, 1972, p. 46]." Hence, a mathematical system
is often accepted as the vehicle par excellence for the reduction of the whole
to elementary parts and relations. The use of a mathematical system as a vehicle
of reductionism or elementarism is, in fact, one of the major traditions of Western atomism going back to Pythagorean philosophy (Wartofsky, 1968); the
other being the physical atomism of Leucippus and Democritus. A contemporary example of mathematical atomism is evident in Pylyshyn's interpretation
of Chomsky's linguistics.

"Chomsky's work is permeated with the belief that the secrets of the universe . . . are as Galileo said, 'written in the language of mathematics . . .'
(This) means that those aspects of the universe that are ultimately comprehensible . . . are comprehensible precisely because one can see in them a structure
that is *essentially mathematical* [1972, pps. 547–548]."

An awareness of this problem of formalism was demonstrated in Piaget's
metatheoretical considerations of the "limits of formalization" (1970a, p. 32).
In these considerations, Piaget discussed Kurt Gödel's discovery that formal
systems which are rich enough to contain elementary arithmetic are themselves
incapable of demonstrating their own consistency and are basically incomplete.
Piaget's claim was that the discovery demonstrates the impossibility of a mathematical or logical atomism. The basic idea is that the systems or structures at
any given level are incomplete and consistent only in terms of the next higher
(more general) level. But this is, in fact, a restatement of the very assumption
of holism and a reaffirmation of the primacy of the abstract. It is doubtful that
any solid elementaristically oriented scientist would accept such a view. Indeed,
it is axiomatic that he would not and, therefore, the constant and ubiquitous
tension between holism and elementarism continues.

A final requirement for the holistic structuralist program is the consideration
of the relation between *diachronic* and *synchronic* dimensions of the basic activity. The diachronic refers to the growth or development of the phenomena under
consideration. It is, in essence, the organization, or order, of the phenomena
through its history. The synchronic refers to the momentary organization or
structure (see Piaget, 1971). The issue of significance is whether it is more appropriate, with reference to explanation of the phenomena, to posit a single general structure or system that remains invariant across history or to represent the
event as a series of ordered structures. For example, is the course of human

behavior best understood by a single structural system or by a series of structures that themselves have an order? Many modern theories of information processing, Chomsky's linguistic theory, Gestalt theory, and Lévi-Strauss choose the former alternative while Piaget maintains the latter.

In summary, the philosophical priority of activity over objects generates a holistic structuralism that is a metatheoretical program for understanding, and it entails: (1) a specification of the activity; (2) a representation of the organizations of forms (structures); (3) an ordering of the general forms (if the diachronic dimension is accepted); and (4) analysis of subsystems or structures in the context of the more general structures. This, of course, is not the complete program for understanding because in itself it does not come to grips with the empirical world or world of the senses. This will be further elaborated as Piaget's specific theory of cognitive development is outlined as a particular representative of the general conceptual program of holistic structuralism.

Piaget's Theory of Cognitive Development as a Holistic Structuralism

In addition to content which consists of the child's understanding of physical concepts of space, time, object, number, causality, and the like, Piaget's theory of cognitive or intellectual development is composed of three major components or dimensions: (1) a functional component, (2) a structural component, and (3) a stage component (Overton, 1972). The functional component, as stated earlier, reflects Piaget's basic commitment to activity. Indeed, the very definition of intelligence within the system involves activity rather than static states. "In telligence is an adaptation" (Piaget, 1963, p. 3) and "adaptation" along with "organization" constitute the two given biological unchanging and always present functions or activities of the system. "Adaptation," in turn, is defined as the more specific twin activities of "assimilation" and "accommodation," and intelligence is further defined as the relation of equilibrium between these activities. Thus, in conformance with the holistic structuralist program, Piaget takes the phenomena of interest and begins by *asserting* or *specifying* the functions of the phenomena (the growth of intelligence) under study. The difference between such an initial step, and an approach such as Guilford's (1967) is obvious. Guilford, and others in the psychometric tradition, although discussing "the *structure* of intellect," begins with attempts to break this object (intelligence) into its smallest component parts.

In addition to specifying the activities (functions) of organization and adaptation, as well as the constituent activities of assimilation and accommodation, Piaget further posits the "equilibration process" as the active developmental dimension that accounts for the order (diachrony) of the forms which are described by the structural dimension of the theory. As he describes it, "the development of cognitive functions consists, above all, of a process of equilibration [Piaget 1967, p. 107]." Going beyond the metatheoretical holistic structuralist program and into the level of theory, the various activities provide the primary explanatory concepts for the specific ontogenesis of the particular structures described by Piaget. That is, the answer to the question of how cognitive structures develop is that they develop through the activities of assimilation and accommodation. The answer to the question of why there are successive new cognitive structures is given by the equilibration process which asserts that structures are directed toward the highest level of equilibrium possible (Piaget, 1967).

With the specification of activities as assimilation and accommodation along with the equilibration process it should be clear that any stability or being must be found in becoming, and this leads to the structural component of the theory. In fact, structures are defined as *"the organizational forms* of mental activity" (Piaget, 1967, p. 5 emphasis added) and as self-regulating *systems* of transformation (Piaget, 1970a). The holistic commitment is announced time after time as he stresses that:

"Wholeness is a defining mark of structures . . . all structuralists . . . are at one in recognizing as fundamental the contrast between *structures* and *aggregates,* the former being wholes, the latter composites formed of elements that are independent of the complexes into which they enter. To insist on this distinction is not to deny that structures have elements, but the elements of a structure are subordinated to laws, and it is in terms of their laws that the structure *qua* whole is defined. *Moreover, the laws governing a structure's composition are not reducible* to cumulative one by one associations of its elements: they confer on the whole, as such, over-all properties distinct from the properties of its elements [Piaget, 1970a, p. 6–7, emphasis added]."

Also, and more tersely, "structure is a totality; that is, it is a system governed by laws that apply to the system as such, and not only to one or another element in the system [Piaget 1970b, p. 22]."

The primary specific structural concepts employed by Piaget in the theory are "schemes" ("the structure or organization of actions . . ." Piaget, 1969, p. 4); "operations" ("the form of internalized actions . . ." Piaget, 1960, p. 33); the organization of operations into logico-mathematical "groupings" ("a certain form of equilibrium of operations . . . organized into complex structures . . ." Piaget 1960, p. 36) and the "group" ("the 4 group, combining inversions and reciprocities into a single system . . ." Piaget, 1969, p. 140). Each structural concept is employed to represent the stability entailed in actions (either overtly or in thought) such as searching, manipulating, combining, separating, relating, and so on.

The next task is that of ordering the general forms or structures, and this is carried by the stage component of Piaget's theory. To order the forms requires the introduction of a principle of order, that is, the equilibration process, which defines the direction (from less to greater mobility and stability of forms) and provides a criterion for the assertion that the various forms are distinct. The criterion of distinctiveness is the particular law of the whole or systemic properties of each general form. Thus action schemes obey laws of coordinated actions, schemes of thought entail laws of symbolization, concrete operations involve logical reversibility, and formal operations demonstrate combinatorial laws. Another way of stating this is to say that each general form is a level of organization that has distinctive systemic properties (not reducible to other levels), and the levels are arranged, not according to time, but according to their mobility and stability. When this part of the metatheoretical program is translated into the theory itself, it defines levels of organization or general forms as stages and yields the theoretical "sensori motor," "preoperational," "concrete operational," and "formal operational" sequence.

It should be noted here that the general holistic structuralist program requires only the representation of structure while a diachronic interpretation requires levels of organization and their order. The specific structures and stages, on the other hand, are theoretical and empirical concerns. Thus, for example, it would be possible for empirical inquiry to determine that few individuals demonstrate the behaviors related to the formal operational structures. Such findings would, from within a holistic structuralist perspective, lead to the conclusion that either the particular structural representations chosen by Piaget are inadequate or that there are no new organizations beyond the concrete-operational level. Acceptance of either alternative would truncate Piaget's particular theory but would leave the holistic structuralist approach untouched. Similarly, the theoretical description of even more advanced structures beyond the stage of formal operations (see Riegel, 1973) would be a theoretical elaboration (provided it occurred within the context of the equilibration process) of Piaget's specific theory, not an attack on structuralism.

On the other hand, any *assertion* that the structures and stages of structures are *simply* descriptions of complex behaviors that can ultimately be shown to be the products of the combination of simple elements reflects an elementaristic structuralism (see Bowers, 1973). Examples of this latter approach, in addition to the previously mentioned work of Guilford are: Gibson's (1969) perceptual theory, which places structure external to the organism and maintains that the perception of structure is ultimately a result of discrimination learning; Gagne's (1968) learning theory, which similarly asserts that higher order cognitive structures (higher-order rules) are ultimately a result of discrimination learning; and Mischel's (1973) personality theory which, while accepting ''self regulating systems and plans'' as significant explanatory constructs, eventually maintains that these and other similar constructs ''cannot be adequately understood without linking them to the cognitive social learning conditions through which they developed and are maintained . . . [Mischel, 1973, p. 278].''

The analysis of subsystems or structures in relation to more general structures, the fourth requirement of holistic structuralism, occurs in both the diachronic dimension and the synchronic dimension of the theory. That is, diachronically, higher level structures are assumed to subsume and transform lower level structures thus forming hierarchical systems of structures. Synchronically, at each level or stage of structures there is an analysis of the specific structure and substructure relations. For example, at the stage of formal operational structures, Piaget (Inhelder and Piaget, 1958) includes analyses of the relationship between the superordinate INRC, a 4-group, and subordinate operatory schemes as well as the relationship of these to more subordinate classificatory operations.

This brief review of the major dimensions of Piaget's theory is undertaken to demonstrate the influence of the holistic structuralist program or theory formation and to suggest differences between this program and an elementaristic structuralist program. Each program is fundamentally designed to understand and explain phenomena, and thus each program defines particular tools of explanation. It still remains to relate the holistic tools of explanation, as reflected in theory, to the empirical world. When the requirement of the representation of structure is translated into the defining of specific psychological structures, and stages of structures in ontogenesis, a number of empirical tasks emerge. For example, as we suggested previously, it is an empirical question whether the specific structures described are adequate representations of the activity. Thus, Lunzer (1965) has maintained that the INRC group does not seem, in any clear sense, related to the scientific activities of the adolescent, and Riegel (1973) has proposed a further set of structures beyond adolescence. Similarly, it is an empirical question whether the specific structures form the particular invariant sequence suggested by Piaget (see Flavell and Wohlwill, 1967).

Furthermore, and most important, as the metatheoretical ideal of structures are translated into the specific structures of ontogenesis, the assertion is generally made that there is, in fact, an empirical progression from one set of structures to the next level or stage of structures. This, in turn, opens the issue of the role of empirical determinants in such a development. From the elementaristic structuralist and nonstructuralist viewpoint there is but one tool of explanation, that is, the stimulus, or antecedent event. Order is ultimately reducible to such events. From the holistic structuralist perspective, the order of development and the order of momentary behavior are conceptual representations, and these representations are themselves necessary explanatory tools—similar in nature to Aristotle's final and formal causes (see Overton and Reese, 1973)—which are not reducible to antecedent events or stimulus conditions. Stimulus conditions as well as biological conditions, from within the holistic perspective, play an important but limited explanatory role. That is, empirical events ranging from training programs to social conflicts, to biological and hereditary events, explain the rate and ultimate level of development but not the order of development. As we stated previously, in Piaget's theory, for example, the explanatory "how" of development is answered by the activities of assimilation and accommodation—in complex interactions with the external and internal environment—and the explanatory "why" is given by the activity of equilibration.

This discussion of explanation leads us back to an important question that was raised much earlier in this essay, that is, the question of why one would choose to embrace a structuralism. From a holistic structuralist perspective, the answer involves a commitment to the idea that understanding and explanation requires more than simple empirical determinants; that explanation requires the conceptual introduction of order as a primitive construct. From an elementaristic viewpoint, a structuralism is merely the temporary acceptance of order or a certain degree of complexity which will ultimately be explained by the single explanatory tool of the nonstructuralist, that is, stimulus conditions (see Skinner, 1974).

Now that the multiple meanings of structuralism have been elaborated and the program of holistic structuralism has been described in the context of a particular theory, we can concentrate on an exploration of general system theory. As will become evident to us, identical distinctions will be found in both areas.

GENERAL SYSTEM THEORY

"A whole which functions as a whole by virtue of the interdependence of its parts is called a *system,* and the method which aims at discovering how this is brought about in the widest variety of systems has been called general system theory. General system theory seeks to classify systems by the way their components are *organized* (interrelated) and to derive the 'laws' or typical patterns of behavior, for the different classes of systems . . . [Rapoport, 1968, p. xvii]."

As this definition indicates, and as numerous other sources confirm, general system theory focuses on organized wholes or systems and explores the nature of their organization. And as Ludwig von Bertalanffy, the generally acknowledgcd father of general system theory, has pointed out, "problems of order and organization appear whether the question is the structure of atoms, the architecture of proteins, or interaction phenomena in thermodynamics (1968a, p. 31)." But "organization," whether at these levels, or at the levels of linguistics, psychology, or anthropology, is also the very definition of *structure*. Thus *general system theory is itself a structuralism*. That is, there is a commitment in this approach to going beyond the observational level and representing the assumed underlying organization of the phenomenon of interest.

Furthermore, as with structuralism itself, there are two divergent forms of general system theory and, not surprisingly, one form—Bertalanffy's—starts from assumptions of the primacy of activity and holism while the other begins from assumptions of the primacy of the static object and elementaristic reductionism. Bertalanffy (1967a, 1968a) refers to these two trends as the *"organismic"* and *"mechanistic"*, respectively, these being labels that refer back to the basic world views within which the trends are formulated (see Overton and Reese, 1973; Reese and Overton, 1970 for an elaboration). Well-known examples of the mechanistic trend include computer simulation approaches, information theory, decision theory and cybernetics, as well as a number of approaches that attempt to impose a mathematical elementarism on various systems (see Klir, 1972 for examples). In the following discussion, we focus on the organismic trend and, specifically, on Bertalanffy's interpretation, while introducing mechanistic considerations as counterpoints of reference.

Bertalanffy's own endorsement of the basic prerequisite of holistic structuralism, that is, the primacy of activity, is clearly articulated in his statement that:

"In the last resort, structure (i.e., order of parts) and function (order of processes) may be the very same thing: in the physical world matter dissolves into a play of energies, and in the biological world structures are the expression of a flow of processes [1968a, p. 27]."

The same commitment along with an explicit acceptance of holism is clearly expressed in his summary of the basic principles of an organismic conception:

"The conception of the system as a whole as opposed to the *analytic* and *summative* points of view; the *dynamic conception* as opposed to the *static* and *machine theoretical* conception; the consideration of the organism as a *primary*

activity as opposed to the conception of its *primary reactivity* [1960a, p. 18–*19*]."

But if general system theory is a structuralism and Bertalanffy's organismic approach is a form of holistic structuralism, it must also be recognized that it has a unique status and makes a unique contribution to the process of understanding. General system theory is, in fact, not a theory at all, at least, not in the narrow sense of that term which entails a particular content or class of events. On the other hand, general system theory is not in itself either the philosophical prerequisite for a structuralism nor the program generated by these prerequisites. Rather, general system theory exists between these two realms. It is a general *interdisciplinary model* which has been formulated in the context of the prerequisites, but rather than being a specific application of the program of structuralism, it attempts to delineate the significant features of all structures, organizations, or systems. Thus it is a general model of organization that, as Rapoport suggested, attempts "to prepare definitions and hence classifications of systems that are likely to generate fruitful theories in the narrow sense [1972, p. 45]." More specifically, general system theory explores structural similarities or *isomorphisms* in various fields of understanding and attempts more precise definitions of structural concepts such as "wholeness," "organization," "teleology," "differentiation," and "directiveness."

The status of general system theory, therefore, is that it is more general than any content area and more specific than the philosophical and metatheoretical assumptions of structuralism. Its value is that it attempts to provide conceptual clarifications about the nature of various systems. In doing this it highlights similar issues that exist across various fields of inquiry, that is, it acts as a vehicle of integration, and provides the conceptual support for elaborating issues within various fields. It is particularly important to recognize this status and value because too often the criticism has been put forth that general system theory has no scientific value because it is not directly applicable to specific empirical problems. Quite simply, the "theory" was never designed for *direct* application, and criticisms of this kind represent a misguided operationalism that depreciates the role of the conceptual (see Bertalanffy, 1962a for other criticisms of general system theory). In the discussion that follows, some of the major concepts of Bertalanffy's approach are described and, where appropriate, the role that these concepts have played in more specific theories and issues are suggested.

Closed and Open Systems

At the foundation of all other distinctions within general system theory is the view that it is reasonable to represent two primary classes of systems, that is, closed and open systems. A closed system is one that is functionally isolated from its environment or, at most, exchanges only energy with the environment. Open systems are those that are characterized by import and export of material as well as energy. Bertalanffy described a gas within a container versus a flame as simple prototypical examples of the closed and open systems, respectively. The gas is totally characterized by the variables of enclosed volume, pressure, and temperature. The temperature and pressure are the same throughout the container and if any external event disturbs this *equilibrium*, the system will, according to the second law of thermodynamics, return to its most probable state.

Closed systems, then, are organizations that are adequately explained by the second law of thermodynamics. This maintains that events tend toward highly probable (diffuse) states or to maximum *entropy* (a measure of probability). Once an event reaches this state, it is at equilibrium. A point of major significance is that it is precisely these systems that are most amenable to mechanical analyses. They are understood according to the analytic ideal previously discussed. Thus, the whole is analyzed (reduced) into individual components and functional relations between them. The relationship between parts of these systems is one of *simple complexity* in the sense that *interactions* between parts may be treated as *trivial* or *decomposable* without doing violence to the system. In addition, the relationships between parts are treated as *linear* or *summative*. In considering the solar system, for example, it is acceptable, for both theoretical and practical purposes, to treat the orbits of the planets totally in terms of the sun and the planet under study while ignoring the complex interactions occurring between the many planets.

Open systems, on the other hand, are systems that through a constant interchange of material and energy with their environment build order and organization. This does not necessarily contradict the second law of thermodynamics but, instead, represents a more general case in which:

"We have not only *entropy production* owing to irreversible processes taking place in the system; we also have *entropy transport*, by way of introduction of material which may carry high free energy or 'negative entropy.' Hence, the entropy balance in an open system may well be negative, that is the system may develop towards states of higher improbability, order and differentiation . . . [Bertalanffy, 1967a, p. 76]

Open systems do not tend toward a state of rest or equilibrium as is the case with closed systems, but they *may* attain a *steady state* that remains constant in time while processes of transportation continue.

In contrast to closed systems, open systems, because of their inherent activity and capacity to build organization, cannot be explained in terms of simple linear causal chains, that is, the twin assumptions of trivial interactions and additivity are not tenable. Rather, the relationship between parts in an open system is one of *organized complexity*, which is characterized by reciprocal or dialectic causality (Overton, 1973; Overton and Reese, 1973). Reciprocal causation of parts yields "strong interactions" (Rapoport, 1966) that are "nontrivial" (Simon, 1965) or nonlinear.

Before we proceed to examine some specific issues that have benefited from the closed-open classification of systems, it will be helpful to be explicit about the "reality" of the classes themselves. It would, of course, be most convenient if one could in some way actually observe members of either category. However, it must be remembered that systems are representations and representations derive, at least in part, from world views. Furthermore, world views purport to account for everythhing and not simply a limited field, for example, closed or open systems. Thus, from a mechanical world view, with its primary static objects and explanatory tools of elementarism or elementaristic structuralism, significant systems are represented as closed and descriptions of open systems are held to be special cases, ultimately to be subjected totally to analytic procedures. An example of this strategy is found in the work of Ashby and cybernetics generally. Bertalanffy (1962a, 1967a) pointed out that Ashby's "machine with input" and other cybernetic models are mechanical conceptions exactly because causality in those systems is represented as unidirectional and linear. The introduction of feedback loops, however complex, does not change this ideal. Rather it simply makes the linearity circular in nature. On the other hand, organismically defined open systems are represented as manifesting the reciprocal causality that was previously suggested.

From an organismic world view, with its primary activity and explanatory tools of holistic structuralism, a similar if inverse strategy is employed. In that instance, open systems are represented as the general ideal and closed systems are represented as a special case. As Bertalanffy articulated the situation, "closed systems . . . represent a special case; for one can always arrive from the theory of open to that of closed systems by equating entropy transport terms to zero, but not vice versa [1967a, p. 74]." The major point at issue here is that ultimate decisions as to the validity of one or the other approach will be a historical judgment made on the basis of fruitfulness and not on the basis of an ultimate, arbitrary reality. Until these decisions have been reached, each perspective will continue to claim the total field and the tension between them will continue.

There are many examples of ways in which open and closed system accounts have been used for further conceptual clarification in diverse fields of inquiry. In addition to the two recently edited volumes mentioned previously (Buckley, 1968; Klir, 1972), *General Systems*, the annual yearbook of the Society for General Systems Research, provides a wealth of examples. Bertalanffy, himself a biologist, primarily explored biological issues in his early works (1960a, 1962b), and in later studies he focused in greater depth on psychological theoretical problems (1959; 1967a,b; 1968a,b). The heavy emphasis on living systems in Bertalanffy's work stems from his position that such systems are uniquely characterized as open. In the material that follows we describe several examples of the role of open system concepts in psychological issues.

An early, if somewhat inaccurate, analysis of personality theories as illustrations of a range of partially to totally open systems was provided by Allport (1960). The major value of this article, which considered stimulus-response theories as the most closed of the theories, is that it interrelated theories, systems, and the issue of being and becoming. Thus Allport demonstrated that to the extent that theories are based on minimum criteria of system openness "they emphasize stability rather than growth, permanence rather than change. . . . In short they emphasize being rather than becoming [1960, p. 304]."

I have analyzed the traditional nature-nurture issue in the context of strong interactions that are descriptive of the organized complexity of open systems. Taking a developmental perspective, I proposed that "the continual reciprocity between genetic and environmental activity occurring before conception, through to the time of testing . . . would constitute a strong interaction, not decomposable [Overton, 1973, p. 86]." This, in turn, leads to a breakdown of analytic attempts to partial out additive components of heredity and environment.

Perhaps one of the best examples of the potential impact of systems concepts in the elaboration of theoretical issues is demonstrated in a series of interchanges between Piaget and Bertalanffy at a World Health Organization conference (Tanner and Inhelder, 1960). The issue involved Piaget's attempts to elaborate, within his holistic structuralist perspective, the concept "equilibrium." Early in the discussions Piaget proposed that the stability of structures and the several stages of structures be thought of as forming a series of steps or levels of equilibrium. Each level of equilibrium would be characterized as a closed system subject to the second law of thermodynamics, although the total form of the system (diachronic dimension) would not follow this law and would instead be characterized by the equilibration process.

Bertalanffy objected that such an equilibrium or *homeostasis* is never characteristic of a spontaneously active system and thus its introduction would imply the acceptance of a mechanical model of man. Bertalanffy further pointed out that active, in other words, open, systems such as the human organism may reach a *steady state*, but in this "time-independent state" regulations are constantly maintained through ongoing reciprocal interactive processes. It is only in closed or partially open systems that regulation occurs through simple feedback mechanisms that, as described previously, are complex forms of linear unidirectional causes.

Piaget recognized the merit of Bertalanffy's argument and since that time has maintained the label "equilibrium" but has asserted that it refers to "stable states in an open system" (e.g., Piaget, 1967; 1971). Also, however, Piaget seems to maintain an ambivalence in his understanding of this view. On the one hand, he has accepted both Bertalanffy's distinction and Waddington's (1971) concept of "homeorhesis." This refers to the idea that what is stabilized in an active system is not a particular value (homeostasis) but, instead, is "a particular course of change in time" (p. 366). On the other hand, Piaget (1971) has also demonstrated a very favorable attitude toward cybernetic feedback systems as basic to the regulations attained by structures. It is this type of ambivalence that has led some individuals to assert that there are strong mechanistic trends in Piaget's theory (see Wilden, 1972; see also chapter . . . "in this volume) or that the theory loses its dialectic origins and becomes static (see Riegel, 1973; Wozniak, 1973; see also chapter 2 in this volume) as later stages of development are considered. Although, if all factors are considered, such criticisms do not seem to reflect Piaget's general approach accurately, they do describe some apparent inconsistencies which require further theoretical elaboration on Piaget's part.

Equifinality, Levels of Organization and Anamorphosis

The open system concepts already described are designed to provide definitions or explanations—in the sense that the subsumption of a specific concept such as "wholeness" and "organization" (reciprocal causality yielding organized complexity) and "differentiation" (entropy transport and negative entropy) becomes feasible. They do not in themselves, however, explain "directiveness" or "teleology." That is, although the idea of entropy transport establishes the possibility of differentiation in a system, it does not introduce a factor that *requires* increasing differentiation. Stated differently, the described open system concepts do not deal specifically with the diachronic dimension of holistic structuralism. Although they account for the order of a system, they do not account for development, or the order of ordered systems.

Bertalanffy has, in fact, been criticized for not introducing a developmental direction into general system theory (Kaplan, 1967). This criticism, however, rather misses the point. Bertalanffy did not deny the importance of the basic idea of diachronic structuralism; that there is a direction to development and that this direction proceeds from initial states of globality to increasing states of differentiation (Werner, 1957), or from less to higher equilibrated states (Piaget, 1967). However, he believed that it is the task of general system theory to provide an account or law for this direction. None has been found as yet.

"Anti-entropic processes are, according to irreversible thermodynamics, *permitted* in open systems, but the latter presently do not contain a law indicating their direction. (The attempt known as Prigogine's theorem, stating that open systems tend toward states with minimum entropy production, holds only under rather restrictive conditions.) [Bertalanffy, 1967b, p. 133, emphasis added]."

As a result, the contribution of general system theory to the diachronic dimension of holistic structuralism has been rather fragmented. The commitment to this dimension is evident in the concept "anamorphosis," which refers to the idea of a spontaneous "transition toward steady states of higher order" (Bertalanffy, 1967b, p. 128). However, this statement does not elaborate anything beyond the general structuralist view of a diachronic dimension itself and the specific theoretical principles of Werner and Piaget. The approach lacks a detailed explanation of the spontaneous transitions. The "states of higher order," on the other hand, are adequately accounted for by principles involving "levels of organization" (Bertalanffy, 1960a, Ch. 2).

Bertalanffy's *principle of progressive mechanization* expresses the idea that while systems are not machinelike they can, to a certain extent, become so. In the course of the specialization of parts that arises out of the undifferentiated wholeness of any open system, the parts lose some of their potentialities and other parts come to dominate the activity of the system.

"Such centers may exert 'trigger causality,' i.e., in contradistinction to the principle, *causa aequat effectum*, small change in a leading part may, by way of *amplification mechanisms*, cause large changes in the total system. In such a way, a *hierarchic order* of parts and processes may be established [Bertalanffy, 1967b, p. 131]."

The hierarchic order is a representation of the various levels of organization. Thus "states of higher order" refers both to a hierarchy within individual systems and a hierarchy across systems (see Whyte, Wilson and Wilson, 1969). For example, in Piaget's theory a structural hierarchy is formed of action schemes at the end of the sensorimotor stage; a structural hierarchy of first-order operations is formed at the concrete operational stage—including the incorporation of sensorimotor structures; and a hierarchy of second-order operations is formed at the formal operational stage. In addition, this series itself forms a hierarchy with sensorimotor structures forming the lowest and formal operations the highest levels of the organization.

A concluding concept that is also relevant to the issue of direction, teleology, and development, is *"equifinality."* This refers to the fact that the same end state or goal may be attained despite different initial conditions and different routes. Bertalanffy denies any vitalist interpretation of this and insists that it is a necessary consequence of processes which occur in open systems as they attain steady states. "The steady state finally reached is not dependent on the initial conditions but only on the ratios between inflow and outflow, building-up and breaking-down [Bertalanffy, 1960a, p. 143]." Bertalanffy also pointed to an important theoretical application of this concept when he proposed that Piaget's stages (levels of organization) be interpreted as equifinal steps (Bertalanffy, 1960b). This account still does not explain the spontaneous transition from one steady state or stage to the next. It does, however, provide an explanatory base for the often cited observation (at least, among nonbehaviorists) that there do not seem to be *specific* experiences that can account for development (see Wohlwill, 1970; Overton and Reese, 1973). Development, within any stage, according to the concept of equifinality could be due to any number of different conditions and, hence, any search for particular antecedent conditions would be fruitless.

Conclusion

This essay explores some of the relationships between general system theory and structuralism, particularly as they are each concerned with issues of development. The description of these relationships requires the recognition that each perspective assumes two forms. One form is conditioned by a mechanical world view which asserts the static object as primary in understanding and, hence, results in an elementaristic interpretation. The second form is conditioned by an organismic world view which asserts activity as primary and, therefore, results in a holistic interpretation. From this analysis it is suggested that holistic structuralism is the superordinate model that generates a program for understanding. Bertalanffy's holistic general system theory, in turn, represents an attempt to more precisely define concepts of holistic structuralism and one that ultimately leads to the production of specific theories such as Piaget's theory of cognitive development.

CHAPTER 5

Piaget and the Structure as Law and Order[1]

ANTHONY WILDEN

When remarking on the fate of new movements, William James once commented that their arrival is regularly greeted with combined apprehension and misapprehension by the proponents of the then dominant paradigm, is furiously attacked, and eventually is explained away.

Inevitably, as a new approach begins to gain influence, there are complaints about the "new jargon" and the difficulty of understanding it, attacks on the writing style of its advocates, and aspersions cast on its ancestry. Whether the movement lies in the field of praxis or of theory—whether it is political, social, or philosophical—the axes of the counterarguments are principally concerned with form rather than content: the critics tend to decry methods and methodology (or the lack of it) and they accuse the movement's advocates of lack of logic, subjective bias, irrationality, emotionalism, impressionism, and the like. However, once a new approach becomes established the counterarguments then shift from suggestions of impending disaster to lengthy explanations of why there is nothing really novel in the new movement.

With social movements, where time reveals their cogency and justness, the process of reaction differs somewhat in its details, but the pattern is the same. Once denials that the state of affairs is what it is have passed through the stage of attacks on the "lunatic fringe," a form of acknowledgment occurs that is merely a more complex form of denial: the cause at issue may be just, but its advocates are too extreme. Its advocates fail to deal with "both sides of the question"; they are suspected of "trying to take over"; they are "overreacting"; and they are in any case "trying to go too far too fast."

[1]For an earlier and in some respects more detailed critique, see Wilden, 1972e, pp. 302–350. Part of the research incorporated in this paper was supported by the environmental systems project directed for the National Science Foundation by W. E. Cooper and H. E. Koenig at Michigan State University. Quotations from English translations of foreign sources (especially Piaget, 1970b) have been modified where necessary.

Past and Present ● The brief experience of the French "structuralist" movement, has not been essentially different from the process described above. However, although we may smile at the truth of James's observation, the critics' demonstration of antecedents is also valid. Where it is lacking as a demonstration is that, because truth is an artifact produced by the nonlinear process through which the instrumentalization of theoretical and pragmatic reality is continually reundertaken by societies in history, the newly discovered antecedents of the new movement in no properly historical sense preceded its emergence. What is said or done in one sociohistorical context cannot have the same meaning or significance as in another, and neither saying nor doing necessarily implies recognition of what is said or done. Hence, the apparent paradox that the antecedents of the new movement did not exist before it. They came into existence with and because of it, arriving "after the fact."

The demonstration does not, therefore, demonstrate what it seems to, that is, a collective "compulsion to repeat," an eternal return in history. Instead, it exemplifies the dialectical nature of human time and human reality: that process through which the pragmatics of life and meaning are repeatedly reordered through systemic emergences akin to "quantum jumps" (Wilden, 1972e, pp. 351–377, 248). This point does not, of course, invalidate the necessity of a continuous archaeology of the past in societies like our own where alienation and exploitation have made academics and scientists necessary. If anything, it reinforces this activity—and not only because the representation of the past in our society goes far beyond the requirement of a myth of origins to explain the present and predict the future (common to all societies), and becomes a rationalization of the activities of a tiny minority.

Just as the discovery of the information-processing capacities of DNA and RNA irrevocably changed the biology of the past, present, and future, so also the American past took on a new signification with the discovery of the American present in the decade that began in 1965—and the entire history of the species was irretrievably reordered by the tortuous revolution in the deep structure of Western society that we call the advent of industrial capitalism.

Deep Structure ● With this caveat, then, we seek to provide an overview of a movement that is still relatively unknown in the English-speaking countries. We shall give particular attention to its representation in the work of someone whose major research preceded its emergence but who claims direct kinship with it: Jean Piaget.

Our task is to consider structuralism at the level of its own epistemological *deep structure,* and in terms of its function inside and outside the boundaries it ascribes to itself. In so doing, we leave aside the *surface structure* of a set of often heterogeneous ideas expressed by a number of different people with conflicting or even opposing positions and, instead, examine some of the common logical and other positions they actually share. The result is that we are soon ensconced in some of the most respected traditions of the theory of knowledge and the science of the nineteenth century. An attempt to deal with the deep structure of the movement—by analogy with the deep structure of a language (which all native speakers employ in speaking without conscious knowledge or understanding of it)—will hardly do justice to the individuals involved. But, then, one of the most profoundly programmed of the assumptions that many structuralists share with the society as a whole is precisely the systematic—but nonsystemic—epistemological individualism that has bowdlerized most social science since the Renaissance.

Analytics and Dialectics ● Much has been made by some commentators, especially anthropologists, of a supposedly radical difference between the style of French theory construction, said to be "rationalist" and "dialectical," and the "analytic" or "empiricist" tradition of the English-speaking countries (Piaget, 1964, p. 119). The assumption of such an epistemological opposition is an indicative example of the failure to distinguish deep and surface structure in philosophy and social science, as well as of a failure to recognize that dialectics does not define a type of logic but rather, a type of ongoing systemic organization in time. The two "schools" are, in fact, united in their acceptance of the fundamentals of the international discourse of science and, above all, of its digital rationalism (Wilden, 1972c, pp. 413–427). The difference between them seems to be that empiricists, like all organisms, live and move and have their being by means of an epistemological construction of the various levels of reality but that most of them would rather not talk about it. The French intelligentsia, on the other hand, seem to the empiricists to talk about it all the time.

Hence, it is the reader familiar with Freud's version of the utilitarian pleasure principle and its direct connection with the psychological basis of modern economics, or with the liberal-conservative political theory of John Locke (Wills, 1969), or with Fechner's attempt to translate physics into biology, or with the long tradition of one-dimensional equilibrium theories in social science who does not find the theoretical base of structuralism as strange as it may have once appeared.

OVERVIEW OF THE STRUCTURALIST PARADIGM

General Characteristics. ● A number of significant characteristics are shared by all these approaches to the socioeconomic ecosystem and the individuals within it. They are, in general, anticontextual and monoplanar, tending consistently to flatten out the hierarchies of order and organization—both ontological, that is, necessary, and historical, that is, contingent—in the biosocial universes. They also tend to establish identities between systems of fundamentally different types by confusing levels of organization; and they set up boundaries in the relations between systems, subsystems, and their environments where, in fact, there are none, while ignoring others that do exist. They tend to use the expression "system," not for a multidimensional organized complexity that is the logical and ontological prerequisite of its "parts," but, instead, for an aggregate of atoms and relations called "organisms" or the equivalent. They confuse the linear causality of physics with the contextual constraints and controls limiting the activities of goal-seeking systems in society and in nature; and they fail to distinguish between succession, development (biological, individual, socioeconomic), evolution (natural and social), and revolution. In general these approaches share with Newtonian mechanics a preference for harmony, balance, stability, and symmetry ("Action and reaction are equal and opposite"). One significant result is the general failure to deal adequately or legitimately with change or with history: all that is not the product of gradualism, great men, genetic programming, or better ideas is the work of outside agitators disturbing something like the natural order of things, the palindromic harmony of the spheres (Wilden, 1972d).

In other words, the privileged world model underlying these and similar approaches is that of the macroscopic physical universe, at whose particular level of complexity the dialectics of ecosystemic communication and exchange do not appear (*pace* Engels—and, of course, Hegel and Lenin—on the "dialectics of nature").

Insofar as this general critique applies to the work of the structuralists, it is not meant to imply that their approach has not provided important insights into collective and individual behavior—Lévi-Strauss's striking analysis of the function of "incest" and exchange, for example, and the new meaning he has brought to the analysis of myth; Piaget's (incomplete) theory of logical-cognitive maturation (Riegel, 1973b); Godelier's elucidation of the double structure of contradiction underlying the analysis of *Capital*; the correlation between metaphor and metonymy in language and condensation and displacement in Freud by Jakobson and Lacan; Bourbakian "parent structures" in metamathematics; Lacan's insights into what he calls the Imaginary (mirrorlike) structures of opposition and identity between human beings; Jakobson and Troubetzkoy's work in phonology (Lane, 1970).

Ideology ● These are insights into sub- or microstructures that may or may not legitimately invite wider applications. The structuralist promotion of digitalized and dualistic symmetries, identities, and oppositions smacks too readily, however, of long dominant patterns in the liberal ideology inherited from the seventeenth century bourgeois revolution in England, and these analyses do not necessarily entail or even encourage any radical break with the dominant epistemology and accompanying ideology in our society. The significance of this observation should surely be self-evident when we consider the events of the last decade or so, for the simplest way to reinforce the deep structure of a social system is to preserve it by change, specifically by allowing for widespread variations in the surface structure (like the many messages possible in English), variations that are, however, dependent on and derived from a general code or repertoire of possibilities which has not changed in any of its essentials.

The dominant values of a culture are reinforced by the invention of a counterculture, for instance, whenever the second is merely a surface-structure subset constrained by the deep structure of the first. Similarly, in spite of many variations, the epistemological foundations of the structuralist paradigm seem to remain subordinate to the general value system represented in the contemporary discourse of science, constrained as it ultimately is by the particular kind of deep-structure commodity relations and exchange values peculiar to industrial capitalism, state and private.

Binary Oppositions ● Originally, the common denominator in what came to be called structuralism was the reference to a supposedly scientific model of structure, drawn from linguistics and derived in part from the pioneering work of Ferdinand de Saussure. This linguistic model was primarily phonological. It, therefore, dealt only with the syntactics of the sound structure, cutting off the analysis of a particular level of selection and combination in language from its systemic relation with the semantics and the pragmatics of language as a whole, to say nothing of the way it divorced linguistics from discourse on the one hand, and from communication, on the other. In this it shared the methodology of quantitative-statistical information theory (Shannon). But it was nevertheless promoted as a model for the analysis of any and all activities in the human sciences. It was supposedly at the base of Lévi-Strauss's analysis of kinship and myth (1958, 1969b), and the mystique generated by the linguistic model was long played on by Lacan, in his important but excessively hermetic rereading of the Freudian texts.

Nevertheless, the basic inspiration of Lévi-Strauss was as closely associated with the beginnings of formal systems, information, and cybernetic theory in the 1930s as with linguistics as such. Its linguistic aspect lay primarily in the methodological tool of the "binary opposition" that apart from being the basis of the digital reversibilities in mathematics, could be employed in a very limited number to account for the acoustic infrastructure of the phonemes in any language. Its translation into the analysis of the algebraic structures of kinship systems, and thence into the analysis of myth, now of course seems like a foregone conclusion (Piaget, 1970b, pp. 18–28, 106–119), and Lévi-Strauss's promotion of the category of opposition as the "fundamental structure" of just about everything has had an extraordinary influence. This is in spite of the fact that (1) he repeatedly confuses the discrete elements already given in discontinuous codes of communication with the nondiscrete differences of continuous or analog codes; (2) he often creates oppositions out of elements that are not of the same logical type and whose relation does not, therefore, have the unidimensional character he ascribes to it; (3) he tends regularly to confuse the symmetrizing "identity of opposites" in Hegel's dialectics with the quite different (because hierarchical) "unity of opposites" in Marx (as does Lenin); and (4) he fails to deal convincingly with the fact that all binary relations are necessarily subsets of triadic ones in which the mediating element (e.g., money in the case of commodities) is not of the same logical type as the dyads whose relation it makes possible.

Although languages are said to "evolve," the changes they go through bear no proper resemblance to natural evolution nor to human history, in both of which we discern an overall process of increasing complexity or organization. In contrast, in linguistic evolution the changes in structure exhibit no particular directionality, and the degree of complexity of a language has never been shown to be related to the complexity of social organization. Neither the synchronic nor the diachronic models of language can be used as adequate models of social or individual states or changes (Riegel, 1974). The inadequacies of most analogies drawn between linguistic or mathematical systems and social and organic systems are the result of a misconception of their common denominator: communication and exchange (Wilden, 1972e, pp. 9–13, 340–341).

Moreover, the myth of the "fundamental nature" of the one-dimensional binary opposition, supported by analogies with the digital computer and the supposedly purely digital (on/off) behavior of the neuron, happens to support the ideology of "fundamental oppositions" in Western society: man/woman, reason/emotion, mind/body, culture/nature, organism/environment, capital/labor, self/other, individual/society, and so on. It is not that these relations do not actually exist as conflicts stemming from the organization of our present system, but that they are neither fundamental nor symmetrical.

Nevertheless, the digital category of bilateral opposition takes on an ontological character in the work of Lévi-Strauss and others. Little or no attempt is made to deal with it from the perspective of a logic of hierarchies (logical types), nor to separate the logical and ontological categories of difference, distinction, opposition, contradiction, and paradox in communication from each other (Wilden, 1972e, 1974a)[2]

Psychoanalysis: Lacan ● Lacan has no difficulty in finding any number of binary oppositions in Freud, the most interesting being the relation between the sounds "o-o-o" and "a" and presence and absence in the play of Freud's grandson, recounted at the beginning of *Beyond the Pleasure Principle* (Lacan, 1966, 1968b; Wilden, 1968). Taking an essential clue from Lévi-Strauss's analysis of the unconscious as a discourse (1958, pp. 198–199); and from his conception of the "symbolic function" in exchange, Lacan has been pursuing an analysis of the "structure (or logic) of the signifier," that is, an analysis of the exchange of signifying units between persons, including the phallus as a "symbolic object," as if they were phonemes or morphemes or both. However, this for all its interest has simply tended to reinforce the material and ideological collusion in our present society between knowledge, power, and words. The phallus is said to be a signifier *(signifiant)*, the "signifier of signifiers," in fact, the reference point for all other such exchanges. Correlatively, the woman is a "lack," providing an essential "empty locus" in the system, one necessary for exchange and circulation to be possible (Wilden, 1972e, 1973b).

The Physicist Model ● Piaget's "genetic structuralism" is similarly, if less obviously, beholden to the same kind of collective value system. In Piaget's case, however, the privileged model has many of the characteristics of the phonological one without being a language; it is mathematics. Interwoven into it are other characteristics derived from phenomenology and his early career as a zoologist: principally his failure to employ an ecological conception of system-environment relations; his tendency to treat the organism and/or person as an entity (rather than as a micro-ecosystem in a whole complex of other ecosystems); his energy-oriented underlying viewpoint (and, hence, his failure adequately to appreciate the role of information and noise in ontogeny, evolution, and ecology); his almost purely digital conception of logic, thought, and communication; and his striking concern to validate a Newtonian model of

---

[2] As Marx put it, speaking of the splitting *(Spaltung)* of commodities into the double form of use value and exchange value: "This double, differentiated *(verschieden)* existence must develop into a distinction *(Unterschied)*, and the distinction into opposition *(Gegensatz)* and contradiction *(Widerspruch)*" [1973, p. 147].

repetition, dynamic equilibration, and symmetry. Besides these factors, one can distinguish the strong Cartesian influence of the subject-object epistemology employed in phenomenology and Freudianism. This in its turn contributes to Piaget's misconstruction of a cybernetic model of "self-regulation."

In the sense that Saussure's structural linguistics can be interpreted to involve a model of "dynamic equilibrium" or "steady state" (Wilden, 1972e, pp. 321–322; Ardener, 1971a), the structuralist appeal to a phonological model is not a fiction. Linguistics has long been concerned to establish similarly physicalist laws for language, namely, Martinet's use of the "law of least effort," derived from optics (and providential theology), to establish a so-called "economy" or principle of "efficiency" in language, as a concomitant of "stability." (The counterpoint here is that no such principle can be discovered operating in living systems. On the contrary, in natural ecosystems, and I suspect human ones also, it is redundancy and enormous "waste" of effort that are the concomitants of long-range stability. Efficiency tends to be disastrously destabilizing in the long run.) Hence, like Cournot's "social arithmetic" (Newman, 1956, pp. 1200–1216, 1267) or the "social physics" of the eighteenth century, the underlying model involved is not much more than a complex transformation of the seventeenth-century physics of "clear and distinct" entities, related to the conception of the social system as a "veritable organized machine" (Saint-Simon, Bernard)—even if the machinery is often described by organicist metaphors or by a mixture of the two.

The Myth of Science ● Given the extraordinary and yet perfectly explicable persistence of mechanical materialism in the life and social sciences—with their two singular bases: biology and psychology—a persistence that can be shown to bear a direct relation to the characteristics of the socioeconomic deep structure (Wilden, 1974a), and given the structuralist translations from this level, it is hardly too much to suggest that far from being in one of its forms the science of myths, structuralism is in many respects simply a new version of the myth of science.

By this I mean the mixed metaphors that confuse, confound, or ignore levels and orders of complexity in the world, producing a body of "human science" where values and hypotheses, derived indirectly from the social discourse and most directly from the supposed law and order of the physical universe, are projected through a screen of objectivity onto the socioeconomic and psychosocial universe. This is a form of reductionism or scientism in which what is called objectivity is in the last analysis a metaphor of the collective subjectivity of a particular product of history: the abstract set composed of the representatives and the representations of a singular race, sex, and economic class.

EPISTEMOLOGICAL SHIFTS

Structuralism, information theory, cybernetics, communications and general systems theory have all been contributions to and symptoms of a twentieth-century shift in the way we conceive of living and social systems—and, consequently, also in the way we conceive of our relations to each other. Some of the specifics associated with these labels have been the direct products of war—submarine hunting, the radar gunsight, missiles, the entire discipline of operations research or systems analysis—but the general change can be viewed more relevantly as the derivative of as yet little understood economic changes on a global scale.

The increasing size and complexity of business corporations, as well as their organization in tiers, trees, pyramids, and more intricate topological structures would naturally lead to the systematization of a body of theory designed to explain and control organization. Similarly one has only to consider the relatively sudden discovery by the industrialized nations that the pursuit of individual economic independence leads ultimately to increasing degrees of collective interdependence to realize that we would necessarily come to live in an era when some form of systems ecology would be applied to any and all complexes of system-environment relations. The shift is thus both a mirror of contemporary socioeconomic reality and an illumination of it.

Open Systems ● For the past half century there has been a distinct movement away from talking about biological and human relations in the terms of aggregates, entities, atoms, individuals, closed systems, linear causality, equilibria, force, and energy (Ruesch & Bateson, 1968; Whyte, 1962; Buckley, 1967, 1968). We now find a new vocabulary, which is much more than a simple change of terminology: wholes, interdependent structures, open systems, feedback, teleonomy, ongoing process, constraint, relations between relations, information and communication. The traditional and quantitative unidimensionality of the epistemology of the life and social sciences is being replaced by the multidimensional viewpoint of levels and orders of communication, complexity, and organization—all of which necessarily involve a comprehension of qualitative considerations as a prerequisite for any quantitative analysis.

This shift has not been based on linguistics, although linguistics has profited from it. It is far from being integrated into any of the forms of structuralism: anthropological, philosophical, psychological, psychoanalytical, or literary. In spite of all they say about relations, contexts, and semiotics (the production, consumption, and exchange of signs), the structuralists have not thus far fully recognized the necessity of utilizing the distinction between energy-entity models and informational-relational models in any theory relating to the life and social sciences; and some of those associated with the movement (e.g., Julia Kristeva) seem to have remained imprisoned in a master-slave relationship to what they believe to be an ideal model: the methodology and epistemology of "hard science."

Lévi-Strauss ● Lévi-Strauss has proved to be an exemplary case in point, repeatedly appealing to this model. He regularly uses mechanical-organicist metaphors for all types of structure, and he consistently employs mistaken analogies between mechanical and/or entropic processes and social or mythic structures. He compares "cold" or relatively static societies with clocks, and "hot" or "historical" societies with steam engines.[3] He also equates social struggles with energy gradients, and physical entropy with social disorder, implying at the same time that socioeconomic differentials cause a movement toward randomness in social systems (1969a, p. 39). It is more accurate to say that a society, at the moment of its greatest internal disruption, is not so much characterized by lack of organization or order as by the rigidity and inflexibility of *over-order*.

Lévi-Strauss seems to conceive of all possible structural models as no more than mechanical or statistical—the first involving the equilibria and inertia of isolated or closed physical systems ("organized simplicity"), the second modeled on the "unorganized complexity" of thermodynamic systems tending toward states of disorder (Simonis, 1968, pp. 172–176). The systems with which he deals are, on the contrary, examples of the organized complexity of open system-environment relationships—relationships constrained and controlled by information, and tending to maintain organization (neutral entropy) or to increase it (negative entropy). Their behavior is a function of a necessary and multidimensional relation to a set of contexts (environments, levels of complexity in the environment as a whole). These systems require that they be categorized by the type and level of their capacity to produce, reproduce, and process information (their relative semiotic freedom), rather than from a monoplanar energy–entity perspective. Insofar as it involves isolating open systems from their

[3]The confusion here is quite complicated. Both machines are closed and entropic; neither contains any internal principle of change. They have only three possible states: stable equilibrium (stopped), dynamic equilibrium (repetition), and breakdown. Moreover, a stationary steam engine is a cybernetic machine with closed-loop negative feedback between input and output (via its governor), whereas a clock is a classical machine involving zero feedback. Lévi-Strauss was still using analogies between kinship systems and clocks or force-pumps in 1966 (preface to the second edition of the *Elementary Structures of Kinship),* and in 1971 he was still referring to the brain as a machine and to the myth as an object. In the last volume of the *Mythologiques* (1971) however (pp. 560–561, 615), he does at least limit his version of structuralism to those supposed entities to which it has always applied: "mathematical entities, natural languages, musical compositions, and myth" (p. 578).

environments without adequately acknowledging the locus or the level of the closure—methodological or otherwise—the approach of Lévi-Strauss ultimately comes to share the traditional perspectives explicit and implicit in the thought-models of American and British social and economic science. This is inevitable, of course, given that for Lévi-Strauss, ethnology is in the last analysis psychology (1966, p. 130; 1972a; Piaget, 1970b, p. 111).

Energy and Information ● Although the organic and human worlds are ultimately subject to the laws of the physical universe, they also obey laws that have no application in physics or chemistry. For whereas the classical physical universe is a universe primarily of matter-energy, the organic and human universe is one primarily of information.[4] Whereas the theoretical world of physics is one of essentially closed or isolated systems controlled by the lineal causality of gradients of energy potential, the organic and socioeconomic world is one of open systems organized in ecosystems.[5] These open systems are fueled by energy, but their metastable processes and organization are constrained and controlled by the communicational relationships of the feedback of information between the subsystem and its environment within the wider ecosystem. In the physical universe, all change and movement is ultimately subject to the second law of thermodynamics, the law of (positive) entropy, which is a statistical synonym for disorganization, disorder, and degradation. In the organic and human world, however, we find that the way in which information controls, triggers, stores, or organizes matter-energy, represents a process of negative entropy (improbable order). The organic world borrows energy from the positively entropic physical universe to maintain or increase its organization and order. In this world, change may be in any direction and is not immediately connected with the entropic degradation of energy potential or gradient so that the system comes to a stop for lack of available free energy. This process of maintaining

[4]The simplest and most adequate definition of information is variety (pattern, organization), imprinted or borne on a matter-energy base (sets of "markers"). In this there is no intrinsic difference between information and noise (Ashby, 1963, pp. 186 187). For the system involved, however, information will represent structured variety, and noise, unstructured variety. As a general rule, the more complex the system, the wider the range and the types of variety it can process, transmit, and exchange.

[5]In thermodynamics, an isolated system makes no matter-energy exchanges with its environment. A closed system is open to energy import only; an open system exchanges both matter and energy with its environment. The term is used here to refer also to systems that involve information exchange with their environments. For most purposes the solar system may be considered an isolated system; the planet earth is a closed system; organisms and societies are open systems. Open systems may also be described as metastable. They import and process external order—matter, energy, and information—in maintaining their internal order, that is, the energy levels and structures that make them different from their environments.

organization is, of course—and just like the human race itself—on a microsco-
pic scale compared with the probability of entropy in the cosmos as a whole.[6]

Homeostasis and Morphogenesis ● Systems that involve nontemporalized
maintenance of organization—that is, systems in which the relationship between
system and environment and the adaptive changes of one to the other are not
essentially affected by time or by the temporal sequence of their interchanges—are
usually called homeostatic or morphostatic. They simply attempt to maintain their
structure in the face of any kind of disturbance. Systems that can maintain their
range of adaptive flexibility in relation to a temporally ordered environment by
means of evolutions or revolutions, that is to say, by changing structure or
organization in the face of externally or internally generated disturbances or both,
may be called morphogenic (Maruyama, 1963).

   All such negatively entropic systems are goal-seeking (teleonomic rather than
teleological) and more or less adaptive. The attainment or nonattainment of their
goals is not ultimately governed by the efficient causality of the "forces" that
act on them, but by the hierarchies of constraints placed on their gamut of possibilities by the ecosystem in which they exist and without which they could
not survive. In such systems the whole is greater than its parts, since it is distinguished from the aggregate of its parts by its organization. But it is also true
that the parts are potentially "greater" than the whole, in that their possibilities
of action, taken in isolation, are theoretically (but never actually) of greater
freedom than they are within the whole. It is this purely theoretical possibility,
combined with the human capacities of simulation, which makes possible the
perennial attractiveness of anarchism (explicit or implicit) in our atomized society, as well as the persistence of both liberalism and conservatism (Wills, 1969).

Bioenergetics ● The life and social sciences have taken over from the social discourse the technological and physicist model of an entropic universe of matter-
energy and applied it—through such closed-system and atomistic metaphors as
"instinct," "autonomous ego," "inhibitory response mechanism," "object relation," and so on—to the negatively entropic organic and human world of semiotic systems open to matter, energy, and information. The underlying model
is derived from a bioenergetic epistemology (Bateson, 1972): that of a universe
directly ruled by the gravitational-electromagnetic interplay of attraction and re-

---

   [6]In relating and distinguishing the interconnected realms of matter-energy and information, it
is useful to make a methodological distinction between three kinds of entropy: energetic entropy
(involving energy gradients), material entropy (involving distributions), and informational entropy
(involving living structure and organization). Whereas matter-energy is always conserved, there is
no such law directly applicable to structure, variety, or information. These forms of order are continually created and destroyed in biosocial ecosystems, whether in metabolism, in the reproduction
of life, or in the production and reproduction of human subsistence and social organization.

pulsion in a world of "objects" and "fields" containing "forces" (e.g., Newton's *vis insita*, which he eventually identified with God). (See Piaget, 1964, pp. 172–174, for the analogy between the dynamic equilibrium of physics and chemistry and his conception of psychological equilibrium.)

Either/Or • Associated with the deep structure of this epistemological model is an "either/or," analytic logic, based on the digital symmetry of opposition and identity, which still retains its hegemony in the schools and in our daily lives (Wilden, 1972e, pp. 202–229). It is now complemented by an ideological correlative promoted by the counterculture: an equally unidimensional logic of "both-and." This is usually said to be "non-Western," and is often associated with a Buddhistic "world soul" or the Chinese metaphysics of yin and yang. Logic and living reality are, of course, *both* "either/or" *and* "both-and," but the dialectical perspective, like the Chinese in some respects, recognizes the hierarchical relationship between them, which makes both and, not a competitor or correlate of either/or but, instead, a relation of a higher logical type. (As such, an uncritical both-and perspective will rationalize and justify the relationship of both master and slave, both predator and prey, just as does the liberal ideology of "both sides of the question.")

This outlook has retained its dominance in our society for at least the past three centuries because it serves a necessary political and economic function. We can expect it to change only when the deep structure of our society does. In all cultures, myth, religion, ritual, belief, science, metaphysics, magic, theories of the cosmos, and theories of knowledge necessarily serve the informational function of controlling the organization of some level or part of the system: the disposition of the matter-energy available to it, its processes of communication and exchange, and so on. It is consequently no accident that the traditional epistemology, which is historically coterminous with the rise and expansion of the capitalist socioeconomic system, expresses and supports the separable and equal personal responsibility (symmetry), the "equal opportunity" (to compete), and the necessity of production for the sake of production ("progress") as they are manifested in the commodity relations of Western society. In the world of physics, of course, all elementary particles are created equal and no one group of particles exploits the others; hence, the similarities between physical theory and the neutralization of hierarchical relations by the dominant ideology are hardly surprising.

GENETIC OR OPERATIONAL STRUCTURALISM: PIAGET

As the axis of this critique, I have chosen Piaget's 1968 résumé, of which there is a freewheeling and sometimes deficient translation (1970b). This is an important book, notably because of Piaget's wide-ranging knowledge of American and British structural perspectives, not to mention his use of Bourbakian structuralism in mathematics. The translator's persistence in giving him behind-the-scenes help to explain himself is not, in general, so misleading as to destroy its usefulness to anyone interested in the subject, to which it is undoubtedly the most lucid introduction available at present. As an exposition, its major deficiencies involve unrecognized confusions about the type of structure under discussion, an altogether cursory reference to Marx and the question of superstructure and base, and an almost complete failure to deal with Freud, from whom many of the basic tenets of Piaget's perspective are derived.

I do not dwell on agreements here, whether with Piaget's outline or critique, but concentrate instead on differences, especially when they concern Piaget's uncritical acceptance of a number of dubious or untenable assumptions about human and organic systems, assumptions so "self-evident" to the scientific discourse of our era that the time, place, and rationale of their invention seems to have undergone a collective repression.

Self-Objectification ● When one discovers Piaget describing the development of the child purely in terms of organic development, for instance, or when one realizes that for Piaget child development requires the child to learn to view his/her "self" as an object in a world of "interpersonal transactions" which is ruled by intellectualist conceptions of "progress" and intelligence, one begins to wonder whether the theory is not, in some significant but surreptitious respect, a rationalization of modern alienation. Objects—the translation of realities into things—like commodities and the answers to IQ tests—have clearly defined boundaries, whereas children and selves do not.

Indeed, the theory of the "ego" or "self" developed by Lacan—to whom Piaget gives the usual ritualistic but inconsequential mention (pp. 86–87)—implies precisely such a critique of Piaget's conception of children and their relation to the world. Lacan would probably say that Piaget is, in effect, recounting in an uncritical fashion the way in which self-*and*-other relationships in our culture are constituted as paranoid and reified relationships of *either* self *or* other, relationships in which we learn to treat ourselves as objects the better to treat as objects the others who began by treating us, in infancy, as objects.

The theory of the self-objectification of the subject in Piaget's work is one of the more obvious results of the way in which the theory involves an unrecognized and artificial closure of the system under study from its socioeconomic context. Piaget defines the environment of the child basically as "psychobiological" (p. 99). This term makes manifest the confusion Piaget shares with many others in social science, a confusion of levels of organization, specifically between the child as a biological organism, the child as a "psychological" person, and the child as a socioeconomic being. Nowhere in this conception of the child is there any adequate recognition of the fact that the child is born into a social and economic ecosystem, to say nothing of the fact that under our present system, it is necessary to compete with others to sell one's labor potential—and, hence, one's "self"—in order to survive (Nicolaus, 1969). It would seem that the merchandising of oneself as a commodity in our culture is regarded by Piaget as part of the natural order of things (cf 1970a, pp. 59–79), and that this historically conditioned commoditization is in effect what the theory of "self-objectification in interpersonal transactions" actually refers to.

If this is true, then where in the theory do we discover the logical extension and scientific analysis of this situation? Where do we find it explained, for example, why some children must learn to be better commodities than others? And where in the logic of Piaget's structures is there any reference to the striking differences in the socialization of male children—predominantly digital, context-independent—compared with that of female children—predominantly analog, context-dependent? (Bernstein, 1971; Wilden, 1972e, pp. 296–299).

Definition of Structure ● Piaget begins his book on structuralism by defining structure as "a system of transformations," comprising three key characteristics: *wholeness, transformation,* and *self-regulation* (p. 5). Given the ecosystemic perspective of this article, this declaration looks very promising. We are further impressed by his critique of Gestaltism on two important grounds. The first is that the traditional psychological conception of the "good form" represents a type of structure with especial appeal to structuralists seeking "pure structures," that is to say, structures "without history and, *a fortiori*, without genesis, without functions and without relations to the subject" (p. 55). The second is that Gestalt was always conceived as an "objective" and mechanical reality, "out there" in the world, whereas Piaget's own conception insists on an "equilibrated interaction" between perceiver and form, in such a way that any "perceptual act" can change with the effects of memory and maturation (pp. 57–59). The critique is impressive because it appeals to history and to genesis, because it conceives of perception as a system-environment relation and, above all, because it is apparently concerned to deal directly with the problem of understanding change.

Equilibrium, Closure ● However, we have already encountered the term *équilibre*, associated, on the one hand, with thermodynamic and mechanical equilibrium states (entropy, inertia) and, on the other, with a bipolar Newtonian machine, the balance scale (Schon, 1969). Piaget also uses the term "homeostasis'' (often used to describe the "steady states" of "self-regulation"). But the use of this more biological and less apparently physicalist term merely reinforces the restricted conception of change implicit in the term "equilibration."[7]

This terminology reduces change to (nontemporalized) random fluctuations from a norm, or to mere sequences of repetition and oscillation dependent on the system's internal states. It is a similar kind of reductionism—notably the reduction of externally generated oscillations to internally derived repetitions (the "compulsion to repeat," the bipolar pleasure-displeasure principle)—which grounds the theoretical closure of psychoanalytic theory from the social context (Wilden, 1972e, pp. 125–154). Freud's bioenergetic conception of the homeostatic pleasure principle (the "principle of constancy") and his later conception of the entropic "death instinct" (the "principle of inertia") are explicitly derived from nineteenth-century physics (Fechner), and less directly derived from utility theory in economics.

Moreover, Piaget's amplification of his definition of structure, which is founded, he says, on mathematical group theory, confirms our suspicions about the source and function of his concept of equilibrium (or "compensation") and its connection with mechanistic cybernetics. He defines a structure as a "system closed under transformation." It is "preserved or enriched" by the interplay of its transformations which never "lead beyond the frontiers of the structure, nor do they appeal to elements exterior to the system" (p. 5) (Lévi-Strauss, 1971, pp. 560–563). But the only such systems or structures we know of are the isolated systems of classical physical theory (closed to matter-energy import), the methodologically closed structures of mathematics, and cybernetic systems open to energy but closed to information and control (Ashby, 1963, p. 4).

Wholeness ● In analyzing the contributions of Gestaltism to the theory of structure, Piaget remarks that Gestalt "intention" and "signification" are phenomenological equivalents of his own "transformation" and "self-regulation" (p.

[7]Piaget has sought to distinguish his concept of equilibrium from "a balance of forces at rest." He suggests that it is compatible with L. von Bertalanffy's "stable state in an open system" (1964, p. 115; Gandillac et al., 1965). He also compares it fleetingly with the activities of Ashby's homeostat—but this is merely a switching machine, closed to new information, with only two possible states (stability and instability) and no memory (Wilden, 1972e, p. 140). His considered definition is that of a dynamic equilibrium achieved "by compensation between external perturbations and the activities of the subject," such that a maximum of equilibrium corresponds to a maximum of activity (1964, pp. 124–125). These "activities" are then compared to the strategies of game theory. But game theory is not a dynamic theory, but rather a logic of situations. It does not describe temporally organized processes; moreover, its less trivial applied aspects require a number of assumptions derived from the social sciences and ethics (Rapoport 1968b, 1962; Shubik, 1964, pp. 1–77). Hence, Piaget's comparison seems inadequate, if not tautologous.

52). He criticizes Gestaltism's basis in physics (as also Kurt Lewin's electro-magnetic concept of the "field" in his so-called topology), noting that it is Gestalt "equilibration," rather than its law of wholeness, that makes Gestaltism a structuralist theory.

He seeks to distinguish the criterion of wholeness in his own "operational structuralism" (p. 9) from the pseudoholism of apparently structural theories, notably those that involve only a reversal of traditional atomism because they either make the whole the atom or make it a mere aggregate of atoms (e.g., Comte's sociology, Durkheim's "total social fact"). For him the significant reference is not the whole, but the relations within it. Neither the whole nor the part is primary, but rather the "logical procedures" by which the whole is formed. The whole is therefore "consequent on the system's laws of composition" (p. 9; p. 4).

Pseudoholism • Reference has already been made to the dictum that the whole is greater than the sum of its parts. This is not enough to counter Newtonian atomism, however, because it may mean no more than that one sums the parts and then adds to the total the sum of the relations between them, calling the result a "system." This procedure still implies that the parts are somehow primary and that, in effect, they preexist their organization into a system: that is, the substructures in the larger structure possess intrinsic boundaries distinguishing them from each other and from the whole. In the extreme case, the atomistic substructures will be conceived of as entering into and remaining in the system unchanged—except that they now possess relations as well as their individual characteristics, and the system displays "emergent properties." This is a perspective common to many proponents of what is now called general systems theory.

However, this is certainly not true of socioeconomic systems (and probably not of any ecosystem), for here the systemic characteristics of the whole create the socioeconomic characteristics of its parts and the kinds of boundaries between them. The underlying perspective is no more than a displaced version of Locke's social contract—which sets the "individual" in opposition to what organizes him, that is, the system, "society." The confederation of the individuals in society under the contract leaves their "innate" characteristics and "natural rights" unchanged. In Locke's perspective—endlessly repeated after him, for example, by Destutt de Tracy in the early nineteenth century—the most significant of these intrinsic characteristics is private property, a notion specifically based on the idea that the body is "naturally" the private property of the "ego" or "mind."

For several reasons, Piaget's conception of wholeness leaves itself wide open to this kind of critique. One major clue to what "wholeness" and the primacy of the "laws of composition" implies is that the example of wholeness Piaget employs concerns the integers—with their properties of forming groups, fields, rings, and so on (p. 7).

Digital Communication ● Integers in mathematics are discrete elements in a purely digital system of communication and exchange (messages that are dependent on a discontinuous code). The characteristic of all digital systems is that the elements selected and combined to make messages must be separated from each other by boundaries equivalent to gaps—as with the either/or gap between "yes" and "no," or between "one" and "two" in the sequence of the whole numbers, or the similar gap between "sister" and "brother" in a kinship system, or that between the exchange value of one commodity in relation to another.

Piaget misses the point that digital codes involving already-given distinctions (e.g., exchange value) are ultimately derived from coexisting analog or continuous systems of difference (e.g., use value)—difference being the minimum requirement constituting a relation. In such differential systems, symmetries, reversibilities, identities, and oppositions (as well as "not") are logically impossible (Wilden, 1972e, pp. 155–195). And although Piaget does pay lip service to the analog and iconic communication of "affective language" (p. 86), his entire construction of reality, his conception of communication, and his understanding of cognition, reason, and logic are nevertheless reduced to purely digital notions. His substructures and superstructures are digitally conceived as well, with unbridgeable gaps within and between them. These gaps are reminiscent of the double frontiers that replace the single boundaries between nation states: the no-man's-land of the space between the customs post of one country and that of the next.

Transformation ● The second criterion of a structure is transformation. The structural laws of composition or organization within the composite whole are not static relations; they are laws that structure relations and are structured by them. This definition is in keeping with Piaget's concern to develop a constructivist and interactive structuralism, unlike the tendency toward archetypal structures in Gestaltism. The "bipolar properties" of being both structured and structuring is what accounts for the success of the notion because, like Cournot's conception of "order" in mathematical structures, it is a process whose intelligibility is ensured by its own exercise (p. 10; cf. translator's note). His mention of Cournot foreshadows a whole series of themes raised throughout the exposition. Cournot was an early proponent of mathematical equilibrium theory whose attempt to explain (by "rational mechanics") the behavior of supposedly free and equal partners in "duopolist" economic competition is now viewed as an antecedent of modern game theory, which Piaget assimilates to the structuralist paradigm later in his book.

Game theory is not applicable to nonequilibrium and rule-changing or evolving systems, nor to certain common tripartite games involving bargaining and coalitions (Rapoport, 1962). Purely bipolar or dualistic relations between human beings, for example, the supposed identity of opposites between "suppliers" and "demanders," simply do not exist, except as academic theoretical reductions. All apparently dyadic interactions are mediated by specific "others," or else by some or all aspects of the social context as a whole (the Other).

The significance of Piaget's appeal to mathematics and game theory (pp. 104–105) is reinforced by the fact that all of the theories he introduces to support his thesis of "equilibrated transformations," are theories that neutralize the contemporary social context of accumulation and levels of socioeconomic status, and the cumulative effects of power and organization in economic relations of competition. Such relationships are not "free" or "equal," since they involve positive feedback—the more you have, the more you get—weighted on the side of power and the control of organization.

Self-Regulation ● There are two types of transformation in Piaget's view: temporal and nontemporal. This distinction ought to lead to a further distinction between morphogenic transformations, developmental successions, and homeostatic repetitions. The fact that it does not is a corollary of his conception of his third criterion: self-regulation. Self-regulation, in its "perfect" form, is said to embody the three "fundamental principles of rationalism": the principle of noncontradiction ("incarnate in the reversibility of transformations"); that of identity (requiring the "neutral element," in this instance zero, which is the boundary between identities); and the principle that "the end result is independent of the route taken" (associativity in algebra, equifinality in behavior). The definition is not derived from the observation and analysis of real systems, however, but from group theory as the "prototype of 'structures'" (pp. 18–20), a characterization that will later be attributed to the organism. Self-regulation is further defined as entailing the "self-maintenance and closure" of a "bounded substructure" (p. 14). Significantly enough, the relation of such a bounded substructure to a larger structure is not described by Piaget in the communicational terms of an interactive, ecosystemic relationship, but by a political metaphor which certainly suits the historical origins of his epistemology: the metaphor of confederation.

What follows begins to sound like a structural doctrine of states' rights *(conservation avec stabilité des frontières)*. The behavior of a substructure is not "impaired" by its relation to a larger structure; it neither loses its boundaries nor suffers "annexation." On the contrary, the laws of the substructure are conserved "in such a way that the intervening change is an enrichment." Thus certain kinds of common enough change, such as self-destruction, internal disturbance of the bounded structure, perturbations of the ideal of "self-regulated" equilibrium, the crossing of the frontiers or the breaking of the boundaries of a structure, sudden changes of state, and the unpredictable generation of novel structures have no integral place in Piaget's theory at all.

Instead of being explained, these kinds of change are explained away by recourse to metaphors suggesting the "foreign bodies" of the germ theory of disease, by metaphors implying a necessary and natural hostility between "organism" and "environment" (as between "individual" and "society"), or by images that, on analysis, suggest entropic degradation or the interference of a galactic meteor with the smoothly running and reversible dynamic equilibrium of the planets. These implications of Piaget's basis in physical theory are further reinforced by his approving explanation of the Gestaltist rule that gestalts tend to take on the "best" form. For him this provides a "psychological equivalent" of the physicist's "principle of least action" or efficiency (Maupertuis, Planck—also Hero and Pappus of Alexandria and Hamilton) and the more general principle of equilibrium.

Reversibility ● By self-regulation Piaget means a symmetrically reversible system of regulation, a *moteur intime* that is timeless. He believes this conception of self-regulation, equivalent to the "perfect regulation" of a mathematical operation (p. 15), to be "cybernetic." In such an "operational system," errors are excluded before they are made "because every operation has its inverse in the system" (e.g., subtraction is the inverse of addition). Next, he speaks of an "immense class" of temporally oriented structures regulated by feedback, anticipation, and error-correction, which do not meet his criterion of regulation. This class, it develops, includes everything else in the organic world—and obviously the child—except mathematics.

This conception of operational structuralism depends wholly on the either-/or, digital function of identity, which requires discrete elements with well-defined boundaries, and on its correlate, the axiom of noncontradiction (either A or not-A, but not both). Apart from the question of its applicability outside algebraic structures, this conception of self-regulation also rules out of order any but equilibrium states and their associated displacements and compensations, as well as the concept of multi-finality in goal-seeking systems (where different ends may be reached from the same initial states and/or by different paths). It also requires a coalescing under the heading of reversibility, of inversion and negation, on the one hand, and of reciprocity or correlation, on the other. The effect is to one-dimensionalize ''zero'' and ''not,'' and ''not-one'' and ''minus-one,'' by making them into categories of the same logical type (pp. 23–27; Wilden, 1972e, pp. 182–183, 323–324).

The problems presented by this set of ontological reductions and logical identifications are compounded by the fact that the value system laid out in Piaget's first chapter turns out to be the *structure de base* of his theory of the child and the organism, and consequently of his conception of social structures.

Self-Control ● Part of the answer to the problem posed by Piaget's definition of self-regulation lies in simply considering the theoretical and ideological import of the expression itself. On the one hand, it is obviously related to the mind-body dichotomy in our culture, which provides for the moral metaphor of individual ''self-control'' (Wills, 1969). The ''mind'' (''reason'') is supposed to control the ''self,'' that is, the body, the analog domain of ''emotion,'' especially in the liberal conception of the ''self-made man.''

But even if this ideological correlation were irrelevant, it nevertheless remains the case that ''self-regulation'' is a contradiction in terms. Regulation in any valid cybernetic sense can only be a function of an open relation to an environment of information, that is, a function of a relation to an ''other.'' If this were not true, there could be no set of parameters in relation to which the ''self'' or system could make judgements about the appropriateness of its states. Having excluded the mathematician from his mathematics, Piaget cannot be talking about regulation in this sense at all. Rather he is talking about the mechanics of equilibrated and reversible systems like that formed by the planets and the sun, whose macroscopic regularities are not a function of a relation to an environment (as the regularities of organisms are), but in fact are the product of mass-energy factors internal to the system considered as such. Piaget's use of ''self-regulation'' is one more example of his persistent confusion between systems of different types and orders of complexity. The expression becomes scientifically almost meaningless, on the one hand, and purely ideological, on the other.

The Semiotic Function ● Piaget's basic position is more clearly and directly derived from the ''empirical'' (and ''progressivist'' or ''evolutionist'') assumptions of Western rationalism—and above all from their connection with what Dallas Smythe has called the production and consumption of the consumer as an object of exchange—than from the critically scientific study of children. One primary assumption of the theory, like Freudian psychoanalysis, is that the child's first relation is to objects, rather than to information. Since the child is first and foremost a communicator in an ecosystemic universe—both biological and social—the assumption of the primacy of subject-object relations in the ecosystem formed by the child-plus-environment(s) will generate imaginary barriers between its parts (Wilden, 1972e, pp. 212–227). The various and multiple boundaries in the ecosystem will not be represented or analyzed for what they are—*loci of communication and exchange*—but rather as barriers to be overcome. Hence, it will become necessary to invent various "action-oriented" or "intentional" or "semiotic" constructs to bridge the no-man's-land between "subject" and "object" that the epistemological and ideological assumptions have created.

One of those employed by Piaget is the "sensorimotor intelligence" of the child, a form of (internal) activity that "does not involve representation, and is essentially tied to action and coordinates of action" (p. 65). However, the only process that can initiate or coordinate action in any organism is a flow of information. Information necessarily involves simulation (representation) of some kind at all the various biosocial levels of complexity at which it occurs. Whether or not it is recognized for what it is, the flow of information that binds organism and environment cannot be completely ignored, of course, for after all our very lives depend on it. Hence, having denied its existence at one level, Piaget must nevertheless deal with it, sooner or later, at another. This he does by introducing another construct, without any apparent connection with the first: the "semiotic function."

This notion appears with such artifice in the French text that the translator has felt obliged to respond to the way the term fills up the hole in Piaget's conception of reality by filling up a hole in the French sentence (the italicized words do not appear in the French): "As soon as the semiotic function (language, symbolic play, images, and such) *comes on the scene* . . . the child . . . uses reflective abstractions [p. 64]." How and why—and in connection with what—does this function "come on the scene"? We must also ask why the advent of a communicational function is so long delayed in Piaget's theory.

Part of the answer is that in any theory taking the individual organism as its "prototype structure" (p. 45), communication with the environment will almost unavoidably be viewed as a secondary function. Consequently there will be no reason to provide answers within the theory to the question posed—because the closure of the theoretical perspective has itself already precluded the possibility of asking it.

Partly because of his atomistic conception of the self-subsistent individual, Piaget, like many other structuralists, makes language the ultimate model and pattern *(patron)* of all communication. Hence, since language appears in ontogeny long after conception, then communication will also tend to be viewed as a derivative of organic maturation, rather than as constitutive of the entire process of biosocial development: "Without language . . . operations (transformations) would be individual, and they would consequently be unaware of that control process which results from interindividual exchange and cooperation [1964, p. 113]." Biologically, this is nonsense. If information did not provide for organisms to be aware of themselves, of their environments and milieus, and of the relation between the two, there would surely be no life on earth. No "operation" can in any proper sense be "individual," because operations are necessarily a function of relations between individuals—which are themselves complexes of relations—mediated by the system in which they live.

The Cartesian and solipsistic dichotomy on which Piaget's conception is based is presumably derived from the assumption that communication and exchange *within* the boundaries of the organism or the individual are of an entirely different type from communication and exchange *between* organisms or individuals. On the contrary—and this is implicit even in Piaget's truncated theory of (digital) communication (p. 50)—self-regulation in relation to an environment requires information flow (on a matter energy base), and language is far from being the only form of information that regulates and "informs" the relations of the socioeconomic ecosystem.

Instinctual Structure ● Once the structure has been defined as autonomous and implicitly self-subsistent, it has been abstracted from its environment. Since the structure and its "self-closure" are functions of its environmental relations, it will now be necessary to project onto the structure, as inherent properties, all of the environmental relations that it has been divorced from. In order to put back what the theory has taken out, the abstracted structure will have to be provided with an internal source of motive, something similar to the supposed *moteur intime* of so-called self-regulation. Without this internal source the structure would be in equilibrium with its environment, that is, either (thermodynamically) nondistinct from it or simply dead.

In tracing Piaget's conception of the autonomous structure (organism, child), it is not difficult to demonstrate its connections with the seventeenth-century philosophical psychology of the individual as a closed system: Descartes' *cogito ergo sum* (1637), for example, Locke's "little closet shut from light" (1690), or Leibniz's windowless monads (1715). However, unlike Descartes, Piaget cannot appeal to God as the mediator of all human relations to account for the communication between the "clear and distinct" organic substructures of his theory, nor can he appeal to Leibniz's principle of entelechy to relate them. (Only the relation between mathematics and physics exhibits this preestablished harmony: p. 41.) Subsequently, he cannot adequately account for the interactions of his "closed and autonomous wholes" with each other and their environments—and specifically for the child's "intentional acts"—without imbuing them with the biological equivalent of the efficient causality of a Newtonian "force," the instinct (p. 48), more subtly represented as "the instinctual structures" and "the logic of the instincts" (p. 51).

Piaget has introduced the instinct from ethology to account for the fact that organisms, although "equilibrated" ("homeostatic"), differ from machines and solar systems in that they depend on significations and hereditary "indices" (p. 48; cf. also Uexküll, 1965)—that is, on information. Needless to say, the semantics of animal and human communication cannot be adequately explained by reference to the model of efficient causality, force, energy, and autonomous entities at the base of Piaget's perspective. Meaning and signification have rather to do with an entirely different order of complexity: with information, communication, organization, and goal–seeking—in other words, with the reciprocal intentionalizing and selecting activity of the organism and the person in relation to their milieus and environments.

The semantics of the organism are hardly adequately explained by essentially one-way principles of explanation like those that gave rise to the term "instinct." A more promising conception, which speaks directly to the problem of what the term "instinct" has always covered up (by being a reification of a "cause"), is that signification is the goal and the result of the way the system uses meaningless information to organize the logical or physical work to be done in relation to an environment (MacKay). This is no mere substitution of terms. The terms "drive" or "instinct" usually represent constructs that, like the efficient causality of physics, are conceived to involve independence of an environment. They are seen as more or less fixed "powers" inherent in one closed system, which come into play only when that closed system happens to come into relation with another closed system (Kilmister, 1965).

In the context of his other appeals to the energetic concept of force (p. 100)—and even "self-regulation," "reversibility," and "noncontradiction" tend to take on this characteristic in his work—Piaget seems to be reducing the phenomenological concept of the intentionality of signification to a metaphor of efficient (and linear) causality. It is in reality a teleonomic concept, one which reappears in the systems-cybernetic notion of goal-seeking, in the Marxian analyses of the systemic goal produced by the constraints of competition between capitals, in the existentialist "project," and in the Freudian notion of "goal-seeking cathexis" or "investment," which Freud himself relates to signification in his later work.

In all fairness, however, the profound epistemological confusion underlying Piaget's failure to distinguish the physical, ecological, socioeconomic, and psychological levels (or orders) of constraint and control in the universe (Cooper et al., 1973; Wilden, 1974a), leads him sometimes to reverse this kind of reduction. Thus, in speaking of physical and biological structures, he first criticizes and then anthropomorphizes Planck's appeal to final causes to complement efficient causality in the physical universe (the principle of least action):

". . . There are therefore physical structures independent of us, but which correspond to our operational structures—even so far as to include a characteristic which might seem specific to the activities of the mind: that of inclining toward the possible and situating the locus of the real within the system of virtual possibilities [pp. 42–43]."

Elsewhere Piaget suggests that one may use "operational mechanisms of a quasi-Platonic and nontemporal sort" as a "basis" from which real structures—for example, "linguistic structures, sociological structures, psychological structures, and so on"—may be derived (pp. 15–16).

Assimilation ● An earlier definition of meaning reinforces the judgment that Piaget's failure to provide a methodological analysis of the different orders of complexity leads him to repeatedly practice the "antistructuralist" and "mechanistic" reductionism that he criticizes in other approaches to organic structure (pp. 44f). In a previous work (1952, pp. 189–195), sensorial images, perceptions, "indications," and signs are treated as if they are entities to be ingested: they are "objects for assimilation."

"Assimilation" for Piaget is always represented by these energy-entity metaphors. He defines biological assimilation as a "fitting" of the "bodies and energies" in the environment to the requirements of the organism's physicochemical structures, at the same time as the organism "accommodates" itself to them. But organisms do not simply or directly assimilate energy or entities from their environments; they assimilate informed structure—order, organization—which they then destroy and reorganize so as to provide sources of energy and structure for themselves. This principle of *order from order* is the first requirement of organic development and maintenance. It is complemented by the principle of *order from disorder*, which accounts for biological evolution—for example, the disordering or mispunctuating of the genetic message in different ways that produces the new order of a variation, mutation, or recombination—as well as for certain kinds of social change.

Whether he is talking at the level of biology or psychology, Piaget manifests a failure to understand or utilize the crucial difference between energy and information. He one-dimensionalizes word and object, signifier and signified, by confounding the category of organization with the entities that manifest it. In other words, he reduces the organizational category of information (pattern, structure, order) to the matter-energy markers that carry it (Wilden, 1972, pp. 249–250, 400–403).

Minds and Monads ● Piaget is unwittingly faithful to the phenomenologist Edmund Husserl in that his structural perspective recreates the main aspects of the "new monadology" that Husserl put forward in his *Cartesian Meditations* (1929). In Piaget's theory, as in Husserl's, the "organism" is forever separated by an imaginary barrier from its environment. This barrier is imaginary both in the sense that the flow of information between "organism" and "environment" pays no attention to it, and in the sense of Lacan's theory of the imaginary relationships of identity and opposition—the Hegelian "identity of opposites"—between "self" (as object) and "other" (as object) in our culture—especially as this mirror-relation between human beings and commodities is expressed by Marx in the theory of exchange and fetishism in the first volume of *Capital*.

The same dichotomy or opposition between organism and environment is the source of Lévi-Strauss's explicit attempts to correlate what he appropriately calls the "symbolic function" with the "fundamental structure of the human mind." Lévi-Strauss has often said that he is basically a Kantian (1971a). As we know, Kant—among whose categories "organization" does not appear—attempted to show how the perceived structure of the cosmos is the result of categories of the "mind." The way Kant approached the problem of what is real and what we perceive as real is, however, the unavoidable result of his atomistic conception of the individual. For him, the "individual entity" (the "mind" or the "I") is explicitly made equivalent to an elastic ball cannoning around in a Newtonian universe peopled by other similarly conceived autonomously bounded structures.

Neither the "mind" nor the "I" are entities or individuals. The first is a systemic category; the second is a linguistic one.[8] If Lévi-Strauss (1971, p. 561) did not go on to compound the confusion by correlating "mind" and "brain" as individual entities, he would merely be playing on the semantic confusion that generates the fallacious oppositions between "innatists" and "en-

---

[8]In linguistics, terms like "I" are "shifters." They do not mean or signify "any-thing"; they simply designate a locus in the discourse, or indicate the position from or to which the message is emitted.

vironmentalists.'' For, as White (1956) points out, when a mathematician insists or denies that mathematical categories such as the integers are "in" the mind, the word "mind" is often being used to mean both the skullbound "brain" and human "culture." However Lévi-Strauss's conception of structure has as its paradigm a displaced form of the individual. This leads him to project an entity-oriented conception of the brain/mind onto culture. Insofar as the brain is an organic complex, the mind is not the brain, but rather a set of relations that intersect in individuals (hence, the idea that we each have "our own mind"). As a result, "culture" ceases to be merely "psychobiological," as in Piaget, and becomes in essence a mere reflection or representation of the structure of "reason." "Mind" is rather to be defined in the communicational sense of "system-*plus* –environment," for only in goal-seeking open systems can the logical and ontological category of mind exist. In this informational sense, "mind" and "culture-as-an-ecosystem" are synonymous: a "unit of mind" (Bateson, 1972) is formed whenever, and at whatever biosocial level, a differential system-environment relationship of communication exists.

Although Piaget refers to the phenomenological concept of intersubjectivity, his epistemic and existential "subject" is really a Cartesian solipsist, an "I that thinks"—alone. He represents the subject as an object in a world of objects, which are there simply to be pushed and pulled around (matter energy), and not also to be listened to and communicated with (information). (Quite apart from the relations of the child with other subjects.) Piaget's child is, in effect, another monad, but with little holes in it to let things in and out. Moreover, the projection into the "subject" of the environmental relations that constitute his subjectivity means that this monad is implicitly endowed with the "inherent human nature" (attacked on page 106)—since the metaphor of innate human nature in Piaget is the "bounded substructure" or the "autonomous structure." "To be real," he says, "a structure must, in the literal sense, be governed from within" (p. 69). But we ask, with a deliberate naiveté: *In relation to what?*

Piaget's Conception of Relation ● Partly in reaction to the phenomenologists' slogan: "To the things themselves," the whole structuralist movement has relied heavily on an appeal to the relation rather than to the entity: "Not the things, but the relations between things." However, given that the epistemology of classical science, for all its evident atomism, is nevertheless a theory of the relations between things, such an appeal may be no more than an introduction to old wine in new wineskins.

Piaget's misconception of relation is rather well brought out by his references to the operation of the genes. In spite of his references to Waddington's "cybernetics of epigenesis'' (pp. 49–51), he thinks of gene complexes as entities separate from their environments and related to them by efficient causality. Consequently, his attempt to explain structuralism in biology eventually is reduced to another transformation of the atomism he is attacking. The genes are not ''aggregates of individuals'' but, as Dobzhansky says, they involve ''gene systems.'' The genes perform ''not as soloists, but as members of the orchestra.'' Piaget's approving reference to this image is revealing. An orchestra plays according to a set of coded instructions, but what it produces has nothing essential to do with the nature of, the presence of, or the reaction of the audience. Simple experiments, such as the rotation of the leg nodules in the developing newt, show that changes in a level or a part of the ''environment'' result, through the relation of feedback and constraint, in changes in the products of the program of the ''system.'' When a 180° rotation of the newt's right front leg nodule produces, not an upside-down right front leg, but a left front leg, we realize that the gene system's ''tune'' has been altered by the reaction of its audience. As Bateson puts it (from whom the example comes): ''A gene is presumably to be regarded as a question to which the answer is provided by its neighborhood.'' This example alone makes Piaget's definition of self-regulation—the ''inner drive'' of the organic structure—as a process of transformations that generate ''elements still belonging only to the structure and conserving its laws'' (p. 14) of questionable application in the life and social sciences, whatever may be its obvious relevance in mathematical group theory.

If a structure is ''a total system of self-regulating transformations'' as defined at the beginning of the book, then ''the organism is therefore the prototype of structures'' (p. 44). It is here, of course, that the structural criterion of a supposed ''internal self-government,'' as well as the repeated confusions between logico-mathematical, physical, organic, and socioeconomic structures, have their sources. In an earlier work (1964, p. 1), Piaget specifically identifies the ''person'' with the organism that bears it. He goes on to describe psychic development from birth to adulthood as directly comparable to the organic growth of the individual—forgetting perhaps that whereas organisms can make only physiological adaptations to their environments, people may well undergo the equivalent of ''genetic'' mutations in learning and consciousness, if the filter of their self-image and ''knowledge structure'' (Boulding) becomes sufficiently disordered by events.

The confusion in levels of organization involved here is that of identifying the skinbound biological individual with the psychosocial and socioeconomic person, and of reducing the apparent boundaries of the one to the supposed boundaries of the other. However, by more carefully considering the status of boundaries in metamathematics, Piaget might have avoided—as in the case of his "confederated" structures with stable frontiers—a tendentious logical and ideological confusion. He confuses the person-as-commodity (a digitalized discrete unit of *exchange value*) with the person-as-a-human-being (a complex of shifting analog differences in the continuum of *use values*). Such a confusion would not be possible, in most "anthropological" societies untouched by wage labor, where "I" refers not to a bounded entity, but to a complex of communal relations—but Piaget relegates such societies as roundly to the domain of "backwardness" as does Lévi-Strauss (e.g., pp. 116–119; Lévi-Strauss, 1971, p. 569).

To deal only with the logical question, the error consists in attributing the boundary between two subsystems or substructures at a given level to one or to the other or to both. In contrast, as with the membrane of a cell, whatever distinguishes the inside from the outside cannot logically belong either to the inside or the outside as such. Its status is more like that of a Dedekind "cut" in the continuous sequence of the real numbers.

The cut itself belongs neither to the set of the numbers below it nor to that of the numbers above it. It is, in effect, an empty set, a pure difference or structured *topos*, devoid of numerality or dimension, with no location *in* the sequence it divides. At the same time, the cut is the paradoxical locus that links the sequence together; it is the place where one may distinguish "one side" from "the other side" and, hence, cross over. Such digital cuts or distinctions in a continuum of differences, along with Leibniz's principle of identity for which they provide, are the prerequisite for any mathematics that employs the principle of contradiction (Frege, 1959). This is not, however, any excuse for confusing the topological or thermodynamic boundary between one neighborhood and another with a real barrier (Brown, 1969, Wilden, 1972e, pp. 183–190, 122–124; Tribus & McIrvine, 1971).

Piaget has, in effect, done what he has already explained (p. 57) we all do in our daily perceptions: we make a digital distinction between "figure" and "ground" in the continuum of differences offered and then make the boundary between them into a property of the figure (cf. p. 105 above).

In spite of the conception of an "equilibrated interaction between organism and environment" on which Piaget claims to base his "cybernetic structuralism" and theory of child development, he has opted for a primacy of the organism—complete with its "intrinsic" boundaries—over (and against) its environments. This in its turn corresponds to confusing the "mind" or "I" with the "self" or "ego," and then confusing the product of this confusion with the individual body-image (Lacan, 1968a, 1968b). The problem is that of making relations into entities, or of projecting them into entities. Consider, for example, how in our day-to-day conversation we commonly talk about our own "insides." By this we are usually referring to the alimentary canal, which in fact is outside the boundary of the skin membrane, that is to say, is part of our environment.

Just as he fails to apply his stated model of the system-environment relation in any concrete way to mathematics and its structures (Wilden, 1972d, 1972e, on the relation between Gödel's Proof, metacommunication, and paradoxical injunctions in logic and in life), so also Piaget has explicitly excluded it from the one system-environment relation on which his entire theory ultimately depends: that between the child and the experimenter in the laboratory (Gandillac et al., 1965, pp. 37–61; Wilden, 1972e, pp. 318–320, 347).

Apart from the fact that he explicitly refused to consider to what extent the mere act of posing questions and problems to a child inevitably involves teaching, Piaget also failed to allow for the effects of the adult's role as a mediator and generator of the child's social (and "experimental") performance. Like Freud, he confuses the "reality principle" with the "performance principle" (Marcuse). In considering cross-cultural and cross-class applications of his method, he fails to analyze the possible relation between "retarded" development and "failures of communication" that involve differences of perception. What is missing here, also, is an understanding of the way in which the several levels of *learning how to learn* (Bateson, 1972, pp. 279–308) may in many instances have the desired effect of ensuring the reproducibility of the observations involved, but for the wrong reasons.

It is not surprising, therefore, that Piaget should also fail to discern that the problem of the prototype structure is not posed at the level of the organism, nor even at that of the population or the gene pool (pp. 49–50) but, instead, at the critical conjuncture of relations between relations: the ecosystem.

THE STRUCTURE AS LAW AND ORDER

Contingency and chance have a peculiar value for Piaget, especially since his rebuttal of the theory of random variation and "natural selection after the event" in contemporary neo-Darwinism involves a critique that is a representation of key aspects of the theory itself (pp. 45–46). He attempts to reduce all the various types of variation in evolution to genetic recombination—but this itself is fortuitous for the ecosystem in which it occurs.[9] The "contingent emergence" of a new structure, he says, "is pretty much in contradiction with the idea of structure, and certainly with logico-mathematical structures" (pp. 60–61; also pp. 128–131, 49–51, 89; cf. p. 20 on the Heraclitean flux).

Development ● It is not easy to make sense of this refusal of contingency unless one recognizes the primacy given to organic development and the epigenetic formation of structures in Piaget's work. Organic development involves controlled and programmed change, and its goal is, of course, the "homeostasis" of the mature organism. Here all structural change ceases, and change becomes mere fluctuation and repetition. Thus he speaks of three periods of child development as "successive processes of equilibration," as "progressions toward equilibrium." As soon as equilibrium is attained at one point, "the structure is integrated into a new system-in-formation." The goal is "an ever more stable new equilibrium of wider and wider extent. [1972a, p. 65]."

This approach tends to preclude certain kinds of learning in the individual, and above all that which takes place when "knowledge structures" are unexpectedly disordered and reorganized in one's life experience. At the least, it relegates such changes to the domain of unwanted and unwarranted intrusions into the orderly progression of Piagetian structures—a process which, in the individual, simply stops dead in early adolescence. It is perhaps this above all that indicates the fundamentally antidialectical—or purely Hegelian—character of Piaget's approach.

Order from Disorder ● In contrast, evolutionary theory seeks to explain contingency. Different kinds of variation, essentially in the sense of random disorderings and reorderings of the genetic message, produce novel reorganizations of specific structures, of which an infinitely small number prove to have survival value in their ecosystemic relation to the environment. These novel structures can be conceived of as the result of the introduction of noise into the transmission of the genetic information, with the effect of producing order from disor-

[9]Piaget remarks that Waddington has demonstrated the inheritance (or "fixation") of acquired characteristics through genetic assimilation (1970b, p. 50). In an earlier attack on mutation and natural selection (1964, pp. 134–135), he restates his claim to have demonstrated this thesis in 1929. Both cases suggest a confusion on his part between a surface structure of adaptation or assimilation, which simulates Lamarckism, and a deep structure which is Darwinism—the changes being explicable as gene redistributions or mutations (Waddington, 1968, p. 20; cf. Bateson, 1972, pp. 253–258, 346–363). Moreover, Piaget's own example is rebutted by his own statement that the "Lamarckian" forms he studied did not lose their "acquired characteristics" when transplanted into an environment where they no longer needed them. I find it difficult to understand why he takes these bizarre and lopsided positions on evolution.

der. If selected to survive, then the product of this novel kind of variety incorporates the noise as information—as a memory trace, as a form of writing—in its own reproductive instructions. In the same way, before the evolution of specific socioeconomic structures which generate their own internal noise, and which are therefore susceptible to processes of constant morphogenesis or permanent revolution (such as those of recent human history), such logically external events as the accidental invention of the wheel served the same creative purpose of reordering the memory trace of the socioeconomic system, of changing its instructions for reproduction. Agriculture, writing as such, the control of fire, tools, and so on must have been invented many times and in many places without passing from the status of noise to that of information. Once incorporated as a memory trace, however, these inventions resulted necessarily in a quantum jump in the level and in the kind of organization of the biosocial ecosystem in which they occurred, as well as in a reorganization of the logical typing of the relations within it.

Peaceful Coexistence ● It is, therefore, not surprising that Piaget finds Parsons's equilibrium model of social systems so pertinent to his own views:

"By defining the structure as a stable disposition of the elements of a social system, which escapes the fluctuations imposed on it from outside, Parsons was led to state precisely the theory of equilibrium. . . . As for functions, they are conceived as intervening in the adaptations of the structure to situations exterior to it [p. 102].

We are not about to argue that adaptive and environmentally related self-regulating systems do not resist change, often through processes of redundancy in their information transmission. But Parsons's model hardly applies to socioeconomic systems like our own, which resist the effects of change by both generating and incorporating it.

It was after all Parsons who said in 1951 "Order—peaceful coexistence in conditions of scarcity—is one of the very first of the functional imperatives of social systems." But as Buckley has pointed out in his trenchant criticism of Pareto, Parsons, and other proponents of the equilibrium model (1967), in such models of "consensus," all tensions, deviations, conflicts, and contradictions are necessarily and a priori defined as deviant intrusions from outside into the harmony of the system. It is, of course, organization itself that produces deviances and contradictions, just as one of the stable products of "self-regulation" is variation.

Violence ● From this perspective, any "nonprogrammed" or "nonnormative" change must come from outside the system. It must be external or accidental or "irrational" noise. For the equilibrium theorist, it must therefore be equivalent to violence—and implicitly deplored as such.

An understanding that this disturbing violence which is projected outside the given system by the equilibrium theorists could be the internal product of the institutionalized violence of the system itself—the ecological, psychological, economic, and physical violence by which the modern socioeconomic system, in particular, maintains its precarious "equilibrium"—is effectively excluded from the theory by the artificial closure of the system from its real contexts, including the natural environment.

Positive Feedback ● It is clear from all that Piaget says about cybernetics that there is an internal connection between his refusal of natural selection and random variation in evolution, his attempt to avoid dealing with sudden change (Waddington, 1968, pp. 32–41), his mechanical conception of equilibrium, and his conception of feedback itself (pp. 45, 49).

Piaget, like most structuralists, thinks of all feedback as only single-level and negative, corresponding to the reduction of deviations between input and output in the direction of stasis. Although some form of negative feedback is the overriding control device in all open systems in nature, positive feedback—the amplification of deviations in the direction of change—is also common, e.g., a forest fire, the "population bomb," organic and economic growth, enzyme action, investment at compound interest (Maruyama, 1963). Positive feedback describes the characteristics of systems in a runaway relationship to their environments, as is true for our present economic system. All such systems are eventually controlled at some point or other, by second-order negative feedback. The runaway multiplication of bacteria in a nutritive solution, for example, maintains positive feedback until it has consumed its environment (the solution)—at which point it has succeeded in consuming itself. Since all natural and social systems exist in similarly entropic environments of a limited supply of "free" energy and available ecospace, then if they destroy their environments, they inevitably destroy themselves.

I have not been able to find any serious consideration of such relations in Piaget's work, whether in the sense of the escalating pathologies of communication in human relations (as analyzed by Bateson's double-bind theory of schizophrenia, for instance),[10] or in that of the "self-amplifying" structures of our present economic system—notably the exponential increase of productive capacity that continues behind the single-level, positive-negative-feedback fluctuations

---

[10]These pathologies depend on the same monoplanar and either/or logic as that described by the Piagetian structures.

of the business cycle ("booms" and "busts"). Such relationships have an intimate connection with the morphogenic restructurings of which only ecosystems (and not organisms) are capable. We are already experiencing some of the feedback effects of the noise we continue to dump into nature (e.g., air and water pollution). In socioeconomic systems, moreover, the second-order negative feedback that may eventually be applied to escalating deviations produced by the system's internal relationships is the constructive destruction we call revolution: the replacement of the old order by a new one.

Conclusion

For the early Parsons also, all feedback is purely negative and in only one dimension, just as it is for the "gradualism" of Marshall's equilibrium theory in economics, based on the principle that "Nature does not make leaps" (pp. 103–106). As Buckley points out (1967, pp. 16, 23–31), Parsons's definition of social order has little to do with the concept of organization in systems theory. In the final analysis, "order" for Parsons means "institutionalized patterns of normative culture," that is, the ideological and economic values of the *status quo*.

In this sense we may legitimately suggest that the structuralist concept of order is above all law and order, and that for this perspective all unexpected change can only be explained as the work of outside agitators. This perspective fails to consider that dialectical systems create their own noise, and that a reservoir of internal noise is, in fact, essential to the long-range flexibility—and therefore to the long-range survival—of natural and social ecosystems. Above all, by implicitly treating noise and positive feedback as processes requiring *neutralization*, this approach misses their potentially creative import. As Bateson has said: "All that is not information, not redundancy, not form and not restraints—is noise, the only possible source of *new* patterns [1972, p. 416]."

Hence, in what Piaget refers to as the authentic "analytic" structuralism of Lévi-Strauss, we are not surprised to find several examples of the same Parsonian model of equilibrium, couched in the same bioenergetic language of mixed metaphors. According to Lévi-Strauss, "mechanical feedback" will restore the "previous harmony" (by which it is "governed" and to which it is "subjected") of a totemic social structure that has been "exploded" by the "shock" of demographic change: "It will orient the disordered organ or mechanism in the direction of an equilibrium which would at least be a compromise between the system's former state and the disorder introduced from outside [1966, pp. 67–69]."

Explanations of organizational stability through time and synchronic "steady states" are obviously essential in psychological and socioeconomic theory, and the work of the structuralists will contribute to this end. Such explanations will require a refinement of still ill-defined ecosystemic concepts—such as redundancy, constraint, flexibility, resiliency, ecological efficiency, and hierarchies of control—which seek to indicate how such systems maintain an adequate "function space" of relative semiotic freedom for their present and future activities.

It is unlikely, however, that the incorporation of an understanding of the various typologies of stability into a dialectical theory of the pragmatics of ecosystemic communication and exchange can be achieved by recourse to a bioenergetic conception of "equilibration," replete with the whole perspective that the very choice of this metaphor entails. In the social sciences, "equilibration" is surely one of those comforting but dangerously reductionist theoretical shortcuts, with built-in ideological entelechies, whose own degree of semiotic freedom or requisite variety is too restricted to match that of the universes to which they are applied. But, as with the divine providence of the classical economists—and the "efficiency" that replaced it—such notions fit too cosily with the moral imperatives of established social and family structures to be easily given up.

CHAPTER 6

The Origin of Interactions: Methodological Issues[1]

MICHAEL LEWIS AND SUSAN LEE-PAINTER

Any discussion of structuralism must eventually be concerned with observations and measurement. The purpose of this article is to generate thought on how to transform our concern for structure into an empirical language. Measurement issues are never just methodological play; they always contain theoretical importance. Unfortunately, measurement issues rarely receive proper attention, since theorists are not concerned with empiricism and the empiricists are rarely concerned with theory.

Although we cannot bridge the gap between theory and empiricism in this brief study, we present a starting point for a subsequent inquiry. We discuss the relationship of cognitive structure and the interaction between the organism and its world. We hold closely to the conviction that these cognitive structures are both *caused* by this interaction and at the same time *are causing* these interactions. To understand these structures we must consider the nature of the interaction. For this purpose we examine first Piaget's view of interaction and then develop our own interactional interpretation. Finally, we discuss models of interaction that are currently used in research and the empirical bases of these models and their outcomes.

AN INTERACTIONALIST POSITION

Piaget has called attention to the processes of assimilation and accommodation as the basic processes in the adaptation of the organism to his world. Cognitive structures are formed as a consequence of these processes, and what is assimilated and accommodated to is influenced by the cognitive structures that are formed. Thus, what is assimilated and accommodated must change, since the new structures alter the organism's world. Within this model there exists continually an interaction between the organism's state of being and the world—the

[1]This paper was supported by a grant from the Office of Child Development (OCD-CB-187) and by a grant from the Spencer Foundation.

consequences of which are these structures. Piaget seeks to explore these structures and their change with age.

The cognitive structures in general, but especially in infancy, are not easily defined. Since they refer to organizational properties, they are neither functions nor content; they are variant as a function of development but invariant with respect to specific age, time, place, and culture. As Flavell (1963) has pointed out, in Piaget's earlier work the structural properties were defined in nonmathematical terms such as egocentrism, lack of need to reconcile opposing impressions, and the like, but he has more recently used mathematical terminology. This is most obvious in Piaget's monograph (Piaget, 1970b) where he defines structure as a totality, transformable, and self-regulating.

Piaget questions whether "structures" are real or are only a method to analyze reality. Piaget does not answer this dilemma, and we are not concerned with it at this point. Rather, we consider the nature of these cognitive structures. Our consideration involves two approaches—first, we investigate whether cognitive structures are invariant (age not considered), and second, we investigate the nature of cognitive structures outside of the logical-mathematical or Newtonian framework.

Outside the Genevan literature, the term "schema" has been used often synonymously with cognitive structure (Kagan et al., 1966). Previously, however, schema has been used to refer to two distinct structures—one we shall call action schema as in seeing or reaching and the other we shall call schema for a face that would be similar to a memory schema or neuronal model (Lewis, 1969; Lewis, Wilson & Harwitz, 1971). Schema in both these senses usually are considered to be formed out of particular experiences, and thus are variant. This is especially true for the memory schema or iconic representations. This is in disagreement with those who hold that the cognitive structures and their development are invariant. In the present discussion we use cognitive structure and both types of schema to mean relatively persistent organized classification of information, a model that the organism uses in arranging information.

By design, genetic epistemology has been restricted to particular cases of the organism's interaction with the world. In the select choice of the aspects of knowing we may have deduced a model which, although applicable for some forms of knowledge, is inadequate for others. Piaget has chosen to observe phenomena that are invariant, both with respect to time, place, culture, or specific individual characteristics. Mass, weight, and volume as content and their associative cognitive structures may well be invariant, but these structures may be different from those in the social-emotional realm.

In Piaget's model, cognitive structures—we might refer to them as ways of ordering and obtaining knowledge—are a consequence of the interaction of the adaptive functions and the world. However, while cognitive structures are a consequence of this interaction, the structures themselves are invariant except with respect to age and except that they follow an invariant developmental sequence. For example, for an infant past two years, object permanence is an invariant schema. Whether we talk about a preindustrial society (a stick hidden behind a rock) or an industrial society (a paper clip under an envelope), object permanence and the process by which one learns about the permanence of objects, is invariant. Thus, independent of the content or nature of the experience, the organism's knowledge of permanence is invariant. The issue becomes simply this: Does experience facilitate schemata development while the schemata themselves remain invariant, or does experience provide the material of the schemata themselves? It is our belief that although the processes may be invariant (such processes as assimilation and accommodation), it is important to consider the world to which the infant adapts, for surely different worlds must lead to different requirements and, therefore, structures.

Although Piaget believes in the necessity of experience (action in the world *is* rather than *facilitates* knowledge), he still maintains that cognitive structures themselves are invariant. Because of this view, Piaget's model has been referred to as preformationist (Beilin, 1971).

In our present discussion for the purpose of increasing the range of considerations, we take a radical interactionalist view—namely, that experience is both necessary for and the material of knowledge.

Although the introduction of this type of variance into cognitive structures greatly complicates the task of understanding the developmental process, we have little choice. If cognitive structures are a consequence of interaction for adaptation, it seems reasonable to suggest that the cognitive structure is influenced by the nature of the interaction itself. This kind of theorizing suggests an explanation for several divergent phenomena. First, it may help to explain individual and cultural differences in thought processes (Cole, Gay, Glick & Sharp, 1971). Second, it may explain why certain kinds of structures or groupings of structures are no longer capable of maintaining equilibrium. That is, if the world in which assimilation and accommodation take place changes, then the old structures or groupings are no longer adaptive in dealing with what is presently occurring. Thus instead of emphasizing the genetic underpinning (although always in interaction with the world) as the pressure for consistent change, we evoke the consistent pressures of the world. Although these pressures are not specifiable at the moment, neither are the genetic substrates that evoke the consistency both across the developmental sequence and people. We choose then to avoid relying on an approach that presupposes some type of pre-wiring of the sequences and, instead, argue for an environmental organismic interaction in the process of development.

The effect of the infant's environment may make even greater difference when we consider other cognitive structures, those that do not fit under a Newtonian framework, that is, mass, weight, volume, and the like, as well as noncognitive structures. By noncognitive structures we refer to the socioemotional domain and to such aspects of knowing as feelings. The infant and young child certainly develop structures about their social world through assimilation and accommodation. Unlike the logical-mathematical structures, the specific structures created through the interaction of the child with his social world are as yet undefined, but there is reason to believe that these structures are affected by what the infant assimilates and accommodates to. For example, each time an infant vocalizes its mother vocalizes back while for another infant vocalization produces a smile or look. For these two infants their vocalization produces two worlds—one of vocalization, one of smiling. What is the effect on the child's resulting cognitive and noncognitive structures? Can we maintain that the resulting structure, infant action-outcome, will be invariant under either condition? Is it possible that in both examples the infant develops the knowledge of his mother (through responsivity toward him), but the nature of that knowledge is related to the specific behaviors directed toward him. Presumably, the structures, especially those in the socioemotional realm of knowing, must be affected by the environment in which the structures are formed.

If we are interested in finding out the nature of the structures, it is necessary that we view and understand the kinds of variances, as well as invariances, that exist in the infant's social and nonsocial worlds. That does not mean that structures are exclusively determined by the outside any more than they are exclusively determined by the inside. What are the socioemotional dimensions to which children need to assimilate and accommodate, and what are the resulting structures? Several structures of this kind are apparent. One invariance in the socioemotional domain is the initial helplessness and dependency of the infant on caregivers. Such a dependency exists across cultures and time. A second invariance is gender differentiation. In all human cultures there have been men and women. Finally, there exists in all cultures differentiation in the various ''work'' activities people perform. These are just some of the socioemotional dimensions that result in specific structures.

It is not our intention to elaborate a system of these structures. Rather, what we present is an empirical procedure to investigate the interaction between the child and its social world, that is, a tool that might enable us in any given situation to detect these structures.

MODELS OF INTERACTION

We need a methodology for exploring interactions and, more specifically, interactions between the infant and its social world. We avoid looking at the infant and its caregiver separately, but rather look at them in conjunction. Thus, we present a counter-position to the prevailing view—that of the study of individual elements of this interaction. Our discussion begins with a description of various models of the caregiver-infant relationship. Next, we present some measurement procedures that form a part of the model. Thereby, we elaborate an empirical attempt to analyze the specific problems of interaction between infant and caregiver and to suggest an empirical method for studying interaction in general.

Element Model ● The first model, and that most widely held today, might be called the element model. It reflects the dualism between the organism and its world. This model focuses on two elements and asks about each one of these elements. In most instances, we study what the environment does, usually the mother; the thicker arrow reflects this bias. In our example—see Figure 1—one of the elements is the infant, the other the environment. More specifically, the infant element is a set of infant behaviors that vary as a function of age. The environmental element can either represent things, such as toys or objects (as defined by the adults). Alternatively, the environmental element could be people. The arrows in this case represent the direction of study. This model characterizes studies that ask how much of what kind of behavior occurs. If we ask it of the infant we ask specifically, for example, how much smiling or vocalizing does an infant produce in an hour or two of observation. For the environment we usually refer to people. In some sense these examples reveal the illogic of this model. No one is interested in how many times the cradle rocks in two hours since we realize, although never state explicitly, that the study of that element in the model makes little sense unless we study it in interaction with other elements, namely the infant. Thus we usually study, on the environmental side, only people. The question we usually ask, for example, is: How much does the mother talk to, or look at the infant?

The element model can become interactive when we look at either individual differences or developmental consequences. When we begin to ask about differences between the sexes or social classes in terms of either the infants' or care-

FIGURE 1.　Element model.

givers' behavior, we may be implying that the middle class infant does something more (in terms of frequency of behavior) than the working class infant because the caregiver does something different. Interestingly, caregiver differences are usually not considered to be caused by infant differences.

Instead of interactions, some investigators prefer to talk about basic biological differences. Thus one infant cries more than another because of some "basic" biological difference between them and not because of differences in interactions. Again, caregiver differences are not usually relegated to biological causes. Consequently, individual differences not considered a function of an interaction are asymmetrical with respect to the model, biologically caused for the infant, learning caused for the caregiver. Only the interactional position is symmetrical to both elements.

Developmental Element Model ● Besides individual differences one can study developmental differences. In a developmental model, shown in Figure 2, we observe that there are infant behaviors at times $I1$ and $I2$ and environmental behaviors at time $E1$ and $E2$.

By using this model, one finds another asymmetry. What is usually studied is the caregiver's behavior at time $E1$ and the infant's behavior at time $I2$; for example, the amount of mother's vocalization when the child is three months old ($E1$) and infant's language ability at two years ($I2$). This type of study, correlating these two events, is interactive in nature. Observe, however, that neither infant behavior at $I1$ nor environment at $E2$ are studied, nor for that matter is $I1$ correlated with $E2$—thus the asymmetry in what is studied. In general, the asymmetry represented in this model centers on the failure to compare the infant's effect on the caregiver; however, even these comparisons would not render the model totally interactive.

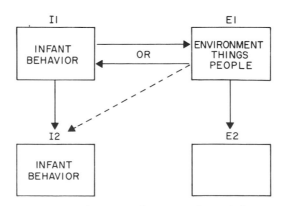

FIGURE 2.   Developmental model.

With reference to Figure 1, one could argue for an interactive approach by looking at specific behaviors. Thus categories such as nonresponded to infant cries could be coded, as could maternal smiling at infant's vocalizing. In some recent studies some of these selective behaviors have been considered (cf. Moss & Robson, 1968; Tulkin & Kagan, 1972).

Interactional Model ● Although the above approach applies interactive principles more than a simple element model, it does not reflect the strongest possible model. Rather than a static representation, a flow diagram is more appropriate to express the dynamic behavior sequences that unfold in a dyadic relationship. The model in Figure 3 schematizes this type of dynamic. Here a proportion of both infant and environment (in our studies usually maternal) behavior cannot be specified as to interaction both as initiated or response behavior. That is, we assume that all behavior is interactive, but we cannot observe the nature or direction of the interaction (MX or IX). Of greatest concern is the circled portion of the flow model. Consider a specified infant initiation; this act can lead to an unspecified maternal response (MR) which terminates the series. Alternatively, the specified infant initiation can lead to a specified maternal response which then acts as a specified maternal initiation. This outcome has two alternatives, either leading to an unspecified infant response (IR) and termination of the interaction or to a specified infant response. This specified infant response in turn becomes a specified infant initiation which then has two alternatives. Thus the flow can continue to cycle as long as the infant and maternal behavior remains specified (i.e., remains directed toward and effective on the other). As soon as this process ceases we are led into either a (MR) or (IR) and termination of the sequence. As we would expect, either person's response also becomes the stimulus initiator for the other (response = initiator in the flow diagram).

By using a flow diagram we become aware of, at least, two difficulties with interactive models. The first is concerned with point of entry into the flow. Our point of entry may mislead us into thinking that a particular behavior is an initiator of a series when, in fact, it is only a part of (in response to) a larger interaction. For example, let us consider the looking relationship between child and caregiver. We may observe a series in which there was a maternal vocalization toward infant, an infant look at the mother and, finally, a maternal look at the infant. If we enter at "infant looks at mother" and mother then looks at infant, we might be misled into believing that it was the infant who initiated the interaction. Point of entry is a very important issue and must be dealt with in some manner.

The second issue is concerned with the nature of the sequences described by

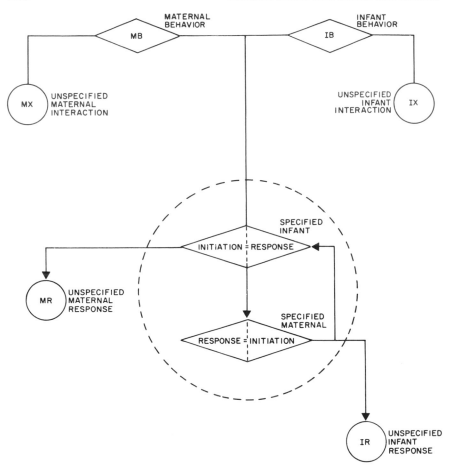

FIGURE 3.   Interactive flow model.

the model. Assumed in this model is that the last behavior of one person is responsible for the next behavior of the other person. This type of sequence is Markovian in nature, since it assumes that it is only the last event that affects the next. There is no reason to believe that this must be the case, and it is necessary to introduce a composite or some set of the previous behaviors into the flow model. We do not wish to imply that it is only the last event of one member that is solely responsible for the other member's behavior. Moreover, since both dyadic members are capable of mental operations, like memory, we must consider that memory can be used in responding to past events that were not necessarily those of the *most* immediate past. This would suggest that the

Markovian model assumptions should become less valuable the older the infant in the dyad.

In a recent paper Lewis and Lee-Painter (1973) have discussed these models in detail, presenting various empirical data to highlight each one of them. The reader is referred to these for a more complete discussion. It is interesting, however, that the use of various models leads to very different conclusions even when the data are collected on the same dyadic relationship. Thus Lewis and Wilson (1972) found no maternal differences in the overall amount of vocalization that middle class and working class mothers exhibit toward their infants. However, amount of vocalization is a noninteractive measure; it is only the amount of behavior emitted by one of the elements. When a more interactive measure was used, important differences appeared. For example, when one looks at the amount of vocalization the mother did following an infant's vocalization, one finds that there were significant social class differences with middle class mothers vocalizing significantly more often as a consequence of their infants' vocalizations than working class mothers. We suspect that this may have implications for subsequent communication and linguistic skills. However, these differences would not be apparent if we had not looked at vocalization from an interactive perspective.

EMPIRICAL METHODOLOGY

Having outlined some of the alternative models of analysis, we must discuss how interactional data can be collected. There are probably a variety of equally good approaches; however, the one outlined below has been found to be successful with very young infants and their mothers.

The mother-infant interaction data were collected using a checklist sheet with a fixed 10-second time base. A 10-second period, after preliminary investigation, was found to be an optimal unit with regard to both the shifts in behavior of the child and the mother, and the recording speed of the observer. Infant behaviors scored, for example, were vocalization, large body movements, fret/cry, feeding, quiet play, noise/nonvocalization, smiling, and looking at mother. Maternal behaviors consisted of touching, holding, vocalization, looking, smiling, playing with, caregiving (such as washing and changing of diapers), feeding, rocking, reading or watching television, and vocalization to others. Each 10 seconds the observer checked off the occurrence of both infant and mother behaviors. Thus, if an infant vocalized and this was followed by the mother vocalizing back to the infant, the observer would check a "1" in the infant vocalization line and a "2" in the mother's vocalization line. If both vocalized in the same 10-second period but the observer could not determine the nature of the interaction, both maternal and infant vocalizations were scored in the same column. The various levels of analysis follow from our theoretical discussion of models of interaction.

Frequency Distribution ● In this analysis all that is obtained is the amount of infant or maternal behavior that has occurred during the observation period. For example, how much vocalization, smiling, touching, fret/cry has occurred in two hours over five different situations such as feeding, changing, and so on. These types of data are those most reported in mother-infant studies for they are the easiest to obtain and score. They are usually considered interactional, since they were obtained while the infant and mother were together and thus assumed to be causal. The manner of the causality and their true interactive quality, however, is highly limited. For example, although we know that girl infants do more of something (for example, vocalize) and boy infants less, and we know how much they each do, we can still *not* answer the question of what causes this behavior and what is the consequence of this behavior on the child's world. Frequency data reflect for the most part the implicit assumptions of the simple element model we discussed in reference to Figure 1.

Simultaneous Behavior ● It is not possible always to describe the exact flow of an interaction, and as an approximation to these it is possible to record simultaneously occurring maternal and infant behaviors. By using a 10-second observational interval it is possible to obtain this type of interaction data. One level of this type of analysis is to obtain the number of 10-second periods in which there was simultaneous behavior for infant and mother. This provides information about the amount of mother-infant interaction, and by looking at the ratio of total frequency of behavior to simultaneous behaviors a general interactivity score can be obtained. Likewise, this similar analysis can be applied to each infant-maternal behavior so that a matrix of maternal and infant behaviors can be obtained. In this model, behavior occurs in relationship with other behaviors. Although the exact flow of the interaction cannot be specified, the time-locked quality of the behavior insures a more interactional position.

There are some difficulties with this type of analysis. For example, the time period selected for such an analysis should markedly affect the interaction results. Too short a time base and very few behaviors would be classified interactive, while too long a time base would include all behaviors in one long interaction wherein specific behavior categories would become blurred. We have chosen for our empirical investigation 10 seconds. It seems to represent a time period that is a compromise between these two problems, as well as being a comfortable time period for an observer both to obtain and record the data. There are, however, two problems with this procedure that must be considered.

First is the consideration that simultaneous·behavior does not indicate any sort of stable pattern of interaction. The collection of a great deal of data should result in the low frequency of occurrence of random simultaneous events. The second problem has to do with cutting of chains of events that would be longer than the 10-second base. The observers were instructed to cross the 10-second periods if they could observe chains that exceeded the 10 seconds. Although long chains of events are not expected at this age (Lusk & Lewis, 1972), this procedure may raise some difficulties when studying interaction at older ages. In our discussion of sequential analysis we deal with this problem directly. However, the whole approach at older ages should be reconsidered, since the behavioral basis of observation should give way to more elaborate behavioral categories.

Directional Interactive Analyses • In this type of analysis we look only at the directional interactive behavior. By utilizing our coding system of "1" and "2" it is possible to determine not only that a maternal-infant behavior occurred in interaction, but the flow of that interaction. For example, an infant fret is followed by a maternal look and vocalization or a maternal vocalization is followed by an infant smile. This type of analysis is described by the model in Figure 3. For example, we obtain all the two-chain infant initiations or infant responses. This would tell us about the interaction and flow of two single behaviors (maternal and infant); however, we know little about what happens as a feedback to this set. For example, an infant vocalizes; this elicits a maternal vocalization. Now by adding the effects of maternal vocalization we can describe this particular behavior chain cycle. It must be kept in mind that behaviors other than vocalization elicit maternal and infant vocalizations. This must be added to the model.

   Although this type of interactional data is most useful in discussing the mother-infant dyad, it is also the most difficult data to obtain. The observation of flow or directional data is relatively infrequent compared with the total amount of behavior elicited, so that only a small proportion of the data can be so scored. Moreover, there is great variability in the amount of directional interaction of specific behaviors, which is probably a function of their differential occurrence rather than their ease of observation.

Sequential Analyses • There are a variety of issues to consider in sequential analyses. When we examine actor chains we can look at length of chain, initiator of chain, terminator of chain, and finally the nature of the chain. The length of an actor chain has to do with the number of actor changes. For example, mother vocalize-infant vocalize; and mother vocalize-infant vocalize, infant smile are both chains involving one actor-change. That is, in both instances the mother did something, and then the infant did something(s) which ended the interaction. Lusk and Lewis (1972) found that this dimension increased with the age of the infant within the first year of life. Initiator and terminator of chain is also an important chain parameter, and relatively little has been done with this dimension. Finally, the nature of the chain has received some attention.

One type of sequential analysis having to do with the nature of the chaining involves the construction of a matrix of transitional probabilities (Freedle & Lewis, 1971). By using a Markovian transitional probability model one can look at sequential analysis. Markovian sequential analysis is unique in that it assumes that only what occurs on trial n can be used to estimate the occurrence of what will occur on trial $n + 1$. There are several ways this model can be of value in the study of interaction. Observation of the transitional probability for each mother-infant pair reveals the ways in which a current state of the mother-infant system influences the conditional probability of the next state. Moreover, by examining the magnitude of the diagonal probabilities, one can get an immediate estimate of the degree to which the infant or mother or both will persist in a particular kind of activity over time.

We do not wish to minimize the empirical difficulties that exist in obtaining interactive data. Certainly the story is not complete. What is important to emphasize, however, is that it is now possible empirically to match some of our theorizing. It is now possible for interactive analyses to be undertaken so that one can observe elements in action as opposed to aspects of the elements themselves. As such, we are moving toward our interactional goals and away from the dualism of our reductionist heritage.

IMPLICATIONS FOR COGNITIVE STRUCTURES

The interactional model and the methodology it generates reveals potentially meaningful individual differences. Some children's worlds are filled with vocalization-vocalization interactions, others are not (see Lewis & Wilson, 1972). Some are touched when they cry, some are rocked, still others are ignored. What shall we claim to be the effect on the cognitive structures of the child? We hold to the strong interactionalist view that the stimulus as well as the context of the infant's cognition are affected by its experience. The important and by no means answerable question is: How? How might the nature of the contingency between the infant's action and the environmental response (also the other way) determine the structures and content of mind? We have no easy answer; however, the recent work of Sigel (1968) may be relevant. Sigel uses a notion of distancing to account for the ability of some children to deal with higher cognitive functioning such as representational thought. By distancing he denotes "behaviors or events which separate the child cognitively from the immediate behavioral environment." Greater distancing leads to more representational thought. Is it possible that different styles of maternal response can lead to more or less distancing? For example, touching in response to an infant's vocalization might be less of a distancing response than vocalization in response. Other distancing responses are looking and smiling. It is interesting to note that vocalization and looking are the responses that do not significantly favor the lower SES mother, while the rest of the behaviors do (see Lewis & Wilson, 1972). As Sigel points out, increasing the distance between self and object may contribute to the development of representational thought and perhaps to cognitive growth in general.

that two year olds who were more distally oriented, that is, looked and talked to their parents rather than touched or stayed close to them, performed better on the Bayley Mental Development Scales (Lewis, Weinraub & Ban, 1973). Attachment behavior expressed at two years by distal behaviors may be another example of distancing. Distancing, expressed by mothers' distal responses to their infants' behavior, would account for the deficit in lower SES children's behavior at ages past two. Why then do lower SES infants show superior performance in infancy? While distancing (vocalization responses, etc.) facilitates representational thought—after two years—proximal interaction such as touching, rocking, and the like, facilitates early prerepresentational thought. This would agree with Geber's (1958) and Geber and Dean's (1957a,b) findings that infants receiving great amounts of proximal interaction are precocious for the first two years and retarded thereafter as compared with infants with less initial proximal interaction. Sigel's hypothesis has some appeal in predicting the consequences of the different social worlds of these infants. Whatever the specific consequences are, it is difficult not to assume that they should have a direct and long-term effect on the child's mental life. Indeed, in a recent study we have found some evidence that the early communication patterns (interactions) of mothers and infants is correlated with subsequent language competence (Lewis & Freedle, 1973).

Thus our methodology has proved useful in looking at interactions. We believe that the effect of the environment makes itself felt by differentially affecting the structures that result from the infant's adaptation to a specific world. The *process* of acquiring meaning may be invariant but the nature of the environment may well determine the *structure* as well as *content* of the mind.

PART THREE

Linguistic

CHAPTER 7

Psycholinguistics: Some Historical Issues

ARTHUR L. BLUMENTHAL

In this chapter we place special emphasis on historical instances of interdisciplinary advances involving linguistics and psychology, which have often revolved around structural issues from the days of James and Wundt to the present. The psychological study of structure in language and in language performance reached its early high point in Wundt's book on language which appeared in 1900. In the two decades that followed the psychological concern with the nature of the effect of language structure on language usage revolved around Wundt's writings.

With the decline and disappearance of Wundt's school, there was a relative void in psycholinguistics that was soon filled by the broad shift toward functionalism and behaviorism. The psychology of language as subsequently represented by F. Allport (1924), Bühler (1934), Kantor (1936), and Skinner (1957) was much more concerned with the activity and interaction of organisms engaged in communication acts rather than with the forms and patterns of the communication medium or the interaction of that medium with mental processes. Just following mid-century, psycholinguistics under the influence of Chomsky underwent a major shift and again adopted the concern of structuralism and mental processes. These historical fluctuations appear to reflect a basic aspect of the study of the psychology of language. It is the difference between the study of the questions of the formal structure of language, on the one hand, and the study of language usage and the process of communication, on the other. Both are clearly relevant for psycholinguistics.

Investigations of language performance and the use of the term psycholinguistics increased suddenly in popularity in America during the late 1950s. This fact has led to the dating of the beginning of psycholinguistics from the time of the Indiana conference on the interdisciplinary study of language in 1953 (Osgood & Sebeok, 1954), a date that is further supported by the common notion that language is so complex that psychologists have only recently been able to approach it because their techniques and procedures have only recently been refined enough to be adequate to the task. But this is not the case, as an examination of earlier research efforts shows (Blumenthal, 1970).

WUNDT'S PSYCHOLINGUISTICS

Wundt's dissatisfaction with the narrow empiricism and physicalism of the mid-nineteenth century caused him to become embroiled in debates with taxonomic linguists toward the end of that century. Yet as a psychologist, Wundt's goal was to give an explicit characterization of the structure and principles that govern the processes of cognition in humans. It was his belief that the study of human language provides one of the best means to knowledge about the mind. As Wundt's psychological and philosophical work matured it became holistic and configurational and represented traditional trends in German idealism that date back, at least, to Kant and Humboldt. His psycholinguistic work was a direct continuation of the program outlined by Humboldt whom he frequently quoted at length on structuralist issues. Many of the topics in Wundt's cognitive psychology and psycholinguistics have emerged again today, for example, notions of creative synthesis, rhythmical grouping in cognition, surface structure and deep structure differences in language, and volitional processes. But his psycholinguistics represents one of the most serious inter-disciplinary efforts in bringing psychology and linguistics together around the concept of structure.

Wundt's Dual System

Wundt's study of mental phenomena elaborated a dual system of the "inner" and the "outer" events. In the inner system of cognitive processes are the principles involving apperception (attention) and judgment. In the outer system, of sensorimotor function, we find principles of association, concerning the effects of frequency, contiguity, and intensity of events. Although he emphatically rejected Cartesian mind-body dualism, Wundt shared with Descartes the problem of how dual entities interact; but here it was the problem of the relation between sensory-motor events and higher cognitive events where the two realms were often governed by different principles, and where the relation between them was viewed as a complex and indirect one and, furthermore, where the methods of study often had to be different for each.

Wundt employed the term apperception to refer to the focus of attention within the field of consciousness. Just as the fovea of the eye may move over the visual field and bring each point to the place most favorable for seeing, so does Wundt's inner (mental) fixation point move over the range of thought taking various points into clearer consciousness. Early experiments indicated that the span of this mental fixation point was about six or seven items or groups. Associated with the phenomenon of apperception were "creative resultants" or those aspects of experience that are organized and structured internally.

According to Wundt, the structures that are the product of the cognitive system are quite different from those that are the product of the external system. Every part of an external structure remains essentially independent so that when it becomes dissociated from other elements it retains its identity and remains recognizable. But with events of internal origin the case is very different. The significance of the individual element is now entirely dependent on the whole mental representation (Gesamtvorstellung) of which it forms a part. The number of constituents in any phenomenon of consciousness, whether of inner or outer origin, is limited to the degree that the mental content lacks structure. For example, a list of words grouped into connected phrases is grasped more readily than it would be if the words were unrelated. Wundt and his students produced a considerable range of experimental and observational data relevant to these conclusions. Elsewhere, Wundt himself preferred dialectical over experimental method in the study of the inner or higher cognitive processes that involve concept formation and language. The higher processes, he believed, might be understood by their products, most notably language, and he was thus led into the study of linguistics where his method was more often logic than experiment.

One of Wundt's most ambitious and most controversial research programs was the attempt to identify subjective feelings accompanying apperceptive states. We must be careful here in the translation of the term *Gefühl* which did not mean feeling as arising from external events. *Gefühl* applies to an underlying basic affective level from which emotions, attitudes, and certain other cognitive functions are derived. There are, for instance, feelings of activity, strain, and expectancy that accompany the train of thought. Wundt claimed that the most prominent *Gefühle* during apperception were the feelings of inner activity *(Thätigkeitsgefühle)* that accompany all volitional acts. The study of this phenomenon received extensive treatment in Wundt's Leipzig laboratory and resulted in a tridimensional classification of rudimentary feelings: pleasantness-unpleasantness, strain-relaxation, and activity-passivity. This may remind one of the three dimensions of the "semantic differential" developed more recently by Osgood, Suci, and Tannenbaum (1957).

Wundt's Theory of Language

Wundt's theory of language performance closely follows his psychological analysis and is divided into two aspects: (1) the outer phenomena of sound production and perception, and (2) the inner phenomena of the train of thought. Wundt's analysis of the complex relations between inner and outer systems for psychology in general relies heavily on language. He proposed that through the study of the structure of language this interaction might be better understood. However, to understand language performance in Wundt's terms, it is necessary to trace the mental processes that precede, accompany, and follow utterances. The first difficulty is that these processes are usually extremely rapid and automatic. Nevertheless, a person often censors his own speech and revises it while in progress. Thus speech is often retarded by the preparatory activity for production of appropriate words and inflections.

According to Wundt, we may say that the act of natural speech begins with the apperception of a simultaneous mental representation (Gesamtvorstellung). Then attention isolates some aspect of this impression. However, this is not a strict isolation of a mental element, because the object of attention must retain a sense of relation or belonging to the general impression. In this way (of relational structuring) the mental content is further organized and analyzed into features or constituents all retaining certain structural relations to one another. From this we derive the basis for the relational structure of sentences. Wundt adopted the device of the tree-diagram in his *Logik* of 1880 to describe these mental events—the judgments made and the relations applied between constituents by the apperceiving individual in the act of preparing his thought for representation in speech. This type of apperceptive division, when including the elementary logical relation of the subject-predicate judgment, enables humans to make their unique representation in speech sounds, or gestures, or by whatever means. These means are social conventions, and they are simply signals and cues from which a listener may recreate a similar *Gesamtvorstellung* or whole impression for himself. However, this example is too simple when it is compared with Wundt's involved analysis of grammatical relations and in the sequential ordering *(Gliederung)* of the words or the elements of expression.

In the act of rapid conversation, the analysis-for-production process is often diverted by the responses of listeners. A listener, on the other hand, may believe that he detects an error or may find a point of disagreement with the speaker. This feeling may be vague, scarcely more than would find expression in the exclamation "wrong!" but the listener becomes conscious of a correction or counterargument. An impulsive person might break in when his own thought is unanalyzed and thus will find himself for a moment conscious of what he wishes to say but unable to say it. Or, if interruption is not possible and we go on listening to the speaker, the germinal concept may be lost, and a person "forgets what he was going to say." If we see a child doing something dangerous the impulse to interfere is at first no more than a willed negative: "No!" or a prohibition: "Don't!" The process of analysis of the situation into a fuller utterance follows. Similarly the germinal form of a question may produce speech before the *Gesamtvorstellung* analysis occurs, or before the production of a full sentence. Many interrogative states need only the slightest analysis as shown in the output, "Huh?" indicating, "What did you say?" or, "What is it?"

The apperceptive function of applying grammatical relations (subject of X, object of X, etc.) to aspects of simultaneous impressions are basic tools in the preparation of thought for expression in human language. They influence the direction of the analysis and retain the sense of sentence unity. The aim of the whole process is to enable a listener to use the ultimate end of the analysis, the speech sounds, as cues for creating and organizing his own cognition. We may observe listening and speaking simultaneously in one individual when he censors his own output by matching it with his own germinal impressions, that is, when he stops and exclaims, "That's not what I intended to say," or "Let me start over."

Approaching the study of language comprehension from the physical utterance and the listener, apperception is again the basis of Wundt's approach. The listener must reconstruct an impression from the sequential sound cues, and he must do it quite rapidly or he is lost. For this reason the very attentive hearer's long-term retention of exact words may be very poor, although he may have understood the speaker perfectly. Wundt asserted that this same ability enables the speed reader to grasp whole sentences at a glance. A person with superior reading ability dispenses with detailed analysis and, instead, catches words and phrases here and there as cues to reconstruct the thought. His apperception skill, the ability to organize rough internal impressions, is superior. The attention of the interested listener is similarly active in anticipating what is to come, and it may regress to revise or complete interpretations of what has already been heard. But Wundt notes that where the subject matter is unfamiliar or where the language is foreign and imperfectly understood, then the reader or hearer is forced into a piecemeal, detailed analysis of the utterance.

It is important for Wundt's approach to language that it entails the priority of the sentence, which he defines psychologically as the transformation of a simultaneous mental representation *(Gesamtvorstellung)* into sequentially ordered speech segments that are logically related to each other according to the rules of language. Because the sentence is primary and the word is secondary, word-forms are viewed as the somewhat arbitrary results of the sequential organizing activity.

Wundt's Contemporaries

Wundt's major statement on language came in his two-volume work *Die Sprache* which first appeared in 1900 and was revised in 1904 and again in 1912. This composed the first two books of a longer series—the ten-volume

Völkerpsychologie (Ethnic Psychology) (1900-1920). The study of "ethnic psychology" had become popular in the nineteenth century after it was initiated in Chajim Steinthal's writings. However, Wundt's holistic-organismic approach differed from Steinthal's, which had been based on Herbart's atomistic psychology. But Wundt shared the Humboldtian tradition with Steinthal in recognizing the centrality of language for ethnic studies. Wundt often became involved in purely linguistic questions and undertook studies of several exotic or non-Indo-European languages. His investigation of sign language systems is still one of the best explorations of that topic.

Perhaps a centrally important assertion in Wundt's psycholinguistic writings was that the sentence can never be understood in terms of the physical utterance, that is, as an acoustical event. Many of his linguistic contemporaries had viewed the sentence as a succession or linking of words or as a sound pattern or as a mental representation that is isomorphic to the sound pattern. Such views are predominant, for example, in the most widely used linguistics text of that day—Hermann Paul's *Prinzipien der Sprachgeschichte* (1886). The debate over this issue between these two scholars (Paul and Wundt) lasted for the duration of their careers, nearly 40 years. Several psychologists attempted to resolve the conflict with laboratory experiments without notable success. But Wundt compiled a broad array of arguments against Paul, who was forced into a very defensive stance in the course of several interchanges. Wundt argued that we cannot take the forms of utterances as representations of their underlying grammatical structure. In addition to the structure of utterances, there is the cognitive structure of the "pure grammatical bases" *(rein grammatische Gründe)* of sentences. This structure is not a linear one as is the sequential utterance. Wundt's tree diagrams of sentences were thus not diagrams of utterances but were, instead, devices to illustrate the relational structure that one imposes on any utterance that he comprehends. With those diagrams Wundt illustrated how sentences may appear recursively within other sentences. He also suggested that the best way to uncover the true nature of the relations that hold among constituents is to transform sentences into various forms (active to passive, etc.) to observe how the relations and constituents behave under these variations. All this work was done under the direct influence of Humboldt's writings, the same sections that Chomsky (1966) has pointed out as the intellectual antecedents of the modern transformational generative grammar.

Wundt did not formalize the notion of rule of grammar as has been done recently. Perhaps the reason that he did not attempt to advance linguistics further in this direction is that he was primarily a psychologist and was more concerned with theories of language performance. Moreover, he grew to be out of sympathy with the newer trends in linguistics so that his contacts with linguists declined in the later years. Indeed, the troublesome intrusion of Wundt into the field of linguistics led Delbrück to his famous decision in 1901 that linguistics could and should proceed without the hindrance of psychology. Paul and Delbrück were only two of numerous other Wundtian commentators.

BETWEEN WUNDT AND CHOMSKY

A movement in psychology called functionalism grew in popularity early in the twentieth century, and its influence is apparent in numerous writings on language spanning roughly that of Marty (1908) to Bühler (1934). Marty's long and ponderous writings were largely in the form of polemic, much of which is directed against Wundt's mentalism and "volitional" psychology. Karl Bühler's works were perhaps the most sophisticated of this tradition and also the most difficult. His notion was to describe utterances in terms of situational context, and in this he applied many of the viewpoints of Gestalt psychology, perhaps more than any other psycholinguist has. When a member of the Prague Circle of linguistics, he became heavily involved in their program to delineate independent specific functions of language. Although his works are little known by the later post-midcentury psycholinguists in the United States, his notions are much closer to those presented at the 1953 Indiana conference on psycholinguistics than they are to the earlier Wundtian psycholinguistics.

Functionalism in Psycholinguistics

The structure in Bühler's system is based on the metaphor of control devices, later to be named cybernetics. The communication act, in Bühler's description, has two control elements—speaker and listener. The listener is a control device in that he functions as a *selector* of cues by which he constructs an interpretation. The speaker is also a control element in that he is a structuring station *(Formungsstation)* for the sending of conventional cues. In cybernetic terms there are thus two covarying control factors always present in language performance, one in production and one in comprehension.

Bühler considered the setting outside of the individual to be as important a part of the performance structure as the mental events that accompany speech, and thus he began with a "total performance field." An utterance occurs within a system of three covariants—the speaker, the hearer, and the facts or states represented by the utterance. These three points in the "language field" defined Bühler's three basic functions of language. They were called the expressive function (symptoms of the speaker's disposition), the evocational function (signals for the listener to react), and the representational function (symbols that describe objects or facts).

In the 1930s "the structure of the field" was the foundation of a number of new theoretical trends in psychology of which Bühler's was one. Only then, in contrast to the Wundtian era, this referred not to the structure of the mind, but rather to the structure of external events that guide or shape behavior or experience. Given two speakers of a language, according to Bühler's system, no matter how well one of them structures a sentence his utterance will fail if both parties do not share the same field to some degree. The total field *(Umfeld)* consists not only of the practical situation *(Zeigfeld)* in which an utterance occurs, but also of the symbol field *(Symbolfeld)*, which is the context of language segments preceding the segment under consideration. More specifically, the symbol field consists of those constituents that stand in grammatical relation to the utterance that is in the foreground at any moment. And thus the figure-ground concept is made relevant to syntactic structure. Grammatical structure may be interpreted in the sense of sentence parts that bear various figure-ground relations to one another.

Developmental Psycholinguistics in Germany

A more detailed look at the development of language acquisition research may be informative with regard to structuralist viewpoints. Most historians of psychology date the modern era of child study from the appearance of Preyer's *Die Seele des Kindes* (1881). In this work Preyer reported the results of systematic observations on the first 1000 days of infancy—the most ambitious effort of its kind up to that time. His report appears in three parts concerning the development of the senses, the development of volitional processes, and the development of the intellect, the latter receiving most attention. A large segment of the work concerned the development of language where Preyer made a detailed comparison of the progressive stages of language development with the regressive stages of aphasia and other language pathologies. This anticipated the highly influential study of these comparisons that was made by Jakobson (1941). Preyer concluded that it is impossible to account for language acquisition solely on the basis of learning, and the human learning of language is possible only if we assume that the child inherits some fundamental *structures*. Preyer was thus led to adopt the nativist position.

The quarter century of research on language acquisition that followed Preyer's book culminated in Clara and William Stern's *Die Kindersprache* (1907) which, in turn, was the most influential text for the next generation of developmental linguistics. In comparing the Sterns' work with Preyer's, we discover that language development studies had improved in at least one important respect—they had become more sophisticated in regard to linguistic structure, owing to advances in linguistic thought about the turn of the century. Many early writers on acquisition are easily categorized as proponents of either an "imitation" theory or a "spontaneity" theory of language acquisition. The Sterns showed how each position when taken alone is too simplistic, and William Stern viewed the development of language as an unfolding process similar to the development of an embryonic cell into a complex organism—an analogy widely used at that time. This, of course, may be contrasted with the tradition of mental chemistry where development is the combination and recombination of various elementary units, sensations, or behaviors. In one instance, *structure* is inherent in the process at the beginning, in the other, it is not.

With the genetic model, the *sentence* was conceived as the embryonic language "cell," and the rudiments of syntax were thought to be somehow present in the initial embryonic utterances or holophrases at the outset of development. But the real problem in the study of language acquisition for the Sterns was to understand the interaction of forces, that is, "to what extent internal tendencies and forces are at work during assimilation, selection, and internal processing of externally presented forms [1907, p. 122]."

The Sterns were impressed with the egocentric nature of the initial language patterns in children. They argued that we must not force these language beginnings into the forms of the adult's elaborated syntax and categories. Their emphasis is on the productivity of children's attempts at language. The phenomena of a child's word-orderings were for them fruitful sources of observations on the unfolding of the mature surface structure of language.

The Sterns postulated the notion of a "speech-need" *(Sprachnot)* to account for many of the child's creative productions. When the child has developed a wealth of experiences that run far ahead of language development, it is forced to be productive or inventive to the utmost to make use of its very limited language means. According to Humboldt, this is after all the essence of language, to make "infinite use of finite means."

Although later editions of the Sterns' book is still used today in certain European circles, it is largely unknown in the United States. Yet it is a large compilation of data taken not only from the Sterns' own three children but from many other children representing several languages other than German with very extensive comparisons among the different cases. There are discussions of numerous syntactic constructions as they take peculiar form in the speech of children. Much of this is conceptually related to the language acquisition investigations that are taking place more than 50 years later, especially in America.

One effect of the Sterns' book was that it renewed the general interest in child language during the early twentieth century. The strong incentive for the earlier child language investigations had come perhaps from Darwinian theory. A blend of evolutionism and nineteenth-century romanticism stands out in the proposal that the appearance of language in the child is a recapitulation of the evolution of language in primitive man. Paul (1886), for instance, encouraged the examination of child language development as a means for testing principles of historical language change. Carl Franke seems to have been the linguist who took Paul's suggestion most seriously, for he made a detailed comparison of the development of language in children with the development of language in societies (1889).

Developmental Psycholinguistics in France

Developmental psycholinguistics flourished in its emergence in the French-speaking world. In one example, Oscar Bloch wrote a series of articles from 1913 to 1924 on the development of language in his three children with an emphasis on the syntactic aspects of language. Later Marcel Cohen published a series of insightful reports (1925-1933) that also emphasized grammatical structure phenomena in child language development. The notable aspect of these articles is the view of child language development as a series of overlapping sublanguages. Cohen (1925) explained it this way:

"These (child) languages constitute small systems, the first of very reduced dimensions and the final ones of considerable breadth. As in the evolution of language, any given system is encumbered by the remnants of the preceding system; the beginnings of the system that will follow can also be found [1925, pp. 109–110]."

Cohen claimed that the beginnings of the sentence, which serve to "declare" and "relate," occur much earlier than is generally considered (i.e., in the form of gestures). Cohen asserts that the infant's successive languages thus begin with gestures and facial expressions in the pre-verbal period.

Further influential French work in developmental psycholinguistics during the 1920s came from Paul Guillaume (1925, 1927a,b). Guillaume had a keen interest in the emergence of primitive sentences, that is, those utterances that consist of the first separable but grammatically related parts developing out of the "undifferentiated verbal protoplasm" of the child's first expressions. He had observed his own preschool children for several years, and then made additional observations on children, ages two to five, in a nursery school. As many had before him, Guillaume criticized the division of children's words into conventional grammatical categories. And he repeats Stern's statement that at age one and one-half or two, the child's "verbal unities do not belong to any class of words, because they are not words, but sentences [Stern & Stern 1907, p. 104]." Guillaume discovered that there are two kinds of elements that first emerge from the autonomous word-sentences. These are the names of people and expressions of volition. The structure of early sentences turns the dissection of experience into one part that is concrete and represented, and another part that is lived, acted, or felt. Here Guillaume's view follows an argument made previously by Alfred Binet (1907) that the most primary division of mental life is into objects and acts.

But Guillaume's analysis also seems to share in the Wundtian approach that language production depends on the dismembering of a mental complex. And in this way he proceeds to describe and explain the unfolding of language up to the age of five. Guillaume's articles illustrate a blend of twentieth-century functionalism with Wundtian psycholinguistics. His definition of the sentence closely follows Wundt.

Guillaume strongly argued that we must escape our subservience to the written mode of language because this distorts our analysis of child language. Then he proceeds to show how the elements, recognized in adult language as sentence constituents, gradually detach themselves from the child's primeval unstructured utterances. In this way we observe the surface structure of sentences unfold during the course of only a few months. As others had before him, Guillaume criticized those investigators who analyzed the initial utterances of infants into parts of speech and then used frequency counts in studies of the vocabulary growth in each category (noun, verb, adjective, pronoun, etc). This taxonomic approach was a form of linguistic phrenology that had a strong following among functionalists in France. In America in the early 1900s, such frequency counts appeared in a great wave of investigations.

Developmental Psycholinguistics in America

The first sophisticated, although brief, observation on sentence development reported in America came from Moore (1896). Her description was just a portion of a larger report on mental development in children. She described sequences of expanding expressions (noted at regular intervals of development) which she reasoned as being synonymous with one another because each utterance was an expansion of the previous one. For example,

Developmental stages
1.   *Book.*
2.   *Mama book.*
3.   *Mama sit down, a book.*
4.   *Mama sit down, read a book.*
5. *Mama is sitting down, reading a book.*

All these utterances had the same function and represented the same situation. In effect, they were all subject-predicate representations. Moore's data illustrated the gradual differentiation of the original "embryonic" expression. And in the later thinking of Cohen, Bloch, and Guillaume this indicates a series of sub-dialects that succeed each other while approaching adult speech.

The issue here is akin to the classic debate between Paul and Wundt concerning sentence production. There is a parallel opposition of views in developmental psycholinguistics: (1) acquisition is considered as a building-up process starting from isolated speech elements (Paul), and (2) acquisition is viewed as a progressive differentiation of a primitive whole or of mass-units (Wundt).

At the beginning of the twentieth century, the spirit of the times in America changed radically and became almost completely isolated from previous thought and research as well as from most European research. The new generation of American psychologists apparently had little interest in linguistics. There was only a requirement of convenient units of verbal behavior (namely words) and little concern for the discussions among theoretical linguists about what were linguistically valid units of language. To the nonlinguist (and certain linguists as well), the most elementary and obvious fact about verbal behavior is that it is a string of words.

The study of animal behavior now made rapid gains. Attempts to study language in a laboratory animal, indeed, led to a very different conception of psycholinguistics. There were no longer any subjects and predicates nor apperceptions to worry about because these notions were of little value in generalizing the animal data to human beings.

RECENT ISSUES IN PSYCHOLINGUISTICS

Modern psycholinguistics has to some degree duplicated the Wundtian era of psycholinguistics by calling for a return to the Humboldtian conception of language. Just as in that day, empiricistic psychology is now held to be inadequate for the problems posed by the study of linguistic *structure*. One problem, however, has surfaced more clearly than it did in the former time. It is the distinction between the structure of language as an abstract formal system and the structure of language usage as a constellation of psychological capacities (memory, perception, attention, etc). Today this distinction is known as the "competence versus performance" distinction.

Competence versus Performance

As it was set forth for psycholinguistics by Chomsky (1965), the competence-performance distinction defines the differences between the study of structural systems of the natural languages and that of the structure of psychological mechanisms. In his initial theoretical statement, Chomsky (1957) pointed out that he was "studying language as an instrument or a tool, attempting to describe its structure with no explicit reference to the way in which it is put to use" (p. 103). Unfortunately, the psycholinguists who, at first, avidly followed Chomsky paid little heed to the above remark. And within the structuralist psychological literature there has not always been a clear separation of the characteristics of abstract systems (grammars, algorithms, musical forms, etc.) and the cognitive processes that act on them, learn them, and use them. For this reason the expression "cognitive structure" may mean either (1) the structure of a system of human knowledge or belief, or (2) the characteristics and capacities of a biological performance process including the mechanisms of perception, memory, attention, and affect. Obviously, a cultural system such as language may reflect in its own characteristics the capacities and limitations of its users or inventors. That is, there may be species-specific limits on the forms of language we may use or the types of games we may play, just as there are clearly different limits on the actions of other animals.

Still it is an old observation that there is not a strict structural identity between these epistemological systems and the human cognitive mechanisms. The paradigm example is that of arithmetic vis-à-vis the act of adding numbers. We may be able to add a column of two- or three-digit numbers in our heads, but we cannot so add ten-digit numbers because of psychological limitations, and these limitations have no representation in the "epistemology," that is, in the rules of arithmetic. Similarly, two sentences may be equally perfect in conforming to grammatical rules but because of differences in length or phrasing one of the sentences may be much more difficult to perceive or to produce.

Piaget also establishes this separation between epistemology and psychology (1970), but then he claims a strict parallelism between the two. Not only may studies of psychological performance be enriched by the study of abstract knowledge systems, but also the reverse: the study of psychological performance mechanisms is to enhance the work of epistemology, which is Piaget's program.

The competence-performance distinction is a traditional one in both linguistics (e.g., Saussure, 1916) and in psychology (e.g., Tolman, 1932) although it has not been observed by most behaviorists or by taxonomic linguists. It is not, as Bever has recently claimed, a very recent simplifying assumption that the present linguists have thrown up to "defend themselves against the accumulation of inexplicable psychological facts about speech . . . [1970, p. 342]." In Bartlett's studies of memory (1932) the distinction was recognized as that separating psychology and epistemology. Bartlett commented on restricting psychology to the study of performance as follows:

"In thus restricting himself, he [the psychologist] is casting, or should cast, no reflection upon the other problems set by the epistemologist. They may be more important, as they certainly are more difficult, even than his own [Bartlett 1932, p. 11]."

But more often, twentieth-century empiricist thought has not observed the distinction between "learning" and "knowledge" or between the development of knowledge and the structure of knowledge.

Linguistics versus Psychology

Transformational linguistics has concerned the study of the structure of languages by means of setting up systems of generative rules, whereas with taxonomic linguistics, you have the segmentation and classification of elements and thereby arrive at a taxonomy, rather than a rule system, as the description of a language. With the recent transformational grammar, linguistics appears to have become more psychological because the notion of a rule implies a rule-user, and psychological interdisciplinary activity was thus vigorously stimulated. The taxonomic school, in contrast, was noted for its isolation from psychology, and the periods of most intensive collaboration between psychologists and linguists preceded and then followed the period of dominance of the taxonomic approach (Blumenthal, 1970). This was true even though the taxonomists adhered to a philosophy of science and to a form of behaviorism that was identical to that prevalent in the psychology of the same period, roughly 1920 to 1960.

The earlier isolation of the two fields began to develop following the appearance of a highly influential monograph by the linguist Delbrück in 1901. About the turn of the century, psycholinguistics was an active field with frequent collaboration between psychologist and linguist. But it was the issue of the proper relation of structure in linguistics to structure in psychology that eventually led to vitriolic debate (summarized by Delbrück) and then to Delbrück's judgment that it should matter little to the linguists which psychological theory is in vogue, since a language as an abstract system remains neutral with respect to whatever mechanisms of memory, perception, conditioning, or the like that may be applied to the linguistic system. Thus linguists were freed from the psychological debates of that period by Delbrück's maxim, and they then proceeded to study the structure of French, German, English, and so on without hindrance from the disagreements with Wundt, Külpe, James, Watson, or other psychological theorists.

Today linguistics and psychology are frequent, although often uneasy, bedfellows—but their relationship is somewhat the reverse of that a few generations ago. Linguists had often been submissive to a dominant psychological theory, whether Wundtian (e.g., Bloomfield, 1914) or whether behaviorist (e.g., Bloomfield, 1933). A change to the dominance of linguistics is a rather dramatic aspect of the more recent psycholinguistics. Here psychological proposals are often justified on the grounds that they are based on a particular notion of linguistic structure (e.g., Miller, 1962, Lenneberg, 1967).

This change in dominance occurred in the late 1950s after enough psychologists had become disillusioned with their accounts of verbal behavior and dissatisfied with their lack of sophistication with regard to language *structure*. They were thus primed to be receptive to the developments in linguistic theory (Chomsky, 1957) that offered exactly the type of advances in structural description that they sought. Moreover, with Chomsky's formalization of the notion of grammatical rule, it was tempting to view this work as a description of the rule-user, and thus a number of psychologists were seduced by the formal niceties of linguistic theory.

This drama could only end with those psychologists left in a state of theoretical despair, since Chomsky's work had concerned all along only the study of a purely formal system that ''generates'' structured sequences of items admissable under a set of formal rules. Psychologists had immediately appropriated this formal logic usage of ''generate'' as though it referred to the structure of natural speech production. Formal linguistic theory had been taken as a description of talking, listening, or reading. There had been a blatant search for the nature of psychological capacity in the structure of the stimulus. Language performance models are thus simply a restatement of some type or level of linguistic theory. And any aspect of the linguistic input, whether abstract underlying logical relations or immediate word order, may be made the basis for ''perceptual strategies'' where appeal to mechanisms of perception or memory are made only secondarily and haphazardly as they support the linguistic description. That is, the psychology of language in this case is not derived from any psychological performance structure.

Recent psycholinguists have committed the classical stimulus error in searching for an understanding of psychological operations in the structure of the ''stimulus,'' that is, language. The description of language structure was made the basis for the prediction and explanation of psychological performance. This misses the essence of the competence–performance distinction. In effect, each time a new wrinkle was added somewhere in the linguistic theory, psychologists were quick to run to their laboratories to demonstrate the ''psychological reality'' of the new linguistic formalism. And because it takes a while to design and set up an experiment and then to run subjects, psycholinguistics always appeared to be a little bit behind the work in linguistics, and thus always to have a strangely archaic appearance in the eyes of many linguists.

Lags in Psycholinguistic Research

Consider the nature of the psycholinguistic experiments that define the recent history of this field. In the earliest of these there is a general effort to show that language utterances are not merely strings of responses linked together in chainlike fashion, but rather must be viewed as hierarchical groupings or phrasings of elements. As with the principles of Gestalt psychology, this was to account for the superior perception of, comprehension of, and memory for language stimuli in contrast to strings of nonsense syllables. Yet no sooner was this program underway than Chomsky offered proofs that phrase structure systems were inadequate to account for the structure of language. There then appeared the early formulations of transformational grammar that depicted language as a set of simple "kernel" sentences plus a set of transformational rules that convert the kernels into a much greater variety of complex sentences. Immediately, Miller (1962) and his students at Harvard set out to demonstrate the "reality" of this new formulation with memory tests, perception tests, and reaction time measures. It was reasoned that when a person comprehends a sentence and stores it in his memory he must de-transform it into a kernel plus some transformational tags, and all these are the memory representation that is used to regenerate the sentence when later it becomes necessary to recall it. After much research effort and some ambiguous results, it seemed to remain a possibility that this is how people "process" sentences. But by then linguists had again developed new insights and had made major changes in the theory.

The new version presented two levels of syntax, the surface structure and the deep structure. The surface is the linear ordering of constituents by which the actual sound production of speech is determined. The deep structure is a description of the abstract logical relations among constituents, and it is at this level that the meaning of the sentence is determined. Between the surface and the deep structure you have the transformational rules which convert one level into the other. The thrust of psychological work was now again to demonstrate the psychological reality of the distinction between the two levels of syntax. Typically the actual sentences Chomsky had used for purposes of illustration in his arguments became the test sentences in many a psychological laboratory where subjects memorized them or discriminated them from others, and where the usual critical arrangement involved holding the surface structure constant while the deep structure was varied (or vice versa) such as in the two sentences, *John is easy to please | John is eager to please*. With enough patience and any given laboratory testing technique, subjects can be made to respond consistently in such a way that their behavior will reflect these particular structural differences.

In many of these experiments subjects performed tasks involving lists of sentences that generally were all of similar form, equal in length, and balanced in other ways. This is hardly typical of normal linguistic usage, or conversation, or of the use of language with a communicative purpose. And the type of explanations of normal performance that were developed directly on the basis of linguistic theory were even more awkward and counter-intuitive. For instance, the "analysis-by-synthesis" proposal claimed that sentences are understood by means of a listener's internal grammar which generates potential structures for an incoming string of words until some structure fits, then comprehension occurs. This was proposed even though in many instances a huge number of alternate structures might have to be generated for a given sentence input. Another line of theorizing was found in the "derivational complexity hypothesis." This claimed that the number or complexity of transformational rules relating surface to deep structure would predict the level of difficulty in the comprehension of utterances. It led to the prediction that more time or effort should be expended in comprehending the sentence, *The young boy caught the red ball,* than with the related sentence, *The boy who is young caught the ball which is red.* The first of these sentences is more highly transformed away from its complex deep structure description than is the second sentence. But in psychological tests the greater ease of processing is found with the first sentence (not surprisingly), and this result is exactly opposite to the derivational complexity prediction.

Generally, in situations where psychological results did not bear out linguistic theory, it was the psychological work that was jettisoned and not the theory. This was for the very good reason that the theory in this case was much more powerful than the empirical testing techniques, as most interested parties readily acknowledged. But psycholinguists were thereby admitting the relative impotence of their own field. The theory involved here was, however, a theory of language structure and not a theory of the structure of psychological performance.

We can take the story of the psychologist-linguist interaction one step further with the group of Chomsky's students who are now attempting to develop a theory of semantics to a level of power that obviates the usefulness of a deep structure analysis of syntax. Now we find a number of psycholinguists demonstrating that subjects in their experiments attend more to the meaning of sentences than they do to the syntactic structures. And the structure of semantic "storage" is the object of much current psycholinguistic experimentation.

At one time a separation of syntax from semantics was a well-motivated step in linguistics. It enabled the theoretician to concentrate on a more manageable problem and thus to come up with some significant gains. But this was a formal-theoretical gambit in that field only. It was not intended to describe how people use language. Nevertheless, among psycholinguists there was talk of the verbal input going first to a phonetic processor, then to a syntax processor, and then to a semantic processor, all orderly steps in the act of comprehending language. I submit that a little old-fashioned introspection would find that description, again, to be a counter-intuitive model for the actual structure of language performance.

Conclusion

There is a certain danger in the infatuation with the pure formalism of epistemological models, when in the hands of the researcher whose intention it is to investigate human performance. The danger lurks in the possibility of mistaking instrumental rule systems for theories of psychological performance processes. In regard to these issues, the psycholinguistics of 70 years ago was perhaps ahead of the more recent movements of the last 15 years. The study of the structure of language has made progress. but today the "psycho-" has too often been left out of psycholinguistics.

CHAPTER 8

Structuralism in Linguistics: Methodological and Theoretical Perspectives[1]

SHEILA BLUMSTEIN

Structuralism as a methodology has been applied to disciplines as disparate as mathematics, anthropology, literary criticism, and psychology. The behavioral sciences as exemplified by the works of Lévi-Strauss in anthropology and Piaget in psychology have applied this methodology in their analyses of human behavior, and have, as a result, been able to impose an organizational framework on areas of data that at first appeared unsystematic and random (Gardner, 1973). The source and model for this structural approach have been attributed to the field of linguistics (Lane, 1970).

One could argue that structuralism is as old as the study of language, since any approach to language is of necessity structural in nature; that is, to study any aspect of language implies the recognition of a system and, to some extent, the concepts of regularity and abstraction (Lepschy, 1970). And yet, this conception of structuralism is so broad and nontheoretical that in a larger sense it is trivial. What is peculiar to structuralism in linguistics is a particular view of the language system developed only within the past 50 years; a view, it will be argued, that is considerably more than a methodology, and that in large measure is based on a particular theoretical or philosophical bias.

A brief review of the history of linguistics reveals that despite their interest in linguistic systems, scholars prior to the advent of structuralism had little, if any, conception of language as a structural system. The earliest tradition of linguistic analysis and description dates back as early as the fourth century B.C. to the Indian Grammarians. Pāṇini, the grammarians' grammarian, wrote a grammar of Sanskrit with the explicit goal of establishing the morphology (word structure) and the phonology (sound structure) for the preservation of this

[1] This work was supported in part by USPHS Grants NS 10776 to Brown University, NS 07615 to Clark University, and NS 06209 to Boston University.

obsolescent but sacred language. His grammar was not a grammar in the conventional sense. Rather, it was an algebraic description of the structure of Sanskrit—it was abstract, exhaustive, had internal consistency, and reflected economy by means of ordered rules applied to basic or underlying abstract forms. This then would seem to be one of the first truly structural approaches to language, since it was based on many of the criteria essential to the structural methodology—namely, analytic, descriptive, abstract, economical, internally consistent, and mathematical. Unfortunately, the roots of Western grammar derived not from the Indian tradition but from the Greek tradition. Instead of describing language as the Indians did, the Greeks speculated about it (Waterman, 1963).

The Greek tradition dating from the fifth century B. C. reflected two basic approaches to language. First, it was studied along with philosophy and metaphysics as a means of speculating about the nature of the world; second, it was studied to interpret the literary texts of the Classical Greek or Latin authors. Thus, for the Greeks, language was not considered a system to be studied of and for itself.

The approaches to language developed in the Alexandrian period changed little in the period of Latin supremacy, as the Romans accepted the intellectual legacy given them by the Greeks. Although the Medieval and Renaissance periods witnessed a tremendous increase in the study of other languages, the methods of analysis and interpretation were those of the Ancients. Thus, from the fourth century B. C. until the eighteenth century, few philosophical or theoretical changes occurred in the study of linguistic systems (Waterman, 1963).

Nevertheless, with the increased study of languages other than Greek or Latin, there grew an awareness of other linguistic systems, and an interest in how these systems evolved. This interest in the evolution and relation of linguistic systems dominated linguistic research in the nineteenth century. It is probably no accident that this approach was popular not only in linguistics but also in the other social sciences as Darwin's *Origin of Species* appeared in 1859. Not only did it put this approach on a sounder scientific footing but it also promoted the search for the "laws" of evolution (Lyons, 1968). Language was now studied in a new perspective—it was considered by scholars to be in a constant state of flux, with a history and development that could be studied systematically and rigorously. These scholars called the Neogrammarians or Junggrammatiker sought the sound laws underlying linguistic systems and vociferously defended the claim that "sound laws have no exceptions." The strength of this approach was its reliance on physical phenomena and its insistence on methodological rigor. However, this approach was singularly atomistic and was preoccupied with isolated features rather than the entire system, resulting in a concern for form rather than function. Linguistics thus became a rather barren, purely descriptive science (Waterman, 1963).

LANGUAGE AS A STRUCTURAL SYSTEM

It is apparent from this very brief review that prior to the twentieth century, linguistic analysis in the Western tradition had little regard for structuralism. Language was not studied as a system qua system, independent of its history. It was not until 1916 with the appearance of Saussure's *Cours de Linguistique Générale* that the first truly structuralist approach to language was elaborated. Saussure applied the rigorous scientific methodology of historical linguistics to the study of language systems independent of their history, that is, synchronic description. As a result, the conception of language as a coherent and orderly system susceptible to analysis and understanding became a tenable notion. It was due largely to a group of scholars called the Prague School linguists that Saussure's views on structuralism in language were further elaborated and developed.

For the Prague School linguists, language was a structural, functional, and dynamic system. It was structural in the sense that it was a self-contained system comprised of elements defined and evaluated only in terms of other elements of that same system. It was functional in the sense that it existed as a system only to fulfill a purpose, namely to communicate about extralinguistic reality (Vachek, 1966). Finally, it was dynamic in the sense that the system was ever changing, ever affected by the "dynamic tensions" existing among the elements of the system. Because of these dynamic tensions, the linguistic system was considered teleological, as gaps and asymmetries in the system would constantly strive for "renewed stabilization" (Jakobson, 1971, p. 2).

Roman Jakobson, one of the founders and leaders of the Prague School, is perhaps the example par excellence of the application of structuralism to language. Both in his analyses of linguistic structure, and in his investigations of poetics, aphasia, and child language, Jakobson reflects methodologically and philosophically a uniquely structural approach. For Jakobson, language is characterized by a system of relations determined by minimal elements that derive their meaning only from the significant relations they hold with other elements in that same system. For example, in describing the sound system of English, the distinctive feature *voice* (characterized articulatorily by the relative onset of vocal cord vibration and the release of the consonant) exists only because there is a distinctive or meaningful contrast between voicing and voicelessness; compare the words *sue-zoo,* the difference between these two words is signaled by the phonological feature [voice], z is [+voice], s [−voice] (Fig. 1).

FIGURE 1.   The concept of the distinctive feature.

Jakobson was the first linguist to extend this notion of binariness—that is, the presence or absence of a distinctive value, throughout the entire language system (Jakobson, 1971). Not only do minimal elements have significance within a particular level, but they also relate one linguistic level to another—that is, although the feature *voice* may signal a distinction between two words as *sue-zoo* on the phonological level, on the morphological level, the distinction between the voicing of /s/ and /z/ has no distinctive significance as either /s/ or /z/ may signal the plural of a noun—for example book-*s,* dog-*z.* Thus language forms a closed system whose levels and minimal units are inextricably but systematically bound to form a whole, a whole larger than its parts.

General statements that reflect this regularity may be derived from analysis of the system. As an example, let us investigate the noun plural in English (Figures 2 and 3). At first analysis, there seem to be numerous plural forms—compare book +s; dog +z, horse + əz, catch + əz, man-men, child-children, goose-geese, sheep-sheep. However, further analysis reveals that plural formation can be described systematically and simply. Compare the first four words—book, dog, horse, catch. If −s is chosen as the underlying plural form, the proper plural ending can be predicted by considering the sounds immediately preceding. Thus /k/ is voiceless and so is the plural form /s/; /g/ is voiced as is the plural form /z/. Following an /s/ or /č/, the plural form is the full syllable / əz/. Plural formation may then be characterized by a set of rules (see Fig. 2).

These rules will derive the correct phonological form of the noun plural suffix. The remaining words listed are exceptions to this regularity and cannot be predicted by their phonological form. Thus they are marked as exceptions, and the correct plural endings will be included with each word. Notice that the

Plural N $\rightarrow$ N$_{stem}$ + plural

N$_{stem}$	Plural
{bUk}	{−s}
{dɔg}	
{hɔrs}	
{k ae č}	

{s} $\rightarrow$ /z/ // C$_{voiced}$ −

/əz/ // C$_{sibilant}$ −

FIGURE 2.   The plural in English—Solution I.

rules derived apply not only to the words listed but to *all* regular forms of the English language plus any new words that might be introduced into the system—for example, gip, wug, niss. Thus a general process of the English language can be characterized by a set of simple, abstract rules. This then is the essence of structuralism.

STRUCTURALISM AS THEORY VERSUS STRUCTURALISM AS METHODOLOGY

It is important to point out that although this methodology is applied to the linguistic system itself, Jakobson at all times emphasizes the relationship between this structure and human behavior. Thus, for him, the analyses derived reflect something about a speaker's linguistic system and his potential interaction with it. For Jakobson, the notions of distinctive feature and binariness, for example, are not methodological tools but theoretical constructs that can be used to characterize a particular language system, as well as the acquisition of a child's phonology or its dissolution in aphasia. To quote Jakobson:

"The development of child language, the dissolution of aphasic language, and the synchrony and diachrony of the languages of the world all exhibit a sequence of common laws of solidarity. These laws attest to the step-by-step development of the linguistic system . . . and their universality establishes the fixed nature inherent in their order of precedence [1968, p. 64]."

This notion, namely that the structural system derived, uniquely reflects the language system is crucial to the conceptual basis of structuralism, and it would seem makes it much more than a methodological approach to language. Perhaps this distinction between structuralism as methodology versus structuralism as theory can be most clearly seen in the approach to linguistic analysis in America in the mid 1940s and 1950s. This approach to language called American structuralism was developed in part as a result of an interest in American Indian languages and a need for developing field methods and procedures of analyses for working with the language systems of foreign cultures. The procedures developed were based on isolating the minimal meaningful units of the system, and organizing or arranging them in some systematic way. This approach to language was basically nontheoretical. There was no concern for the system as it related to linguistics proper or to human behavior. Rather, American structuralism was above all a methodology concerned with rigorous analysis, based on the methodological criteria used in performing the analysis, and ultimately the organization of the description in some systematic, simple, but insightful way (cf. Pike, 1947; Harris, 1951; Nida, 1965). As an example of such an analysis, let us return to plural formation in English and compare a methodologically oriented structuralist analysis with the first structural analysis presented (Fig. 3).

$$\{\text{Plural}\} \rightarrow z\ni \ //\ C_{\text{voiced}} -$$
$$z\ //\ C_{\text{sibilant}} -$$
$$s\ //\ C_{\text{voiceless}} -$$
$$\text{æ} > \epsilon\ //\ m\text{a}n -$$
$$\ni n\ //\ \text{childr} -$$
$$u > i\ //\ goose -$$
$$\phi\ //\ \text{fish} -$$

FIGURE 3.   The plural in English—Solution II.

Rather than choosing one abstract form from which all regular forms are derived, in this approach each plural form is listed, as are the items that go with each ending. Observe here that all items both regular and irregular are analyzed similarly despite the fact that some of the endings cannot be systematically predicted while others may. Nevertheless both analyses presented here can explain the observable data. Whether or not one abstract form should be used to derive all other forms is not really methodological but again a theoretical question. It implies, to some extent, the preeminence of one form over another (both of which in fact signal the same meaning—in this case, plural) and it implies a process—one item *becomes* or is *rewritten* as another (Hockett, 1954). This so-called item and process or morphophonemic approach was emphatically rejected by the early American structuralists as it seemed to them to impose on the data something that was not determined from the data alone. What they were concerned with was describing the linguistic system, not imposing a theoretical framework on it.

Even if one were to define structuralism as a rigorous methodology, it is questionable whether the application of this methodology will necessarily give a unique solution. This question was of considerable importance in the development of structuralism in America between 1935 and 1955 and succeeded in splitting American linguists into two opposing camps—the so-called God's truth linguists and the Hocus Pocus linguists (Joos, 1963, p. 80). To the God's truth linguist, there is only one unique solution, and only one analysis that ultimately reflects the true nature of the linguistic system. To the Hocus Pocus linguist, there is no unique solution; the linguistic analyses conducted are simply a means of organizing data, and the methodology devised may lead to several solutions to the same problem. Note that for both groups, the same methodology is used analyses are derived from observation and description of raw data, minimal units are established and their relationships are determined. For the God's truth linguist, the methodology or procedure will naturally derive the description logically from the data. For the Hocus Pocus linguist, the same procedures may result in different solutions (cf. Chao, 1934; Bloch, 1941, 1947; Nida, 1948). The differences between these groups then is not methodological but theoretical. It is not the methodology that gives a unique solution, but rather the belief that only one solution exists and the subsequent application of the methodology to that end.

Even the notion of binariness and its importance in linguistic solutions is a theoretical rather than a methodological issue. Chao, one of the opponents of the uniqueness of linguistic solutions has argued that binariness need not be applied to a linguistic analysis as it is purely a methodological principle easily imposed on a structural system, and thus it adds little insight to the linguistic analysis per se (Chao, 1954). Jakobson, on the other hand, argues that the dichotomous scale is inherent to, not superimposed on, the linguistic system (Jakobson & Halle, 1956). The use then of binary features is much more than methodological—it is based on a theoretical bias—namely, that binariness captures something intrinsic to the system that a nonbinary solution cannot.

Thus it seems evident that structuralism demands a certain theoretical bias— namely that by means of a rigorous methodology, one may arrive at a unique solution which is not only economical, insightful and abstract but which also reflects the intrinsic structure of the system being described.

STRUCTURALISM AND TRANSFORMATIONAL GRAMMAR

It was not until 1957 with the appearance of Chomsky's *Syntactic Structures* that we find again a truly structural approach to language. Chomsky postulated a model of language in which linguistic levels were interrelated by a set of ordered, abstract rules. The resultant grammar was based largely on criteria such as internal consistency, simplicity, and abstraction. In a further development of his theory in his later work, *Aspects of the Theory of Syntax*, Chomsky made a distinction between linguistic competence, what a speaker knows, and linguistic performance, what a speaker says. For him, the theoretical model was a model of linguistic competence. Thus the linguistic system qua system was abstracted from the speaker and could be analyzed and described as such. With this emphasis on abstraction, analyses conducted were now no longer based on a rigorous methodology but instead were based on a set of intuitions, intuitions of the linguist about what a speaker must know to create language.

Chomsky's model is based largely on a syntactic framework. As a result, he was not only able to characterize the systematic structural relationships of the elements comprising the sentences of a language, but he could also define the implicit relationships that existed among the set of sentences belonging to the language system. By characterizing the relationships existing among the elements of the sentence, he could define formally such notions as subject and object of a sentence in terms of the internal relations held among the grammatical categories noun phrase (NP), verb phrase (VP), and sentence (S). These relations are defined by the linear order and hierarchical structure of the grammatical categories. The subject of a sentence then can be defined as a NP immediately dominated by S, whereas the direct object of a sentence is defined as the NP immediately dominated by the VP (see Figure 4).

By defining the relationships among the set of sentences of the language, Chomsky was able to capture the systematic structural relations that existed among sentence types as declaratives, passives, imperatives, negatives, and negative interrogatives. Differences among these sentences were conceived as differences in the syntactic organization of the elements comprising the sentence. In the 1957 model these relationships were derived by ordered sets of syntactic rules called transformations; later they were represented by syntactic markers derived in the deep structure that triggered certain transformational operations. Transformations were thus syntactic operations that could permute, delete, or add elements to the basic structure of a sentence without changing its underlying meaning.

With the introduction of recursion in the base of the grammar, the power of the theory increased tremendously. For now the grammar could generate an infinite number of sentences with varied grammatical complexity by means of a finite number of rules. Productivity, the ability to understand and produce an infinite variety of sentences, was now operationalized at the level of syntactic processing.

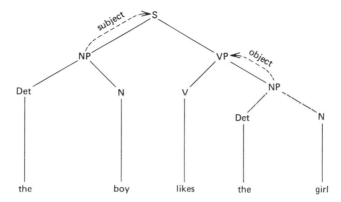

FIGURE 4. The relation between grammatical and functional categories in English.

For Chomsky, syntax forms the core of the grammar. The semantic interpretation of the sentence is derived by the semantic component of the grammar, and is based on the meaning of the underlying elements of a sentence in relation to the deep structure syntactic frame in which they occur. Similarly, the phonological interpretation of the sentence is derived by the phonological component of the grammar, and is determined in relation to the underlying phonological elements of the system as well as the surface structure syntactic frame in which they are found. The phonological and semantic components are thus interpretive components, as they interpret the meaning of the syntactic organization of the system as well as derive their meaning in part from the syntactic relations held within the system. These components as well as the deep and surface structure of the grammar are linked by the transformational components, thus forming a linguistic system that is self-contained and internally consistent (see Figure 5).

STRENGTHS AND LIMITATIONS OF A STRUCTURAL APPROACH TO LANGUAGE

Two important trends have emerged in linguistics as a direct result of Chomsky's theory. Both reflect the results of the application of structuralism to language. A review of these trends may not only demonstrate where structuralism has led linguistics but also may serve as an example of some of the problems and strengths inherent in this approach.

The first trend that has emerged from Chomsky's theory is an interest in purely theoretical linguistics. Theoretical considerations have been divorced entirely from the relationship between language and man. Here the system is stud-

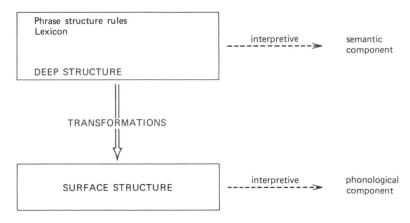

FIGURE 5.   Chomsky's model of language.

ied of and for itself with the primary objective of characterizing formally underlying linguistic relationships. This, of course, is a laudable goal and is in many
ways the essence of structuralism. However, as a result of the interest in formalism, this approach has developed into a complex metatheory based mainly
on an excessive emphasis on the formal apparatus that is used to describe the
system. Thus, in the literature, one finds articles on topics such as the cyclic
nature of linguistic rules, the noncyclic nature of linguistic rules, the application
of rule variables in linguistic analysis, the introduction of disjunctive ordering
in linguistic rules allowing rules to be collapsed and expanded in certain defina-
ble formal ways. To be sure, these linguists are trying to answer questions
about the language system itself. Nevertheless, the formal machinery developed
has, to a large extent, become the major theoretical question. Although fewer
rules may be needed to describe the linguistic system, one may ask at what
cost? The formal machinery has become more and more complex, all in the
name of simplicity. Moreover, it is not clear whether this formal apparatus reflects the actual structure of the system or the structure of the formal apparatus
itself.

This is one of the most important lessons learned from the application of a
structural analysis to a system. Namely, although formalization of underlying
structures may be essential to understanding the actual system to be described,
formalism is *not* the major objective of a structural analysis. Rather, it is the
insight to the structure of the system that a formal approach may give.

The second trend which has developed in linguistics has come from two very
different sources—the first is the theoretical linguist, and the second is the psy-

cholinguist. Theoretical linguists such as McCawley, Ross, and Lakoff attempted to develop Chomsky's generative or transformational approach to language. In their analyses, they found that Chomsky's approach seemed inadequate—that is, they could not account for all of the data within his theoretical framework (cf. Lakoff, 1971; McCawley, 1968). For example, one of Chomsky's major contentions has been that the ambiguity of many sentences may be resolved by demonstrating different underlying syntactic structures, one for each interpretation of the sentence. Take the ambiguous sentence "The shooting of the hunters bothered him." Two syntactic analyses reflect this ambiguity.

In the first (Figure 6a), hunters is the subject of the verb shoot; in the second (Figure 6b), hunters is the object of shoot. However, consider the sentence "The shooting of the target bothered him." This sentence is not ambiguous. Why?, because although people may shoot targets, targets don't shoot anything, that is, "target" is not likely to be the subject of the verb "shoot." This then is not a syntactic question but a semantic one. It is this kind of evidence which has suggested to these linguists that the analyses of sentences in language may be semantically based rather than syntactically based. However, with the priority of the semantic component, linguists have had to recognize the real world. Is the fact that a target or any inanimate subject cannot shoot, a linguistic question or a real-world question? The answer comes from considerations of semantics, at the very least, as well as extralinguistic or real world knowledge and ultimately the speaker-hearer.

The speaker-hearer is the major concern of the psycholinguist. For him, a linguistic theory that is formal and self-consistent but has no relationship to the linguistic structures used by a speaker-hearer or the linguistic system of the speaker-hearer is uninteresting and trivial. Psycholinguistic research in the 1950s and 1960s attempted to determine the relationship between Chomsky's theoretical model and human behavior. Results in general, have been very disappointing. It has been shown that the derivational complexity of a sentence bears little, if any, relationship to complexity for the speaker-hearer. Instead, semantic constraints and semantic complexity have been a more reliable index than the hypothesized syntactically based model (cf. Greene, 1972). Although early work seemed to support the notion that sentence processing time was directly related to the syntactic complexity or the number of transformations needed to derive the surface form of a sentence (Miller, 1962), further work revealed inconsistencies with the theoretical framework (Lyons & Wales, 1966). As an example, the sentence "Bill was hit" is derived in Chomsky's model from "Someone hit Bill." The surface structure form is derived by the applica-

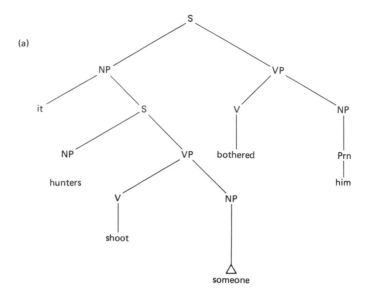

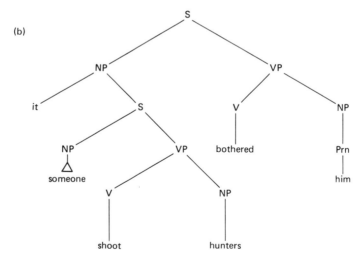

FIGURE 6.   Underlying structures of the ambiguous sentence: "The shooting of the hunters bothered him."

tion of two transformations—passivization, that is, "Bill was hit by someone" and deletion of the indefinite object, that is, "Bill was hit." Theoretically, then, the sentence "Bill was hit" should be more complex than "Someone hit Bill" as two additional transformations are needed to derive the surface form. Not only does this solution seem counter-intuitive, but more importantly, psycholinguistic investigations have revealed that subjects find it easier to understand and process the transformationally more complex sentence (Watt, 1970). In addition as further studies began to investigate *comprehension* instead of *memory* of sentences in language, it was revealed that semantic rather than syntactic factors played a larger role in the subject's performance (Greene, 1972; Slobin, 1971). It is quite apparent then that a self-contained theory that is internally consistent and systematic need not reflect anything about the structure of that system in the context of the real world.

As a result, linguists and especially psycholinguists have realized that language does not occur in a vacuum—it is spoken in a social context, it has psychological and neurological concomitants. It is questionable then whether the isolation of language as an independent abstract system can give us the answers we seek. Can one determine *the* structure of a system independent of the other behavioral systems from which they are derived? Probably not. This is the second lesson to be learned from the application of structuralism in linguistics.

It is because of structuralism that linguists are now able to consider language not as a closed, self-contained system, but as one system, part of and inextricably bound to larger structural systems. Although the scope of the analysis grows larger and, as a result, the application of a purely structural approach becomes more difficult, nevertheless we may not only gain more insight into the true structure of the system under investigation but we may also gain a further understanding of human behavior in general.

CHAPTER 9

Semantic Basis of Language: Language as Labor

KLAUS F. RIEGEL

Most inquiries into early child development emphasize the undifferentiated state of the organism and its embeddedness in the environment. Development, subsequently, is considered as a differentiation of objects and, more basically, of the subject from the object. In accepting such an interpretation—and what choice is there? it becomes apparent how inappropriate a stimulus-response theory would be. Stimuli and responses do not yet exist as separate conditions; they need to be differentiated before any acquisition based on them can be explained. Similarly, associations cannot connect stimuli and responses according to their contiguity, frequency, or recency; everything is connected anyhow. The first task for the child is to recognize some constancies in the flux of his sensory impressions and in the shifts of his motoric expressions.

Many cognitive and philosophical psychologists have provided interpretations of early development similar to the one presented here. Most notably, Heinz Werner (1926) has elaborated the early differentiation (and concurrent integration) of the child's experiences, and Piaget (1963), likewise, has explicated processes leading to schemata of perceptions and actions. In focusing on Piaget's work, we compare his interpretation of cognitive development with the early acquisition of meaning. In both cases, the child is confronted with a flux of events and his main developmental task consists in recognizing constancies in the flux of his impressions and invariances in the stream of his expressions. Only after these constancies and invariances have been recognized and practiced can learning in the traditional sense be considered as a means for acquisition.

In spite of similarities in the goals of cognitive and language development, the task of recognizing constancies in the general physical environment and of invariances in the more specific sound and speech environment points toward basic differences that might have prevented any consolidation of both interpretations. The former constancies might be regarded as synchronic-spatial structures (with the supplementary option of temporal shifts and changes); the latter invariances must be regarded as diachronic-temporal structures (with the rather ad-

167

vanced technological option of fixating them in space through written transformations or on magnetic tape).

Of course, such a contrast overemphasizes the differences. The constancies of objects in space may represent stable states during short periods of time only; the objects change and move. Moreover, the subject through his own movements creates for himself continuously changing impressions of these "stable" objects. When, on the other hand, a person perceives an invariant section within a speech sequence, for example, a word, his percept will activate a conceptual field (Trier, 1931) or network (Quillian, 1967; Riegel, 1968; Riegel & Riegel, 1963) representing his past experiences related to this word. Thus a synchronic structure is brought to his attention that is often identified with the subjective semantic organization of the language. As subsequent units are perceived by the listener, other semantic structures are called on, blending into one another and modifying the earlier structures. The sequential progression across synchronic semantic structures represents the diachronic organization of the language that has been identified as its syntactic order. Because of the sequential blending of the synchronic structures, the distinction between both organizations, again, overemphasizes their differences at the expense of their similarities.

The above distinction, furthermore, holds only for an individual who has already acquired a fair amount of perceptual-cognitive and linguistic experiences. The young child has to generate, first, these semantic and syntactic orders. Of course, we should not neglect the fact that the language of the environment as well as the general physical surrounding already possess a high degree of segmentation and structure. These are either properties of nature (such as the formation of rocks, mountains, plants, animals, including the human and his organs for cognition and speech) or, more importantly, they have been generated through human efforts (such as rooms, buildings, cities, social organizations, language). Students of learning and association have systematically neglected the structural properties of the world and have proceeded as if the child were born into a random world of chaos.

The young child has not yet experienced these outer structures. His development, essentially, consists of recreating these outer organizations through his own activities and on the basis of his own, inner structures. At the same time, these outer organizations will be induced on him through the efforts of the people around him. This group not only includes all persons who are attending him, but the whole contemporary and, in the end, all previous generations who laid the foundation and are continuously creating the physical and social world in which the child grows up. The child through his own activities also partakes in changing this world, at least those sections that are experienced by the persons in his immediate social environment, that is, his parents, siblings, neighbors, and the like. Indeed, the child's activities might produce more dramatic changes in his parents, for example, than the parents are able to produce in the child.

In the following presentation, we outline the processes by which the child recognizes and regenerates some invariant and organizational properties of language. In these efforts, the child will conjoin and contrast recurrent segments of the messages presented to him. For example, the child might hear sequences such as "Drink your milk," "The milk is too hot," "We have to buy some milk," and so on. After repeated exposure to such messages, the child recognizes invariant segments, for example, the word MILK. Using a visual analog, we might think of these statements as written on strips of paper; the child would then bundle these strips together with the invariant segment at the intersection. As we attempt to show, both the identification of meanings as well as the formation of classes can be explained on this basis.

Similar arguments can be made for operations at the phonetic level leading to the recognition of the phonemes of the given language. Although phoneme recognition will be consciously activated only through the intervention of teachers, the recognition of meaningful units, such as words, may be initiated by the child himself. Recognition and transmission of meanings is, after all, the main purpose of language. These operations, furthermore, are not bound to smallest elements, such as letters, syllables, or words, but involve more complex units as well, such as phrases, parts of sentences and, perhaps, whole sentences and expressions. The acquisitions of these units are fused with syntactic developments that cannot and should not be separated from those of semantic structures.

In the main part of the following presentation, we emphasize the acquisition of words, classes, class relations and, generally, of the semantic and syntactic organization of language. The basis for these developments are contextual segments whose smallest units we call simple relations. All of these acquisitions succeed through active operations by the child with and on the relational information given. These operations consist in intersecting or composing (as well as decomposing), conjoining or aligning (as well as separating) of relational information.

We are not able to explain much further how these operations originate in the child. But in the first part of our presentation, we discuss language acquisition as an unadulterated process of activities with little consideration for the products and structures generated. In particular, we compare linguistic operations with those in economy by describing three stages in the development of monetary systems: the barter system, the coinage system, and the debenture system. Similarly, we delineate three levels in the origin, development, and study of language: the protolanguage, the token language, and the interaction language. Tangentially, we also argue that the intellectual processes involved are roughly comparable to three stages of cognitive development as they were originally proposed by Piaget: the period of the sensorimotor activity, the period of concrete operations (including the subperiods of preoperational and concrete operational thinking), and the period of formal operations.

MONETARY AND LINGUISTIC SYSTEMS: A DEVELOPMENTAL AND HISTORICAL COMPARISON

The relationship between goods or merchandise and the labor or activities necessary to produce them has been regarded, at least since Marx (1891), as dialectic: labor that does not produce something is futile; goods that are not produced by labor are miracles. In the following discussions we equate labor with the acts of producing or perceiving speech; merchandise with speech products, such as sentences, words, or speech sounds. Through acts of speech a person increases the individual and collective repertoire of linguistic products. This repertoire is comparable to capital in the economic sense. Capital is only useful for the individual and the society when it is productive, that is, when it is transformed into new labor, speech acts. Traditionally, linguists have regarded language as commodity but not as labor.

The Barter System and the Protolanguage

Our monetary system originated from the one-to-one bartering trade in simple hunting and farming societies. A social situation in which one participant exchanges, for instance, a sheep or a pig for a certain amount of grain or wool seems to have little in common with a situation of linguistic exchanges. The items traded do not have any representational or symbolic value and satisfy direct needs of the persons participating in the exchange. Basic similarities become apparent, however, once we realize that languages also are systems of social interactions in which not the objects but, instead, the labor that leads to their creation and possession is exchanged. Strictly speaking, objects do not play an essential role in such an exchange. Where would they come from, how would they be generated except through the efforts of the participating individuals? It is the labor involved in raising or catching the animal, in the seeding, tending, and harvesting of the crop that is being exchanged. The exchange value is determined by the amount of effort, the quality of the required skills, and the scarcity of the available resources (which, in turn, must be acquired and secured through the individual's efforts).

Many linguists and, especially, psychologists regard sentences, words, or speech sounds as building blocks or objects of language. But language is basically an activity which, in turn, induces or provokes activities in others. This comparison is similar to, although not identical with, Saussure's distinction between *la langue* and *la parole*. The former, characterizing the universal properties of language, represents the total repertoire of forms and the structure that has emerged through the efforts of mankind. Surprisingly, as Labov (1970) noted, *la langue* has been studied by relying on the "linguistic intuitions" of one or a few individuals. A science of *parole,* although never developed, would have to deal with various speech actions in different social contexts.

Language as an activity is revealed most clearly under primitive conditions that are comparable to those of barter trade. Through grunts, cries, gestures and manipulations, that is, in Bühler's (1934) terms through "signals" and "symptoms," one participant might induce the other to recognize a danger, to give assistance, or to coordinate activities. The sounds and movements might be recorded as objectifications of such a primitive language by the linguists, but these transcriptions provide only a distorted picture of the needs and intentions or the activities involved. These activities are meaningful in a given situation and in an immediate manner. In the linguist's description their meaning is bleached; they become abstract and rigidified (see Malinowski, 1923).

Already at this level, language as well as commercial exchanges rely on basic rules. The barter system presupposes property rights. If it is not granted, for example, that the sheep belongs to person A and the grain to person B, no stable exchanges, not even thievery, can take place. In Piaget's sense, this type of commercial activity is comparable to the level of sensory-motor operations. One item is exchanged against another item regardless of the particular shapes in which they happen to be found. Trade does not yet require a knowledge of conservation.

Similarly, proto-linguistic communication presupposes the constancy of expression which, once given, cannot be undone. In this sense they have immediate, existential meaning. Language at the proto-linguistic level is bound to a given situation of high survival but of low symbolic value. Its increase in representational character can be compared with that which occurs during the change from a barter to a coinage system.

The Coinage System and the Token Language

(a) When changing from the barter to the coinage system, communities select one of their major commodities as a standard for exchange. In agricultural societies a certain quantity of grain might serve this function, in stock-farming societies it might be served by the horse, the cow, or the sheep. (In ancient Rome, the word for money, *pecunia,* derives from *pecus* denoting *livestock.)*

Shifts in standard commodities indicate the growing diversification of societies. This growth is determined by variations in geographical and climatic conditions. It has to be brought about, however, by the activities of generations of participating members. Through these activities, society progresses toward more advanced forms of manufacturing and industrial production and, also, toward a division of labor. Developments of this kind increase the significance of natural resources other than food crops, for instance stone, wood, wool, coal, and—most important—metals. Because of their scarcity, compactness, and endurance but also because the resources can be easily controlled by the dominating classes of the society, metals soon became the exclusive standard for monetary systems.

The transition from the barter system to a coinage system is not necessarily abrupt (see Cipolla, 1956). After one or a few items have been selected as standard commodities, the exchange continues to proceed as before. When metals are introduced to serve as standards they continue, at first, to fulfill basic needs of everyday life. For instance, metals such as copper, bronze, or iron are not only used as currency but the coins also serve as standard weights as well as provide the material for the production of tools and weapons. As the society advances, these common metals are replaced as standards for exchanges by others that are less readily available. Subsequently, smaller and lighter coins can be introduced whose mining, melting, and minting are more easily controlled and that do not serve essential functions for tool making but, instead, those of luxury and extravagance. For example, in the Roman Empire, bronze coins with a standard weight of 327.45 grams were substituted by much smaller silver and gold coins. Whereas, the amount of metal of the bronze coins had a direct, nonmediated value for the receiver, rare metals, such as silver and gold, lacked utility. Therefore, refined rules about their use had to be established by the community; the value of the coins had to be guaranteed by the state through laws that set the standards, determined the metal composition, and regulated their distribution. Also, classes of persons, who succeeded in controlling the processing of these rare metals, could set themselves apart as the rulers of their society.

As coins lost their foundation on the concrete value of commodities but gained in symbolic value, the economy expanded rapidly. But through the reckless manipulation of a few and the uncritical trust of many, the changed conditions were selfishly exploited. The emerging histories represent an unending sequence of catastrophies, inflations, and devaluations (Gaettens, 1955). Imperialistic expansions (from the Punic Wars to the war in Vietnam) always outpaced the growth of the economic and monetary systems. Since not enough metal could be secured, the silver or gold content of coins was drastically reduced. Subsequently, coins lost value rapidly until the system had to be replaced at the expense of the working, wage and salary earning population. In spite of these dire consequences, the coinage systems, in comparison with the barter system, offer many advantages that, in particular, shed light on similar implications for language systems.

(b) Coinage systems, especially those based on symbolic instead of pragmatic standards, allow for delayed exchanges, sequential exchanges, and multiple distributions. *Delayed exchanges* provide the possibility that the seller does not need to convert immediately the items received into other merchandise but may store coins of corresponding value until a better opportunity for a purchase arises. Such delayed reactions are of equal significance in the development of language systems. Whereas the nonlanguage-using organism is closely bound to the here and now of a given situation, the use of a language, corresponding in abstraction to the coinage system, not only allows for more efficient communication but also for better storage, especially once a written code of the language has been invented.

In contrast to the barter trade, exchanges do not need to be limited to two persons interacting at a particular location, but *sequential exchanges* are bound to result. A person who wants to buy a sheep but has no commodities that are of interest to the seller, might reimburse him in coins; the seller, in turn, might approach a third person who is willing to dispose of the desired item. Frequently, the chain will extend over many more than three participants. Coins are an efficient intermediary, provided that their value is sufficiently safeguarded by social agreements and rules. The social exchange of goods made effective through the invention of coins has similar implications as the invention of verbal codes for linguistic systems. Once a coding system has been adopted, messages can be more reliably transmitted across long sequences of communicating persons than under the more primitive conditions in which utterances are spontaneously and idiosyncratically produced. In a more remote but also more significant sense, the composition of these messages becomes sequential in nature. Linguistic tokens, such as sentences, words, or speech sounds, are ordered into strings. Nonlinguistically encoded action sequences are hard if not impossible to transmit.

Once a coinage system has been introduced, *multiple distributions* of goods can be arranged easily. A person who has sold his sheep does not need to spend his earnings at the place of the trade but can distribute them across many vendors and can purchase a multiplicity of items. Again the improvements of such operations in comparison to the one-to-one exchanges of the barter trade are comparable to those brought about through the development of language systems. In the most direct sense, a language user can transmit his message simultaneously to a whole group of listeners; in a remote sense, he has multiple ways of expressing his wishes or intentions and can partition his message into smaller chunks that are presented separately. This possibility is especially important for safeguarding the transmission when individuals with varying linguistic skills are involved in the communication process.

(c) The linguistic system that we have compared with the coinage system might be called a token language. It is founded on basic forms or elements, such as words, syllables, letters, morphemes, or phonemes. Aside from determining its elements, the main goals in the analysis of this system consist in the description of its syntagmatic and paradigmatic, that is, temporal-diachronic and spatial-synchronic properties.

A token language system lies halfway between the manifold of phenomena of the experienced world and the single token coinage system of the economy. Both systems are reductionistic. Languages use a large set of tokens, that is, words, to denote the many different objects, events, or qualities. However, every token denotes a whole array of similar items. For instance, the word CHAIR denotes many different objects. Moreover, the relations between tokens and the items denoted are of several different types, indicating actor-action, object-location, part-whole, object-class name, and many other relations. The corresponding monetary systems consist, in general, only of one token, for example, the Dollar, which designates (relates to) every possible item and condition in the same manner. Because, thus, a large manifold is reduced to just a single element, elaborate forms of operations must be implemented. This is done by relying on the complex numerical properties of the system that capture the large variety of items and conditions by assigning to them corresponding variations in the quantity of tokens, for example, Dollars. The emerging structure represents an arithmetic formalism.

In comparison with such a single token system, languages consist of many different tokens (frequently called types) and of many different kinds of relations between tokens and between tokens and the denoted items. Manipulations with these tokens do not include operations of addition or multiplication but only those of order. By applying order rules recursively, a multitude of expressions can be generated; by applying them to different types of relations, this multitude is enriched much further. The emerging structures are topologically rich. These systems rely on cognitive operations that are mastered by older children only, for example, on decentration and reversibility. They remain concrete because the tokens, for example, the words, are thought of as building blocks that reflect directly the conditions of the real or phenomenal world. Just as the coins, these tokens, rather than the commodities that they represent or the labor that produces these commodities, may ultimately come to be regarded as the true objects of the world.

Tokens are selected and retained through social conventions that, moreover, determine the permissible rules of operations. They fail to express the activities and efforts that lead to their creation. As much as the further development of the monetary system advances to a full realization of the transactional character of economic operations, so also does modern linguistics emphasize the interactional character of language. Whereas, traditional linguistics consisted, essentially, in the delineation of linguistic forms and of the rules of their combinations, units such as words, syllables, or letters lose their significance in modern interpretations. What attains significance are clusters of relations representing the activities within and between language users.

The Debenture System and the Interaction Language

(a) Economic history resembles a progression of catastrophies in which, because of ceaseless expansions and lack of constraint, one monetary system after the other has been wrecked. At the terminal points of these progressions, the metal value of coins was reduced out of proportion to its original designation, the confidence in the system was lost, prices skyrocketed, and people were forced to return to the barter system to secure their daily needs. At least from the beginning of the eighteenth century, autocratic rulers began to make a virtue out of the pitiful state of their financial systems by abandoning the backing of the currency through silver or gold and by substituting paper money for hard coins.

The first well documented case of such an innovation is that of John Law on whose advice Louis XV introduced paper money in France. After a few successful years, the confidence in the financial system was lost, leading the nation one significant step closer to the French Revolution. At approximately the same time, Georg Heinrich von Görtz financed the military adventures of Charles XII in Sweden through the issuing of state certificates. After the king's defeat and death these financial manipulations were violently attacked and Görtz was executed. Nevertheless, all leading nations have since then introduced paper money and, more recently, most industrialized nations have abandoned the full coverage of their currency by gold or silver or, at least, they do not guarantee full convertibility. This shift represents the third major step in the development of monetary systems which we will call the debenture system.

It would be misleading to think of paper money only in terms of the common bills issued by national banks. Of course, these documents are the most useful for everyday commerce in comparison with all other certificates and, except for changes affecting the economy as a whole, remain fixed in their values. Similar in kind, bonds are issued and guaranteed by national governments, states, and communities as well as by larger industrial and business organizations. Since their value fluctuates with the condition of the economy in general, and with the up and down of the money market in particular, these risks must be compensated for by the payment of interest. Next in line, stocks fluctuate more widely than bonds. They are backed by commercial or industrial companies but rarely by governments. The last extension in the development of paper currencies consists in the utilization of personal checks. Here, each individual attains the role that formerly only a stable government was able to attain, namely to guarantee the value of such transactions.

The last steps in the development of monetary systems, thus, represent another stage of operations and symbolic representations. Written statements become substitutes for standard units of rare metals which, in turn, served as substitutes for the items to be exchanged or, at first, as direct objects of trade. During the earliest stage in the history of trade, exchanges were tied to the given items and to the persons interacting in a particular locality. With the introduction of coins, exchanges could be temporally delayed, could be executed along extended chains of participants, and could reach simultaneously an array of different vendors. Although this increase in flexibility led to advances in the volume of trade, the expansion remained limited because the total amount of rare metals backing the economic transactions increased very slowly. With the shift toward various forms of paper money, this limitation was abandoned and the monetary system was explicitly tied to the sum total of activities in which a whole nation, an industrial complex or, finally, a single individual was, is, or was to be engaged.

The explicit return to a standard set by the activities and labor of an individual or groups of individuals represents only a superficial shift. As we emphasized previously, the objects of trade have always been the efforts necessary for producing particular goods rather than the merchandise itself. Even the gold and silver accumulated in the treasuries of states represents, basically, the efforts and work by their people. Because of the static character of these financial units it appears, of course, as if the wealth attained had been once and for all removed from the activities that produced it. The deteriorations of such financial systems, whenever the growth in productivity failed to keep pace with the increase in monetary volume, show, however, that such a stability is rather fictitious.

The apparent accumulative and static character of economies based on coins makes them very similar to linguistic systems that emphasize linguistic elements, such as words, syllables, letters, morphemes, or phonemes, and which fail to consider language as a system of activities and interactions. While the proto-economy of the barter trade implies too little symbolization to make it closely comparable to language, the intermediate system of coins, because of its elementalistic notions, is about equally inappropriate for such a comparison. An adequate understanding of language can be achieved only through comparisons with the debenture system, which is based on matrices of transactions instead on classes of fixed elements.

The power of commercial and industrial operations in modern economic systems is not so much determined by the amount of hard currency or cash but by the diversification and the speed with which limited assets are transformed and retransformed. The worth of money is determined by its owner's ability to utilize it productively. Stored money is of lesser value and, indeed, lessening in value as a function of continuing inflation. Although these operations also characterize the more advanced stages of the coinage system, such a system remains more firmly anchored to the amount of cash available to the operator. The opportunity for obtaining loans on written declarations, for investing them immediately in new financial operations, for transferring the profit to cover commissions, and for obtaining new resources for investments characterizes the effectiveness of the debenture system. In the extreme—and there exist numerous documented cases of this type of operation, many bordering on illegality—a financial operator might gain large profits without much or without any firm financial basis, only through quick transactions of fictitious capital. In this extreme form, the debenture system, through the transactions that it facilitates, has lifted itself from its foundation. It has become a pure system of interrelated activities. The cash that, presumably, buys these activities and the products that they generate have become of negligible importance.

(b) In modern linguistics, beginning with Sapir, Jesperson, and the Prague School, the study of transactions, likewise, has overpowered the study of forms. Already Jesperson emphasized that the purpose of a linguistic analysis is "to denote all the most important interrelations of words and parts of words in connected speech. . . . Forms as such have no place in the system [Jesperson, 1937, pp. 13 and 104]." More recently, this idea has been expressed in the transformational grammar of Chomsky (1965), in Piaget's (1963, 1970) cognitive developmental psychology and in the structuralism of Lévi-Strauss (1958). In Chomsky's theory, transformations relate deep structure components to the surface structures of languages. As for Piaget, the language-using individual is actively participating in these transactional processes. These operations are confined, however, to the organism himself. An interaction with external, for example, social forces, is deemphasized if not disregarded in both theories.

Undoubtedly, Chomsky's theory has profoundly shaken the traditional, elementalistic, and parallelistic views of linguists and psychologists with their undue emphasis on external physical stimuli and mechanical physical reactions by, essentially, passive organisms. Piaget, like Chomsky, has strongly emphasized the transactional character of psychological operations. He, indeed, seems to draw the final conclusion of this interpretation by stating that "Transformations may be disengaged from the objects subject to such transformations and the group defined solely in terms of the set of transformations [Piaget, 1970, pp. 23–24]."

Both Chomsky and Piaget have stated their theories in mentalistic and idealistic terms. Although this orientation has set them clearly apart from most American psychologists, they have failed to assign an appropriate role to the cultural-historical conditions into which an individual is born and within which he grows. The environment is regarded as passive. All learning and development is initiated and directed by the organism. To attain his goals, the individual needs, of course, information and material from the outside. There is no place in these theories, however, for an active role of the environment and for a codetermination of an individual's development by other active organisms. It is at this juncture that a comparison with economic theories becomes most pertinent because these theories bypass and advance far beyond modern interpretations of language and cognitive development.

For a complete understanding of cognitive and linguistic operations, we must consider two interaction systems. One relates these operations to their inner basis, to their physiological, biochemical foundation. The other represents the interactions with the cultural-historical environment into which an organism is being born. While the latter system is realized in theories of economic operations and in the symbolic interactionism of Mead, the former system is expressed—although incompletely—in the theories of Piaget and Chomsky. An advanced synthesis of both interaction systems has been proposed by Rubinstejn (1958, 1963; see also Payne, 1968; Riegel, 1973a; Wozniak, 1972).

Rubinstejn extended, on the one hand, the first interaction system by relying on Pavlov's work. He introduced the second interaction system by relying on Vygotsky (1962) and, thereby, on the historical materialism of Marx, Engels, and Lenin. The psychic activities of an organism are viewed as the changing outcome of these two interaction systems: one binding them to their inner material, biochemical foundation, which is described in terms of relations within the nervous system and sensory and motor organs, and the other binding them to their outer material, cultural-historical foundation, which is described in terms of relations between and within the physical and social world of individuals. Behavior is regarded as an activity continuously changing in the process of interactions. It is not a thing-like particle that can be separated from these transactions. Language, similarly, is an activity, founded through the two interactions that, in particular, integrates nervous activities and cultural-historical functions. It should be studied as a process of this kind rather than as a conglomeration of particles or forms that are the rigidified products of relational activities.

To carry Rubinstejn's program to its systematic conclusion, it would be necessary to devise a methodology and theory of relations on which the interactions of the human being and the cultural-historical conditions are based. In other words, the "reflexology" of Pavlov's first signaling system, which explores the interactions of the organism with its inner, biological basis, needs to be supplemented by a "relationology." In the material that follows, a brief sketch of this kind of program for the study of language and its acquisition is given.

SEMANTIC ACTIVITIES: THE BASIS FOR LANGUAGE DEVELOPMENT

Psychologists who are studying language often regard it as one of their most important tasks to define the elements of their analysis. Many of them settle quickly on words or syllables as basic units if not on the infamous nonsense syllable. To linguists, however, words as well as syllables pose grave problems. But their superiority is only superficial, as long as they do nothing else but choose different, although more sophisticated elements for their analysis, such as morphemes or phonemes. Linguists do not always feel compelled to overcome such particle models of language. Of course, once these units have been defined, the scientists will proceed to explain how they are arranged into larger sequences. In psychology, associations have traditionally provided the necessary bonds. Eventually, it was hoped, science would be able to reconstruct the complexity of immediate experience. Although in all these interpretations elements are regarded as prior to their connections, we argue for the priority of relations over elements. Such a shift in interpretation represents a renewed emphasis on the language users and on common, meaningful, phenomenal experience.

Extralingual Relations

Whenever information is exchanged it consists of connected, and never of isolated terms. Thus, when we explain the word ZEBRA to a child, we say "(A) zebra (has) stripes" or (A) zebra (is an) animal," and even if we use nothing but the word ZEBRA we, most likely, point to a "real" zebra or to the picture of one. Thus we are invoking a special extralingual relation between a label and the object denoted by it which we will call "ostensive relations." On some other occasions we may utter single words like GO or STOP, expecting that the child will perform the requested actions. The role of commands and demands has received considerable attention in studies of classical conditioning by Pavlov and is basic to Skinner's interpretations of verbal behavior. However, these "intensive relations" are rarely considered in studies of language development. Finally, a third type of extralingual relations is invoked when a person utters, usually in an idiosyncratic manner, some words or sounds such as BRAVO, OUCH, etc., thereby indicating his emotions or feelings. Many theories on the origin of language, beginning with one proposed by Darwin, have focused on these connotative or "expressive relations." However, with few exceptions little attention has been given to this topic in studies of language acquisition.

All three extralingual relations (ostensive, intensive, expressive) are important for the initiation and control of psycholinguistic performances, but their significance decreases during the later periods of development. The majority of information consists of intralingual relations, for example, relations between words that are one step removed from their nonlinguistic basis.

Mutual Dependence of Elements and Relations

An apparent difficulty in relational interpretations is the circularity of the concepts of elements and relations. But the problem is not different from analytical geometry, where a point (representing an element) is defined as the intersect of two lines (representing relations), and where, also, a line is defined as the connection between two points. Thus, in both cases, it becomes a matter of choice of where one enters the cycle and from what place one begins to unravel the issues.

Traditionally, an elementalistic viewpoint has dominated the natural as well as the social sciences. By disregarding the contextual implications, psychologists, thereby, have brought themselves into the unfortunate position of having eliminated meaning from their consideration, that is, those aspects that ought to be of greatest interest in their analysis of language acquisition and use. Elements in isolation are completely meaningless much like the ideal nonsense syllables of the psychological laboratory. On the other hand, relations, like the reflexes in Pavlov's view, are smallest, although idiosyncratic, units of meaning. Since it is inconceivable that human activity can ever be completely without meaning (at least, from the actor's own point of view), relations represent the immediate information given or produced; elements are constructed and derived.

Intersection of Relations

If relations are combined, two intellectual operations can take place: the meaning of the element at the intersection can be explored (that is, a word can be identified) and/or the free elements of the intersecting relations can be recognized as members of a class. Both processes involve an abstraction from the immediate information given, the relations. Both processes may occur simultaneously. However, if one of the elements or if the particular types of relations are not familiar to a person, considerable time might be required for completing these processes.

Two relations can be combined in no more than four different ways. The first combination aligns two relations opposite in directions. It represents a trivial loop or reverberation. If relations would combine in this manner only, for instance, if the word BLACK would always lead to WHITE and WHITE always to BLACK, then no relational structure would exist. Fortunately, psycholinguistic relations never combine exclusively in this trivial manner but always reveal sufficient variation in their arrangements.

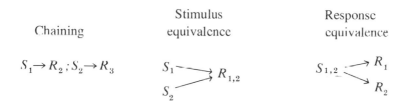

| | Stimulus | Response |
| Chaining | equivalence | equivalence |

$$S_1 \rightarrow R_2 \, ; \, S_2 \rightarrow R_3$$

The three remaining combinations of the two relations shown above are identical with the chaining, the response equivalence, and the stimulus equivalence paradigms (Jenkins & Palermo, 1964). The first attaches one relation at the end of the other. If nothing but those chaining paradigms were prevailing, a language would consist of idiosyncratic strings. More likely, various chains will crisscross each other, thus, lending transient strength to the network of relations of which a language is made up. The last two paradigms, in particular, allow for the identification of the intersecting element and for the recognition of classes. In the response equivalence paradigm, two relations diverge from a common left-hand term, leading, in the sample on p. 183, from HORSE to EAT and RUN. Both right-hand terms explicate the meaning of HORSE. In the stimulus equivalence paradigm, two relations converge on a shared right-hand term, for example, leading from COW and HORSE to RUN. Both left-hand terms explicate the meaning of RUN (see Quarterman & Riegel, 1968; Zivian & Riegel, 1969). If more than two relations are combined, considerable variation in the patterns results. The methodology for analyzing such networks has been considerably advanced during recent years (see Harary, Norman & Cartwright, 1965; Sokal & Sneath, 1963).

Reductionistic and Discriminative Aspects of Language

When a linguist explores an unknown language, he must rely on extralingual relations. Except for the rare case of unequivocal proper names, there will always be a wide range of items that are denoted by a common label but vary in many attributes. If this were not true, the language would be nonreductionistic. Only when numerous items are commonly labeled does a language become an efficient means for communication. Consequently, for any term, the linguist needs relational information under numerous conditions to gain an understanding of the full range of its meaning.

Often, the linguist's task has been compared with that of a child acquiring his first language. Such a comparison would be simplistic if we were to restrict it to information reduction through labeling. Concurrently with such performance, single objects, events, or qualities are denoted by different labels. For instance, a child might be called BOY, LAD, PAUL, SMITH, NAUGHTY ONE, and so on. The choice of the label varies with the situation and depends on the particular discrimination aimed for. An item might be called THING (if there are no other relevant items), BLOCK (if there are also beads and marbles), BLACK ONE (if there are red and white items), and the like. The exclusion or disregard of attributes is often as important as the positive denotation of an item (see Trabasso, 1970). Moreover, the discriminating use of labels makes their application more productive than when their function was exclusively reductionistic.

In terms of our interpretations, the reductionistic character of language is represented by relations diverging from the label and pointing toward the set of denoted objects, events, or qualities. The discriminative character, on the other hand, is represented by a set of labels converging on a single object, event, or quality. Reductionistic and discriminative properties of language coexist dialectically. The same is true for the related issue of identifying the meaning of a word or of recognizing a class. The first implies the focusing on a single term from which several relations diverge; the latter implies the focusing on members of a distribution many of which might be linked to a single item, for example, their class name, and all of which are linked to some shared items, for instance, shared functions, parts, and locations.

Criteria for Classes

Many psychologists regard the stimulus and the response equivalence paradigms as sufficient conditions for the determination of classes. However, these two paradigms represent minimal criteria only because they imply that any two items elicited by a common stimulus or leading to a common response would form a class. They are also abstractions because, in such simple forms, they occur under laboratory conditions only. In concrete situations, a multitude of combinations are superimposed and embedded in one another, making up the complex network of the natural language and, thereby, strengthening the classes at varying degrees. But because of their abstractness, these paradigms, next to simple relations, may serve as units into which this network can be partitioned.

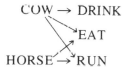

The superposition of the paradigms can be demonstrated by the example shown above. If a child has learned that COWs DRINK, EAT, and RUN and that HORSEs EAT and RUN, he has formed a network of relations involving two semantic classes. COW is a stimulus for three response equivalence paradigms involving the terms: DRINK/EAT, EAT/RUN, DRINK/RUN, respectively. HORSE is the stimulus for one response equivalence paradigm: EAT/RUN. Furthermore, EAT and RUN, respectively, are the responses for the two stimulus equivalence paradigms both involving COW/HORSE.

Undoubtedly, both the classes of right- and of left-hand terms are more firmly established than when only a single response or a single stimulus equivalence paradigm was involved. The strength of classes might, indeed, be determined by enumerating the number of stimulus or response paradigms embedded in the more complex display (see Riegel, 1970). Once classes have attained a certain strength, a child might generate novel utterances without ever having been exposed to them before, for example, in the illustration above, the child might realize that HORSEs DRINK.

Types of Intralingual Relations

Thus far we have discussed general procedures for identifying the meaning of words and for determining word classes but we have not given any thought to the types of relations involved. Apparently, many types of relations are conceivable and, most important, will lead to different classifications. Thus, ZEBRA together with TIGER, CANDY-STICK and BARBER-SIGN are forming a class sharing STRIPES as a common part or quality. On the other hand, ZEBRA will be categorized with ELEPHANT, NEGRO, and NILE, all of which are located in AFRICA. Hence, different relations lead to only partially overlapping categories. This result, in our opinion, is the main reason why philosophers, linguists, and psychologists have failed, thus far, to develop and to operationalize comprehensive semantic interpretations.

The above problems are further complicated by the mutual dependence of classes and general (class) relations. This difficulty is similar to the circularity in defining elements and simple relations. Classes, as we have argued, consist of those elements that share certain relations such as actor-action relations. On the other hand, we might conceive of a class of animals and of a class of actions that, in conjunction, define the general relationship between them. These two ways of looking at classes and general relations correspond to the alternative principles elaborated by Dedekind (1893) and Frege (1903), respectively (see Chapter I, pp. 10–11).

When considering developmental progression, however, it seems unlikely that the recognition of general relations precedes that of classes. Once simple relations are given, classes can be derived; once classes are derived, the general relationship between them can be apprehended. General relationships do not represent anything more than the totality of all simple relations between each member of one class and each member of the other class. Similar to the concept of classes, no surplus meaning ought to be attached to the general relations between classes.

Relying on Piaget's interpretations (Inhelder & Piaget, 1958), we have previously (Riegel & Riegel, 1963) categorized general relations into three groups: (1) Logical relations between linguistic elements made explicit by verbal abstraction, such as synonymity, antonymity, superordination, coordination, and subordination. (2) Infralogical or physical relations between objects, events, or qualities made explicit by abstracting features from these physical items such as parts, wholes, locations, preceding, contemporaneous, or succeeding events. (3) Grammatical relations derived from the phenomenal (surface) structure of linguistic expressions and representing concatenations between the major parts of speech, that is, nouns, verbs, and modifiers.

The above list of general relations is neither exhaustive nor independent. It must be supplemented on the basis of more abstract considerations which lead to the classification of relations into those that are: symmetrical versus nonsymmetrical, transitive versus nontransitive, reflexive versus nonreflexive, and so on. (see Carnap, 1928, p. 21). Our list may also be supplemented by semantic relations discussed in Fillmore's (1968) case grammar and in the developmental studies by Bloom (1970, 1973) and Brown (1973).

Implicit and Explicit Relations

If we receive the abbreviated messages: ZEBRA → ANIMAL, ZEBRA → STRIPEs, ZEBRA → RUNs, we not only have four different words at our disposal but the implicit relational information of superordination, whole-part, and actor-action. The failure of a particle model of language to deal adequately with both semantic and syntactic interpretations is determined by the disregard for this relational information. Thus far, our discussion has been concerned with relations implied in meaningful combinations of words (and, strictly speaking, all combinations of words are meaningful). An implicit relation is unique for the words that it connects; it is general if many words are combined in the same manner, that is, if the left-hand and right-hand elements are members of two different classes.

The transmission of relational information would be insufficiently safe-guarded if no other and partially redundant clues were built into the natural languages. Thus, instead of the abbreviated messages listed above, we usually receive phrases like, "The zebra is an animal" or "The stripes of the zebra" or "The zebra runs." In these examples, the auxiliary IS (used as a proper verb) plus the indefinite article AN explicate the logical relation of superordination; the definite article THE and the preposition OF explicate the infralogical relation of whole-part; only the grammatical relation or actor-action does not receive any further explication except for the inflection, s, marking the verb. We call these explicit clues redundant, because they do not occur regularly in the "telegraphic" speech of young children. Apparently, implicit relational information is prior to its explicated form.

The significance of our last statement is underscored when we realize that many single words have inherent relational features. Such implicit relationality is most strongly exhibited among adjectives and adverbs whose role of modifying nouns and verbs necessitates this feature. Their relationality is further extended through the use of comparative constructions that make this part of speech an exceptionally rich topic for a relational analysis (see Clark, 1970; Huttenlocher & Higgins, 1971; Riegel, 1973b). Also, verbs relating to noun subjects and/or to noun objects imply such relationality, for example, PUSH, PULL, GIVE, TAKE. With the exception of professional and kinship terms, for example, FOREMAN, UNCLE, BROTHER, such implicit relationality is not very common among nouns, however.

Compounding of Relations

With our discussion of explicit relations we have, finally, reached areas of inquiry traditionally explored by linguistics as the foundation of language. In contrast, our own discussion did not begin with an elaboration of these abstract structures but was founded on the concrete experiences and activities of the real child. Throughout, the order of our topics corresponded to the natural order in which a language is acquired. After sufficient relational information is obtained, the child may identify elements as well as classes. Next, explicit relational clues, such as the prepositions, will be utilized and the child will, increasingly, obey the proper sequential order of semantic classes. At this moment the child is still not operating within syntax of the linguists because he has not yet a sufficient grasp of the more abstract grammatical classes nor of the rules of their combination and transformation. He will be ready for these operations when the classes and class relations available to him have become sufficiently general. With few exceptions, semantic classes are subsets of grammatical classes and, without exception, semantics is prior to syntax.

When two or more elements co-occur regularly, the relations involved may begin to function as elements of a higher order. This stratification occurs, for instance, when words are compounded, such as yellow-bird, store-keeper, window-pane, and the like. These conditions can be depicted by bracketing, that is, (YELLOW → BIRD). Subsequently, a telegraphic sentence could be expressed as (YELLOW → BIRD) → SINGS, in contrast to the original formula YELLOW → BIRD; BIRD → SINGs.

The possibilities provided through compounding are not limited to words but lead us directly into questions of semantic and syntactic levels, strata, and hierarchies. The above example represents, indeed, the combination of a noun-phrase, NP, that is, YELLOW → BIRD, with the verb SING. Instead of bracketing, Chomsky has preferred to depict hierarchical organizations by tree diagrams:

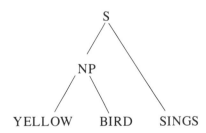

Thus, our example provides the important connection with the topic of syntactic structures and their acquisition during childhood (see McNeill, 1970a,b; Slobin, 1971).

Relations of Relations

In spite of their concern with language structure, psycholinguists have paid little attention to what we might call relations of relations or the logical connections of relations. Two relations, as discussed above, can be monotonically combined leading to the derivation of classes such as "animals" and "animated actions." They can also become part of more complex expressions. For this purpose, connectors must be introduced. Mainly two types of words serve these connective purposes: conjunctions and relative pronouns. In particular, symmetrical conjunctions (AND, TOO, ALSO, AS WELL AS, etc.) and relative (asymmetrical) pronouns (WHICH, WHO, and THAT) express—in analogy to our former distinction—logical relations of coordination and superordination-subordination as in the following examples:

Coordination: (EAGLE → FLIEs) and (RABBIT → RUNs)

Superordination-
Subordination: (RABBIT → RUNs) which (EAGLE → HAUNTs)

     or   RABBIT which (EAGLE → HAUNTs) → RUNs

Asymmetrical conjunctions (IF , , , THEN, BECAUSE, BEFORE, AFTER, etc.) and relative adverbs (WHERE, WHEN, WHY, etc.) generate infralogical relations between relations and represent spatial, temporal, causal, and other physical conditions as in the following examples:

Spatial: (HOUSE → BURNs) where (JOHN → LIVEs)

Temporal/Causal: (CORN → GROWs) after (SUN → SHINEs)

             if (EAGLE → FLIEs) then (RABBIT → RUNs) etc.

In spite of the lack of evidence, these logical and infralogical relations of relations are prior and of greater importance in the language acquisition process than any syntactic structures reflecting formal and abstract linguistic conventions. Since permutations within logical and infralogical structures produce, in most instances, changes in interpretations, such a "syntax" is more fundamental than those aspects of syntax usually analyzed by linguists. The child will have to learn how to operate with logical and infralogical combinations; as a by-product he generates sentences that incorporate words according to their syntactic rules.

Psycholinguistic Systems

If, instead of elements and simple relations, we discuss classes and general relations, we shift from what Chomsky has called finite state grammars to phrase structure grammars. Of course, such an extension is not limited to syntax but, more important from our point of view, holds true for semantic systems as well. Instead of proposing simple relations such as RABBIT → RUNs, EAGLE → FLIEs, and of elaborating different types of combinations, we argue, now, in terms of semantic classes, such as "animals," "food," "toys," "animated actions,'' and the like, and in terms of general relations that not only link but also define these classes. Since there are no nonoverlapping semantic classes, only the most formal and abstract features of the language, namely those of syntax, have been described in an unambiguous manner. But even here, multiple classifications may seem disturbing, but they also guarantee the richness of linguistic expressions and the creative potential of the language.

Rules for combining semantic or syntactic classes are more general than rules for combining simple relations. Although, therefore, the resulting semantic and syntactic systems are more powerful, Chomsky regards them as almost equally insufficient because they do not consider transformational operations. Although transformational systems might be still more comprehensive than the other models, it is readily conceivable that these various semantic and syntactic systems coexist in the child, and that large portions of his language skills might be sufficiently explained by systems of classes and general relations or even by transitional probabilities without invoking more complex operations. The problem of different, coexisting semantic schemata is very similar to that raised in cognitive developmental psychology. As is argued elsewhere (Riegel, 1973) the coexistence and, especially, the simultaneous operation at several levels can be explained only from a dialectic but not from a formal operational perspective.

Inversion and Negation

A language model based on classes and general relations accounts for the well documented generative skills of children (Brown & Fraser, 1963; Stern & Stern, 1907; Weir, 1962), but it does not handle operations of intellectual shifts or reversals (Riegel, 1957) which, recently, have been discussed under the topic of deixis (see Bruner, 1972; Rommetveit, 1968). When we identify an object or a term, we always do so at the expense of others with which the target item is contrasted. Only during the very early stages of intellectual development, that is, during the sensorimotor period in Piaget's theory, does the child focus on singular items. In most instances, the contrastive disregard of information (Trabasso, 1970) is as important as the positive identification of the item itself.

Recently, Olson (1970) has given a cogent analysis of this problem. By hiding a small paper star under blocks differing in several attributes, the verbal identification of the target item varies with the alternatives given. In one situation we might merely say that the star is under the block (if there is only one block within a set of other objects); in another we might say that it is under the black one, the round one, or the large one, depending on the alternatives given. In the language of set theory, the identification of a concept A also involves the recognition of its inverse A', both of which compose the superset B in the form of $A + A' = B$.

The problem becomes more complex if the discrimination occurs along several dimensions at the same time. For instance, if the child has to operate within the dimension of red versus nonred and wooden versus nonwooden, he might again discriminate red blocks from all others or wooden blocks from all others by disregarding each time the second of the two interacting attributes. However, he might also be asked to form combinations, such as red *and* wooden; red *but not* wooden; wooden *but not* red; *neither* red *nor* wooden.

Since psycholinguistic information is mostly positive, our discussion has been somewhat academic. Generally, we describe an item by listing several, preferably, criterial features, rather than by informing the listener what an item is *not*. For example, we are telling a child that a "ZEBRA is an ANIMAL with STRIPES," rather than that "a ZEBRA is *not* a PLANT and does *not* have DOTS." We choose the positive strategy because complementary sets are often ill-defined and vary from situation to situation. Moreover, human subjects seem to be better able to handle positive rather than negative information (see Bourne, 1970; Bruner, Goodnow & Austin, 1956; Wason, 1959; Wason & Johnson-Laird, 1972).

Because of the traditional emphasis on cognition, the role of negative information has been insufficiently explored by psycholinguists. As soon as we focus on language as a means for the initiation and control of nonverbal actions, motivations, and emotions, we are impressed by the significant role of negation in the form of inhibition, repression, and denial. These noncognitive aspects of language provide important connections with other major areas of psychological inquiry, such as physiological, personality, and social research and theories. The concept of negative information also enters into consideration when we extend our discussion of classes to those of ordered relations. Within such models, negations of ordered or partially ordered subsystems represent an operation specifically called transformation.

Transformations

In discussing transformations, it is useful to refer briefly to mathematics where this concept has been rigorously applied. Mathematical systems consist of sets of axioms defining possible operations with symbolic elements, such as numbers. As elaborated by Hölder (1901) and more recently discussed by Stevens (1951), Coombs (1964), and others, the simplest number system defines nominal scales which, when applied to observations, allow for the categorization of items in distinct classes to which, in turn, labels, such as words, letters or numerals may be assigned. Since no order between the classes exists, the degree of transformation is almost unlimited and consists in the relabeling of the classes and their members. Differing from linguistics, however, logical or mathematical transformations keep the significant properties of the system invariant, that is, the classes remain the same even though their labels have changed. When additional axioms on the transitivity of the operations are imposed, ordinal systems are generated. Subsequently, logical or mathematical transformations, in keeping the order invariant, are more restricted than those applicable to nominal systems. Ordinal scales might be monotonically stretched or compressed but the order of any two items may not be altered.

Unfortunately, linguists have used the term transformation in precisely the opposite sense. Linguistic transformations, in producing variance, gain importance the more complex the system is to which they are applied. In categorical systems they lead to the identification of the inverse of classes. In ordered systems, for example, in various types of syntax, they imply rearrangements of these classes which, often, require changes in interpretations. Linguistic transformations deal with the reordering of sequences of classes or, at a lower level, of elements, by which, for instance, declarative statements are changed into questions, passive statements, negative statements, and vice versa, or by which deep structure phrases are converted into surface structure expressions and vice versa.

Conclusion

With our brief reference to linguistic transformations, we return to the main issues of the first part of our chapter in which we seek to demonstrate that a purely transactional analysis is conceivable and has been successfully implemented in economic operations. Language, likewise, ought to be regarded as an activity and not merely as a system of particles or tokens, products, or commodities. Such a conclusion, if accepted, does not contradict our analysis in the second part of our chapter where we emphasize the relational character of linguistic operations. In the summary that follows, we attempt, once more, to show the congruence of these two aspects of language development.

At the proto-economic level, trade consists in the exchange of particular items on a one-to-one basis and is bound to a given situation. Such a system is concrete with little symbolic representation. But the items exchanged are not to be viewed as having thing-like, substantive character; what is exchanged are the activities and the labor necessary to produce them. Similarly, linguistic operations at this level involve extralingual relations between labels and objects, internal states, or—most important—actions. If a comparison with Piaget's developmental levels is attempted, the proto-economic and the proto-linguistic systems are characterized by sensorimotor activities.

The next economic system is comparable to the level of concrete intellectual operations. It relies on standard commodities represented by concrete materials or objects, for example, gold or silver, and allows for a wide range and much more flexible operations, such as sequential and multiple distributions of traded goods, as well as for advance storage and delayed actions. The conceptual danger of a system of this kind lies in the tendency to regard its basic monetary unit as fixed, universal entities. History has repeatedly shown that this apparent stability is easily shattered when the basis of activity, representing the labor and efforts by the participating people, is brought at variance with the standards of the system.

Traditionally, similar viewpoints have dominated psychology and linguistics, namely, the view that language consists of sets of basic units, such as words, syllables, letters, morphemes, or phonemes, from which the more complex forms are derived. Thereby, the view of language as an activity and a process is either disregarded or lost. Just as different currencies represent different monetary systems, so do different sets of linguistic elements represent different languages or dialects. Thus, there exists variability and (linear) convertibility or (nonlinear, transformational) translation. The universal basis of different linguistic systems is represented by the protolanguage of the preceding level with its notion of the identity of operations. Correspondingly, the proto-economy of the barter system represents the universal features of the more advanced trading operations. It is based on property rights. At the second economic level, more specific rules must be implemented determining the standard, the order, and the distribution of exchanges. Likewise, at the second linguistic level, more specific lexicological conventions and syntactic rules of order and restitution are required.

Only at the third stage of development does an analysis of the economic system advance our understanding of linguistic systems to a significant degree. Monetary forms characteristic for this stage and represented by certificates, bonds, stocks, and checks are representational units of exchange. They help us to realize that it is not the objects or any particular material, such as rare metals, that are exchanged but the labor and activities of people producing these objects and operating with these documents. Transactions on such elusive bases require explicit rules of conduct of which only a minor portion concerns the specific relationship of these certificates to the objects of trade. Most of them deal with intraeconomic relations.

The conditions are similar in linguistic operations. Only when we realize that linguistic units, such as words, syllables, or letters, are mere abstractions from the stream of operations that characterizes language, do we gain a full understanding of linguistic systems. These operations constitute the information immediately given through the interrelating activities of communicating individuals. An understanding of these interactions can be gained only if these activities are studied as they are produced and perceived; the products of these interactions are rigidified objectifications that do not capture the constituting activities of languages.

CHAPTER 10

Pragmatic Structures of Language: Historical, Formal and Developmental Issues[1]

WILBUR A. HASS

What can one say about the ways in which a language functions as a means of communication among people? This question is somewhat different from those that are often asked about language: What formalism best approximates all and only the well-formed sentences of a language? Or, how does a language provide representations of states of affairs? For the latter two questions we have a better idea of sensible answers; for the first, we have high hopes.

"Pragmatics" can serve as a label for our attempts to provide an answer, that is, for an account of the way language functions in a speaker-hearer matrix, or, if we prefer, of the way in which people function in a manner dependent on the properties of language as a shared instrumentality for communication. This usage generally follows the syntactics-semantics pragmatics division of Morris (1938; 1946, Ch. 8; 1963) and Carnap (1939; 1942; 1956, app. E; 1963); for detailed definitional considerations in this area see Lieb (1971). "Pragmatics" has figured prominently in various psychological accounts of language (e.g., Cherry, 1961, Ch. VI; Watzlawick, Beavin & Jackson, 1967), as well as in linguistics (e.g., R. Lakoff, 1972) and philosophical logic (e.g., Stalnaker, 1972). Related terms might also be employed: "the new rhetoric" (Perelman, 1970), "communicative competence" (Slobin, 1967; Hymes, 1971), "discursivity" (Parret, 1971), "the psychosociology of language" (Moscovici, 1972).

Pragmatics, I believe, should be based on a search for structure of a kind

---

[1]The contents of this chapter build on work for a book with Carol F. Feldman of the University of Chicago; although she deserves indirect credit for a considerable proportion of whatever good points this discussion contains, any faults are my responsibility alone. Shimer has provided an atmosphere that has allowed me to write with minimal discomfort. The opportunities for study and discussion available to me while I was a visiting associate professor at the University of Michigan (Fall, 1971) are also reflected.

that is analogous to syntactic structure or semantic structure (sometimes called "logical structure," by virtue of a narrow interpretation of logic). What is at stake is the determination of relationships among the principal invariances in communication via natural language. It is this organization of invariances that best characterizes a given utterance, rather than exhibition of whatever physiological or phenomenological correlates happen to be in evidence during production or reception. What is said is thus to be described in relation to other things that might have been said; or alternatively one characterizes the entire ensemble of "sayables." Such an endeavor represents an extension of what has been the typical and successful program of modern structural (in the wide sense) linguistics.

A description of pragmatic structure strives to be, simultaneously, sufficiently rich and sufficiently specific. It should be rich enough to include functions over and above that of representation (designation, depiction), since such a function is merely the enaction of the language's semantics. Also it should not be so inclusive as to make it impossible to separate the functions of language from those of other human acts (say, of "expression" or "instrumental behavior"), nor from those of the communicative behaviors of other species (e.g., greeting, warning, or threatening). To carry out these desiderata involves going beyond social psychology (even though the latter includes, incidentally, human interaction) and ethology (dealing as it does with the whole range of organisms' signaling). In my mind the very holding of a conference on historical and developmental structuralism evidences enough specificity of human language functions to indicate a need for pragmatics.

Another preliminary issue which cannot be pursued here concerns the coherence of the notion of "pragmatic structure." The first of two objections is one of multiplying entities. If pragmatics is a special part of a theory of action (just as a theory of action is a part of an even more general theory of function), are we not in the position of inventing a structure for function? And if function is prior, what is the ontological status of the structure? The second is an objection about self-application. Must I not be assuming that you already know about language function, or else how can what I say to you have a communicative function? What function(s) can be assigned to language which is(are) able to include that very act of assigning? These paradoxical aspects of structural description and reflexivity, however, occur in all studies of human affairs; they seem to demand some kind of developmental or dialectical stance (as we shall note in the last section). For the time being, we can perhaps go on supposing some modus vivendi for pragmatics—as well as for our other actions as students of behavior and experience.

HISTORICAL: THE QUEST FOR A VIABLE PRAGMATICS

A cursory and critical sketch of some antecedents of current pragmatics will show how difficult it is to achieve a rich, specific and coherent pragmatic description, as well as provide a glimpse of some problems that an ideal pragmatics would solve. The descriptions below reflect, not the most sophisticated possible handling of the theory under consideration, but the general tenor of attitudes of proponents of the original theory.

Pragmatism

To begin, let us consider the relation of pragmatics to *pragmatism,* as a general philosophical approach. It was initiated by C. S. Peirce (1878) as a way of dealing with the meaning of concepts or terms. Following its extension by William James (1907) to problems of truth, in a psychologistic and popularized form, Peirce himself resorted to calling his own position "pragmaticism," which he deemed "ugly enough to be safe from kidnappers" (1905). An indication of "American practicality" and a forerunner of operationalism, Peirce's and James' work pointed out ways in which conceptual language functioned in human activity. It changed the emphasis from the way in which a term "stood for something" to the way in which it "allowed a person to do something."

For Peirce, the representative relation between word and thing always hovered in the immediate background; language was fundamentally a kind of sign. But he did produce a radically new definition of "sign":

"A First which stands in such a genuine triadic relation to a Second, called its *Object,* as to be capable of determining a Third, called its *Interpretant,* to assume the same triadic relation to its Object in which it stands itself to the same Object [1940, pp. 99–100]."

Although Peirce relied on representation of the referent by the expression, he clearly had in mind a nonmechanistic relationship, a triadic one, one which was, indeed, by definition inherently recursive. This attitude also found reflection in the way in which he emphasized the progressive and always uncompleted nature of science. Clearly the fixed, one-to-one mapping of classical and empiricist referential approaches has been avoided. Nevertheless, we search in vain through Peirce's papers for a rich account of the full range of the "interpretational" possibilities of language.

James' problem was the opposite one, inability to provide any sort of a priori constraints on the functions of language. He specifies the role of language in terms of personal improvement, the quelling of fears, the exchanges of the marketplace. If a person has the will—and right—to believe anything that ''works'' for him, then, one might justly argue, he deserves to be told anything that works for the speaker. We do not see the ways in which the workings of language are required to meet special criteria, criteria we do not try to find in other ''goals, consequences and facts,'' for example, isometrics, pacifiers, or bearskins.

A similar division in terms of locus of weak point in their pragmatics might be carried out for many recent philosophers who have had fundamental concerns with language. Thus, Cassirer's philosophy of symbolic forms stumbles because of lack of richness (his mention of emotional values in language is never tied into his basically representationalist account of propositionality). On the other hand, the implicit pragmatics of Bergson and Croce may be considered to have erred in the direction of too little specificity.

Major movements in the social and behavioral sciences provide clear demonstrations of the need for a coherent pragmatics. The components of the demonstration, in case after case, can be roughly outlined as follows: First, the movement takes a position that reduces language function to an oversimplified, ill-considered basis (the pragmatics, as actually stated or implied, is grossly nonspecific). Second, the procedures of the movement require a better notion of how language works (the pragmatics needed by the movement to carry out its program exceeds the capability provided by its position). Third, an attempt is made to make do by means of a representationalist view of language (the inadequacies of the movement's pragmatics are filled in by resort to an impoverished ''picture'' account). That is, the movements have promised a radically pragmatistic account of language, but lacking any substantial pragmatic structure, have fallen back on the support provided by an unanalyzed reliance on language as ''sign.'' We now determine how such a state of affairs came about in the cases of Marxism, psychoanalysis, and behaviorism, by a quick examination of each.

Marxism

Marxism gave an account of language in terms of its role in the dynamics of social-economic dialectics. Marx's 1844 manuscripts already use language as an example of a sensuous object and of a social given. In *The German Ideology* we find a clear statement as follows:

From the start the spirit is afflicted with the curse of being burdened with matter, which here makes its appearance in the form of agitated layers of air, sounds, in short, of language. Language is as old as consciousness, language *is* practical consciousness that exists also for other men, and for that reason alone it really exists for me personally as well; language, like consciousness, only arises from the need, the necessity, of intercourse with other men [Tucker, 1972, p. 122].''

As the movement gained a following that required organizing, language came to be treated, in directly political terms, in terms of its ability to facilitate or to impede revolution; the notion of "truth", outside of the communist program, is debunked as an idealist fiction.

But since the class struggle has been at work throughout history without the need for prior awareness or description, what is it that is added when people *tell* others that they have been determined to unite and throw off their chains? What status can be given *Das Kapital* (it strikes one as a queer sort of propaganda leaflet), and by what authority does "the vanguard" speak? Is language to vanish once classes are abolished? One finds an attempted answer to these problems in Lenin's doctrine of the "reflection" of the world in the human mind, and in Stalin's assertion that language, somehow, escapes the dialectic process. These clearly appear to be vacuous and ad hoc hedges, just as Pavlov's remarks remained a vacuous excuse to get at important human phenomena (cf. also Marxist literary criticism, e.g., Steiner, 1967; and Jameson, 1971).

Psychoanalysis

Psychoanalysis begins with the postulate that language derives from and expresses instinctual drives (albeit in a way that may be rather indirect and sublimated). To realize how bald the sexual attribution was, consider the following account of the origin of language cited by Freud in his *General Introduction to Psychoanalysis.*

". . . the first sounds uttered were a means of communication, and of summoning the sexual partner, and that in the later development the elements of speech were used as an accompaniment to the different kinds of work carried on by primitive man. This work was performed by associated efforts, to the sound of rhythmically repeated utterances, the effect of which was to transfer a sexual interest to the work. Primitive man thus made his work agreeable, so to speak, by treating it as the equivalent of and substitute for sexual activities. The word uttered during the communal work had therefore two meanings, the one referring to the sexual act, and the other to the labour which had come to be equivalent to it. In time the word was dissociated from its sexual significance and its application confined to the work [Freud, 1943, p. 149].''

Freud and other analysts have at times made much of the fact that language is produced by the mouth (read: "oral zone"), taken in through the ear (read:

"oral equivalent"), expelled by the body (read: "fecal"), or had "phallic" significance. Language, however, looms much larger in psychoanalytic treatments than one could expect of any set of bodily movements. Sucking, biting, taking in, rejecting, expelling, retaining, intruding, enclosing—these all do have rather specific bodily forms, but one cannot tell the motivational significance of the difference between telling someone "You're wonderful!" and "You're a bastard!" on the basis of the difference in movements involved. Hence, so in practice one must rely on the "symbolic" value of what is said; this seems to take the form of a referential approach, enlarged by a vague set of metaphorlike equivalences (plus whatever else is included in "listening with the third ear"). Most unsubstantiated is why the therapeutic activity of the analyst should take the form that it does: why defenses are to be dealt with verbally instead of by some more direct form of intercourse. Until a more complete view of the way language is implicated in "curing" is provided, it is impossible to defeat the view that "what I did in analysis is to learn how to talk about what's wrong with me." Supplementing the theory by means of an ego-analytic reliance on an unanalyzed "reality" means unenlightening, unless the sphere of "object relations" is considerably clarified.

Behaviorism

Behaviorists have never ignored language; their treatment of it is exemplified in the following:

Man is above all an animal which reacts most often and most complexly with speech reactions. The notion has somehow gained ground that objective psychology does not deal with speech reactions. This, of course, is a mistake. It would be foolish and one-sided to an absurd degree to neglect man's vocal behavior. Often the sole observable reaction in man is speech. In other words, his adjustments to situations are made more frequently by speech than through action of the remaining motor mechanisms. [Watson, 1919, pp. 38–39].

This quotation shows how they have sought to reduce language to movements, of no more inherent significance than their past history, and of no different functional status than other conditioned stimuli or socially reinforced operants. Also, they have had a tendency to use language as an escape hatch, to say that complicated human activity is a function of language (and to leave the matter there)—for example, to reduce conceptualization to verbal mediation (cf. Goss, 1961). Insofar as language has been tied down to anything (anything, that is, other than other bits of language, as in verbal learning), there has been an overwhelming emphasis on reference, as in Osgood's representational mediating response or Skinner's reliance on "tacts." This story has become familiar through a series of scathing criticisms (Chomsky, 1959; Fodor, 1965, 1971). There is little need, accordingly, to argue: first, that the associationist mechanisms have a difficult time even in accounting for reference; and second, that a referential account cannot play the role it must in explaining the aspects of human activity that behaviorists find intractable.

All these approaches, then, have a tendency to find that language is practical in some common way: as a means of social action (*pace* Marx), as an expression of libido and defense (*pace* Freud), and as an acquired adaptation to the environment (*pace* Watson). An internal contradiction arises in the form of a peculiar *ad hominem* argument in which critics' language is viewed as practical in a grubbier way than one's own; the critic is reactionary, defensive, or "superstitious," while one's own statements are, in some mysterious way, simply true.

Logical Positivism

The attempted retreat to representational language has been faced most squarely and carried farthest in the Vienna Circle of "logical positivists." Although they shared with the pragmatists a suspicion that much philosophical and theological language was meaningless, the Vienna Circle, as well as Frege, Russell, and the like had the notion that one should construct an "ideal language." It would be "ideal" in the sense that it would accurately reflect the nature of the world it described, and would rule out metaphysical, self-contradictory, or otherwise undesirable expressions. The goal was clearly formulated in the *Tractatus* of Wittgenstein (who had connections with both Russell and members of the Vienna Circle): the language was to be built up on the basis of sentences whose structure paralleled that of the states of affairs they referred to. This pictorial ideal would purge elements of emotional and practical meaning and would allow direct access to the facts. Natural language might have pragmatic vagaries of the kinds we have been encountering, but they could be kept out of the philosophical workshop.

Wittgenstein eventually rejected this as an ideal for philosophical inquiry. His later recommendation went to the other extreme: "Don't look for the meaning, look for the use." Language, he decided, could not adequately be viewed as representational but, instead, must be considered as a kind of activity (or "form of life"), which could be clarified by reference to "language games," as follows:

"Review the multiplicity of language-games in the following examples, and in others:

Giving orders, and obeying them—
Describing the appearance of an object or giving its measurements—
Constructing an object from a description (a drawing)—
Reporting an event—
Speculating about an event—
Forming and testing a hypothesis—
Presenting the results of an experiment in tables and diagrams—
Making up a story; and reading it—
Play-acting—
Singing catches—
Guessing riddles—
Making a joke; telling it—
Solving a problem in practical arithmetic—
Translating from one language into another—
Asking, thanking, cursing, greeting, praying.

—It is interesting to compare the multiplicity of the tools in language and of the ways they are used, the multiplicity of kinds of word and sentence, with what logicians have said about the structure of language. (Including the author of the Tractatus Logico-Philosophicus) [Wittgenstein, 1958, pp. 11e–12e].

Having rejected his pictorial view, Wittgenstein came to believe that the kinds of language were "countless" and that new uses constantly "came into existence" (1958, p. 11e). He can obviously never be wrong with such a protean view of pragmatics, but this state is obtained only at the price of leaving pragmatic structure unformulated and, by implication, unformulatable.

Analytical Philosophy

It is hardly worthwhile to give up attempts at formulating language functions after only exhibiting a motley sampling of them. An earnest attempt was made by the Oxonian leader of analytical philosophy, J. L. Austin (1961, 1962, 1963). He first noted that for many things people said it was absurd to speak of the truth or falsity of the utterance, but that saying was in such cases *doing* something (e.g., asking, promising). He tentatively set off such cases as "performative," found that they sometimes took the form of first-person-singular subject with present-tense verb, and stated typical conditions for their successful occurrence. However, on closer examination, all instances of natural language were seen to involve performance of acts; in fact, the general act of speaking could be broken down into components: producing sounds, saying words in a grammatical construction, referring to whatever one is talking about, saying something with a certain illocutionary force, and having a certain perlocutionary effect on the listener. Illocutionary acts interested Austin the most, and he developed a five-category classification of them. Comments on and extensions of his analysis may be found in Alston (1964), Searle (1969), and Furberg (1971) as well as in numerous articles. Although one may have doubts about the adequacy of his concept of "performing an act" (cf. Cerf, 1969), it is clearly in the pragmatic tradition ("pragma" being, after all, Greek for "act"). Furthermore, illocutionary force seems to mark off a rather separate and fertile field of exploration, and having a classification is a start toward having a structural description.

Conclusions

We have, then, found a certain movement from analyses of language as merely representational or as involved in action of a nonlanguage sort, to examinations of the inherently linguistic form of some actions. It is becoming apparent that one should seek to understand what people do with language, as a specific kind of praxis, before trying to relate language to other things people do (economically, sexually, or in pursuit of whatever reinforcement)

This concern is increasingly a part of everyday life in this century. Our suspicions about language stem not merely from the feeling that language may be impractical (just a lot of hot air), but from the notion that language is merely practical (in the grubbiest way). To know that language is "about" the world does not, by itself, help much. We need a way of dealing with the properties of language over and above whatever pictorial force it may have, a set of positive criteria for considering the full range of language activity. This need is, indeed, stressed in an election year, when we are inundated with language of a most puzzling sort—not in terms of its syntactic structure nor of what it is about, but of its status as appropriate, worthwhile, effective, salient, and responsible. We have no trouble agreeing that it reflects cognitive development when a child adapts his description of a game to the fact that his listener is wearing a blindfold (Flavell, 1968). How are we to compare what is said about drugs to a supermarket crowd, in contrast with a group of college-student volunteers? On what principles are we to object to calling bombing raids "protective reaction strikes"? Answers, which require far more than a dichotomy between "the truth" and "whatever works," await formulation in a pragmatics.

FORMAL: POTENTIAL EMBODIMENTS OF PRAGMATIC STRUCTURE

No complete, formalized pragmatics exist for us to discuss their structural properties, say, in terms of Piaget's notions of structuralism. Instead of presenting a preformed pragmatics, we are in the position of having to construct it. This may help clarify the nature of pragmatics, but it hardly makes for neatness of presentation. At any rate, we now review some ways, by no means necessarily mutually exclusive, that may be used to describe pragmatic structures for natural language. The comments made are directed toward providing potential answers to the question: How can we say something (anything) about the pragmatics of English that has a chance of productivity and generality? In no case is it certain that we are getting at language universals, rather than facts about a given language.

Model Theory

This way of dealing with pragmatics (best exemplified in Montague, 1968, 1972, and in related but notationally simpler work of Harrah, 1971) has arisen in recent logic out of the success of model theory (and related truth-functional approaches) in specifying the semantics of artificial languages (introductions requiring some background in mathematical logic are Mostowski, 1966, XIII-XIV; van Fraassen, 1971). It originated in Tarski's formulation of "truth" (1944), and rests on the assumption that language functions can be based on the truth of sentences and the designations (or senses) of their component terms.

How this approach works becomes evident when we examine how it deals with deictic expressions (personal and demonstrative pronouns, adverbs of the "here/there-now/then" variety, tenses). These are clearly of pragmatic interest, since their reference changes from use to use—in order to know who "I" is, you must know who is talking, and so on. These have formed a problem for logical analysis for this very reason—"This is Tuesday" is true if, and only if, it is said on Tuesday. Model theory provides an interpretation of these expressions by an extension, rather slight but by no means simple to carry out completely, wherein deictic expressions are mapped onto features of the extralinguistic context, once these have been included in the meta-language (Stalnaker, 1970; Apostel, 1971 and the papers they cite). This technique allows one to construct an account of the interrelation between the directly referential world and the contextual (and deictically referential) world.

For other elements of undeniable pragmatic import, the model-theoretic treatment involves an even more complicated interpretation of the expressions as particular functions of propositional content. Thus questions can be treated in terms of the statements that work as answers for them (Harrah, 1963, 1969; Aqvist, 1965). Commands, requests, and other sentences with recommendatory or moral force can be mapped onto ideal worlds in which they are carried out (Hilpinen, 1971, passim). Modals of necessity and possibility can be treated in terms of possible worlds in which they are true (Kripke, 1963, and his successors).

Such accounts show that with sufficient technical ingenuity one can "analyze away" heretofore puzzling pragmatic aspects of language, by including them under a blanket idea of "satisfaction" (in the abstract form of a mathematical mapping relation). In other words, if we go to the trouble we can avoid any but the most vacuous of pragmatics and, in so doing, gain structures of exemplary complicatedness; the result is that the pragmatic features no longer function in a recognizably nonreferential way. But constructing such a formalism does not show how these elements actually work in natural language; in fact, one could argue that it makes it harder to determine how they function there, by virtue of the elaborate way of hiding what they are used for.

Of course, one wants one's pragmatics to be true (among other things). But this cannot be taken to imply that all the functions of language can best be taken as more or less elaborate ways of packaging the truth. As we mention above, it is the nontruth functional aspects of language that pragmatics needs to emphasize; truth can, for the time being, more or less take care of itself.

To prevent the above discussion being taken as a criticism of logicians, we must emphasize that nonlogicians have often held an even more optimistic view of what a truth-functional analysis of language might accomplish. Sometimes such a program has been explicitly stated (e.g., Davidson, 1967). More frequently, reliance on conditions of truth in accounting for the whole range of language meaning has been implicit, part of a general program that strives to account for words and phrases in terms of their referents, or to account for sentences by translating them into expressions of some variant of predicate calculus (e.g., McCawley, 1970). (Here I claim only that such efforts, however valuable they may be, have been taken as providing for a fuller account of meaning than they can provide).

Even when individuals have deliberately determined on carrying out pragmatics, they have often fallen back on descriptive language. For example, in Travis' (1971) sketch of illocutionary force, only expositives are represented—the most "factual" case—and it is not clear how what he says could be generalized to other acts. Again, Fodor's (in prep.—that is, the draft I have seen) account of sentence meaning in terms of speech-act potential quickly seizes on declaratives used for asserting as paradigmatic. In fact, a whole set of arguments in recent linguistics, about whether transformations preserve meaning, whether surface structure contributes to meaning, and so on, have arisen by virtue of ignoring the inadequacy of representational interpretations of language function. Similarly, many psycholinguistics experiments have been expended to show that people can devise ways of referring that they think will be adequate for the task and the hearer; this is one aspect of pragmatics, but a most limited one.

Game Theory

Here we are concerned with the interactive version of decision theory that involves the analysis of matrices which associate each of a repertoire of moves with its resulting payoff for the players. This formalism allows the vague notion of "rule" to receive two rather definite interpretations: (1) constitutive rules, which define what comprises a move and the repertoire of moves, and (2) strategic rules, which state the relation of moves or move-sequences to their payoffs, or are some function of this relation. (Of course, the surplus meaning of "rule" is not exhausted by employing this dichotomy.)

In simple games it is possible to provide a listing of the moves, a technique that (as Wittgenstein's position illustrates) is hardly open to us in dealing with the functions of language. But talking of moves by itself emphasizes the involvement of activity in language, quite apart from any tie with representation. Also, one may note (after Miller & McNeill, 1969, p. 667) the categorically imperative rule of any game—namely, that you may make any move you would allow another player to make under similar circumstances; that is, the activities of the participants in a game arise out of a shared frame of reference that interprets what is done independently of who does it to whom. Principled limits are thus provided for the basic meaning of an act insofar as it forms a move.

Concerning the payoffs gained through moves and move-sequences, the interpretation for pragmatics is even more problematic. It does not help to observe that we have here a clear reflection of the instrumentalist tradition of pragmatism—one that has been carried to great lengths in operant analysis of behavior and in social-psychological theories of sanctions for role-behaviors. I am unaware of any attempt to specify payoffs for communication in a way that is not ad hoc. It is doubtful in principle whether the payoffs can be specified in terms of a single utility metric, because of the interactive nature of the relation between move and payoff in communicative language (I owe this point to William Livant). And without a unitary utility metric, none of the usual game-theoretic formalism will work.

An illustration of the line of thinking encouraged by a game-theoretic approach to pragmatics is the following.

"Recently at the counter of the university bookstore, I showed some amusement at the presence of some copies of a book entitled *The Wisdom of Spiro Agnew* and said simply, "What's this?" My role at this point was that of a partner using a strategy of overt cooperation. I must confess that I anticipated that the clerk would share my amusement at what appeared to be another one of that kind of book that shows the person quoted as anything but wise. She responded by saying that a lot of those books had been sold but that she did not approve of the constant ridicule of the Vice-President. Obviously the role she had selected for our exchange was that of opponent with a strategy of overt opposition. My response was that I thought that the Vice-President could take care of himself, a statement I intended to make from the role of partner with a strategy of covert opposition. The clerk answered that she knew Mr. Agnew could take care of himself but he still should not be made fun of because we should have more respect for the office of Vice-President and that that respect should keep us from making fun of Mr. Agnew. This statement struck me as made from the role of partner in covert opposition [Ianni, 1970, pp. 104–5]."

What is not implausible as a description of moves loses much of its intuitive support when utilities are added in:

"My opening question from the role of partner with a strategy of overt assistance (P/OA) and the clerk's response from the role of opponent with a strategy of overt opposition (0/00) result in a payoff of 0. The second exchange, where both the clerk and I played P/CO results in a payoff of 1. Notice what the payoffs would have been if the responses had been different. If the clerk had responded to my initial play with the play of P/OA, the payoff would have been 3; or if I had responded to her play of 0/00 with the play 0/00, the payoff would have been −3. [Ianni, 1970, p. 106]."

In concluding this discussion, we briefly comment that the game-theoretic approach is, in our terms, very rich, but has a tendency to be nonspecific. The feature of projectivity, whereby the value of an utterance can be determined on the basis of its components, has also been lost.

Set Theory, Componential Analysis, Dimensional Analysis

As we have indicated above, Austin came to reject the view that some utterances did things while others were only true or false. In examining the ways in which anything that is said in a normal setting has an illocutionary force, Austin provided a program that is meant to span the whole universe of utterances. His partition of illocutionary acts into five classes opens the way to further set-theoretic interpretations. These become interesting insofar as they demonstrate that such acts are not simply chosen from a single repertoire of moves, but have a structure based on overlap and inclusion among categories of acts.

Hints of the presence of these structures can be found even if we restrict ourselves to overt performatives, referring to the "performative force" of the act, as given by the verb employed. First, the same components of performative force that underlie one verb may also be present in another, albeit in another ordering of prominence (as noted for the verbs "criticize" and "accuse," as nonperformatives, by Fillmore, 1969). For example, "suggest" and "recommend" differ most clearly in that the former involves specification of information with implied positive evaluation, while the latter involves positive evaluation with respect to information that is implied to be evident. Thus, if a neighbor is fixing his lawn mower while it is running, one can tell him, "I don't recommend that" but hardly, "I don't suggest that"—whereas "I suggest that you check the choke" works as well as "I recommend that you check the choke," perhaps even better if checking the choke is not to be taken as an obvious possible course of action. This leaves the two with an overlapping use in situations where both evaluation and specification are taken for granted (e.g., a waiter in a restaurant may look over one's shoulder and say either: "I suggest ordering the veal as entree" or "I recommend ordering the veal as entree").

Second, performative verbs can sometimes co-occur, resulting in multiplicity of performative force (the phenomenon was noted by Fraser, 1971). This co-occurrence can take place only if there is sufficient congruence between the verbs involved. For example, it would be weird to say, "I beg that I command you to leave," but "I insist that I recommend that we accept all early entrants" is a candidate for both insisting and recommending. In such cases of co-occurrence, hierarchical ordering of performatives is maintained (which Fraser does not bring out). Sometimes the alternative ordering is not plausible (as in "I recommend that I insist that we accept all early entrants"—which would demand a context in which the speaker was talking to himself in a strange way). In other cases where both orderings of the co-occurrent pair are feasible (e.g., "I admit that I insist that we lost" and "I insist that I admit that we lost.") the order of the acts still makes for different interpretations.

Third, relations of entailment also occur in connection with performatives (cf. Fraser, 1971, again). Even when only one performative verb is present in the sentence, the act being carried out may "imply" an act that makes use of another performative verb. For example, "I promise that I will fix the stove" implies that the speaker would also be willing to say, "I predict that I will fix the stove"—although one does not have "I promise that I predict that I will fix the stove," or vice versa. Often, in these instances, some sort of gradient of strength is involved, as in "I ask you to let me pass the course; in fact, I beg you to let me pass" (where begging implies asking, in its generic sense, but asking does not always go as far as begging).

Finally, in the limiting case, one may be able to envisage an entire "space" for performatives, generated out of performative dimensions (which are not themselves given in the vocabulary of performative verbs). Such a way of conceptualizing data has become popular through the technique of factor analysis and the functionalist tradition in experimental psychology. This form of analysis has been sketched by Searle, in the slightly more general case of illocutionary force, as follows:

"First and most important, there is the point or purpose of the act (the difference, for example, between a statement and a question); second, the relative positions of S and H (the difference between a request and an order); third, the degree of commitment undertaken (the difference between a mere expression of intention and a promise); fourth, the difference in propositional content (the difference between predictions and reports); fifth, the difference in the way the proposition relates to the interest of S and H (the difference between boasts and laments, between warnings and predictions); sixth, the different possible expressed psychological states (the difference between a promise, which is an expression of intention, and a statement, which is an expression of belief); seventh, the different ways in which an utterance relates to the rest of the conversation (the difference between simply replying to what someone has said and objecting to what he has said) [Searle, 1969, p. 70]."

Thus one can infer that speech acts show various kinds of interrelatedness, based on the contrast and congruence of performative verbs. One is further led to believe that pragmatic structure will show (at least) the taxonomic and paradigmatic patterning that is typically found in other parts of the lexicon, for which formal analysis is well underway (cf. Tyler, 1969).

It remains to be seen, incidentally, whether there are any important structural differences among analyses in terms of set theory, componential analysis, and dimensional analysis. For example, if the distinctions were typically continuous (rather than discrete—e.g., binary), completely crossing (rather than merely taxonomic), and unlabeled, one would prefer a dimensional approach. However, for most purposes, given current statistical devices, they may virtually be notational variants. Any of the three might uncover interesting and nonobvious features of pragmatic structures, although projectivity can hardly be hoped for.

Transformational Grammar.

As transformational grammar has moved from Zellig Harris' statement of relations among sentences, through Chomsky's statement of relations between surface structures and deep structures, to the generative semanticists' (cf. G. Lakoff, 1971) statement of relations between surface structures and semantic representations, its structural properties have become more and more unclear and (presumably) involved. If we propose to relate the utterance-in-context with its semantic-pragmatic force, hope fades for an adequate formalism to carry this out in a generative manner; there may be limits on the projectivity we can obtain. But the notion of such a transformational device may still be a tempting, as well as a chastening, ideal.

Because of transformational grammarians' basic concern with a semantic interpretation of meaning and/or with underlying structure which could be related to such a semantic representation, a rule of thumb for progress in pragmatics turns out to be: examine the aspects of syntactic structure that typically have been ignored (relegated to "optional" or "equivalent" status) or have remained problematic at the edge of transformational accounts. Thus, the original "optional" transformations (yielding interrogatives, imperatives, negatives, passives, etc.) are of prime interest because they indicate the communicative stance being taken, and are indeed far from optional. And the same also holds true for the great bulk of the major features introduced transformationally (cf. Hass, 1970, 1971—this point apparently originated with Anderson, 1966). From these major features, one can go as far our as to the differential interpretation of "Well, . . ." and "Why, . . ." as they are used as utterance-introducers (R. Lakoff, 1971).

To comprehend the evident pragmatic functioning of syntactic features, consider the interaction between clausal negation and the selection of predicate components. Klima (1964) reported that "any" replaces unstressed "some" as a quantifier in negative contexts (e.g., "We didn't see any meteors" versus "We saw some meteors"). However, what is at work here is not the presence of an overt negative marker, as in Klima's account; presuppositions of the speaker (R. Lakoff, 1969) can be reflected in "some-any" variation in the absence of any overt negative (e.g., "Do you want any tickets?" indicates that it is less likely that there will be takers than "Do you want some tickets?"). Similarly, "If you eat any kumquats, we'll go jogging" is, other things being equal, more likely a threat than a promise, whereas "If you eat some kumquats, we'll go jogging" is a better candidate as a promise. The distinction is a general one, including all sorts of cases where a "negative context" is balanced against a nonnegative one; other examples are: scolding with "How naughty of you to open any windows" versus praising with "How nice of you to open some windows"; or: "I wouldn't admit having done any work" versus "I wouldn't brag about having done some work."

The analogous distinction arises with all sorts of negative and positive polarity items (a negative polarity item being one that occurs with negatives—for example, "That course isn't worth a damn," as opposed to the strange-sounding, "That course is worth a damn"—while a positive polarity item, the converse, is exemplified by, "I would rather die than teach that course again"). Again, overt negation is not necessary; the same shadings appear with questions (Borkin, 1971) as well as in other instances where the pragmatic force is sufficiently clear.

An example is provided by "emotive complements" (Kiparsky & Kiparsky, 1970), which also provide polarity-determining contexts (e.g., "I'm surprised that it's worth a red cent" and "He was reluctant to believe the story for a minute").

The syntactic variability in all these cases results from the working of a single "hyperbole principle" in the pragmatics of English. Its general form is: "don't miss the chance to go as far as you dare, if it's at all worthwhile." The direction of exaggeration is, of course, different in the case of positive as opposed to negative contexts; in a negative context, minimization takes place, while maximization takes place in a positive context. Exact statement of the principle (Hass, 1972) depends on the formulation of "gradient" (which is not relevant here) and "negative context" (which, as we have noted, must include cases where the negation is implicit and pragmatic, in addition to Klima's positive, semantic ones).

This is one example in which a dimension of pragmatic force (negativity in this case, but certainty, formality, topicality, and the like in others) are need to capture the syntactic features of natural language. It will be interesting to discover if the same dimensions that are at work in the syntactic domain are also at work, say, in the domain of performative verbs, as we discussed above.

DEVELOPMENTAL: DIFFERENTIATING AND INTEGRATING IN PSYCHOLINGUISTICS

In the preceding section we provide some glimpses of pragmatic structure at its most sophisticated. Now we must consider how it gets this way. I view this task as equivalent to formulating the most relevant variants of the orthogenetic principle (Werner, 1948; Werner & Kaplan, 1963; Kaplan, 1968) and considering which of these variants most typifies the empirical data children provide. In other words, in what sense of "simpler" do children of a given age and a given group actually have a simpler pragmatics? The orthogenetic principle suggests that simplicity lies in some simultaneous absence of differentiation and integration on the child's part. We are scarcely in a position to give a full account of the ways in which pragmatic differentiation and integration intertwine, but certain hypotheses that seem to be relatively unnoticed truisms can be stated, and their empirical foundations can then be discussed.

We can begin by considering how the syntactics–semantics–pragmatics distinction itself may be subject to the orthogenetic principle. Insofar as the child is not differentiated, he is not likely to be able to separate semantic and syntactic issues from their pragmatic context; and I suspect that a large number of developmental psycholinguists have come to grief because of this, regarding the resulting "poor data" as a sign of failure of methodology. This does not imply that psycholinguists can stop trying to make syntactic and semantic generalizations at any given age, since we obviously have no a priori way of knowing when the part functions become sufficiently specific to be reflected in experimental tasks. It does suggest that failure to get a child to respond sensibly to syntactic or semantic tasks (to make judgments or to indicate comprehension) is itself a significant finding about how language works for children. By no means should we conceive of syntactic or semantic "rules" as of a fixed, "innate" nature, simply because the child produces (or correctly interprets) sentences that exemplify such rules in adult language functioning. Phonology, syntax, semantics, and pragmatics, as independent competences, must be achieved by the child out of the global matrix of his dealings with language.

Matters are complicated even more by the fact that the different competences also become more interrelated in the course of development. It is not enough to attain accounts of isolated phonological, syntactic, semantic, and pragmatic functions in the child, since they become linked with one another in an increasingly flexible and stable way. For example, if we show that a certain communicative effect can be viably dealt with by a child, and that he can make a certain sort of syntactic judgment, we may find that the syntactic judgment becomes subsumable under the communicative force (e.g., breaking a certain rule of grammar for a certain effect) and/or that the communicative force takes the guise of a syntactic form that did not initially have that force (e.g., obtaining a new effect though a familiar form—e.g., the rhetorical or the testing question).

If we assume reasonably independent pragmatic functioning on the child's part, what would his pragmatics look like. Here we can only speculate on some of the ways in which an overly representationalist view of child language could be corrected.

People often treat children as if "the original word game" (Brown, 1958, Ch. VI) were that of labeling objects with words, as if the child were uniquely interested in the function of naming. From an orthogenetic point of view, this is a most unlikely supposition, if it is taken to imply that the child initially has a single adult function and then comes to add others to it. Examination of what the child is doing leads one to believe that his "naming" lacks the contrastive and componential functions that we find in adult naming. Naming, as the child does it, is not so much a developmental prime as a luxury (a kind of "conspicuous consumption" of language particularly pleasing to intellectualist observers). When children do act as if they are naming, they do so because the stage has been set to encourage this kind of performance. Sometimes adults, whether parents or proponents of some forms of early education, deliberately drill a young child to provide labels for objects (or otherwise encourage him along these lines); under these circumstances the child will quickly discover that "things have names."

There is no reason to believe that practice in labeling, in any principled way, encourages pragmatic development; it might retard that development if it blocked other forms of interchange. However, incidental benefits may accrue to it, insofar as it gains the child access to experiences of a sort that he would not otherwise have, is required for success at later tasks the child will be facing, and encourages the child to use language in additional ways. Arguments that the child is "provided with vocabulary" or "taught to be logical" are pointless until it is shown, respectively: (a) that labeling leads to greater introduction of words than other tasks, and (b) that the standards by which labeling is constrained are more rigorous or important than those found in other tasks. I would suspect that a child could do many other things involving language that would be just as enjoyable and fruitful, and that emphasis on labeling may, if it has any long-range effect, encourage only the most superficial kind of geometrico-technical orientation (which must later, as a form of "verbal realism," be broken down).

At any rate, labeling works only for a certain class of "contentive" elements of the vocabulary, and passes by the acquisition of syntactically structured utterances. In this respect, we can note that changes in the form of the language the child produces and/or understands reflect pragmatic development as well as factors of syntax per se or semantics. Arguments for this point are available elsewhere (Hass & Wepman, 1969; Hass, 1971a, Hass & Hass, 1972). One clear example is found in the acquisition of the passive voice. The syntactic forces that lead to its formation lie in a differentiation of predicate adjectives and in the avoidance of cumbersome left-branching surface structures. Semantically, there is a definite biasing of representations of actions in terms of prominence of agent versus patient or goal, with a congruent process of representational decentration of action-components. The pragmatic source lies in the establishment of means of reflecting topic/comment organization, of which the passive is one (cf. Hornby, in press, and the body of studies cited therein).

Arguing for pragmatic factors in syntactic production does not represent a stance against the postulation of general cognitive-developmental trends and their reflection in the nature of child language. Rather, the scope of cognitive-developmental explanation is expanded. Recent attempts to link language acquisition with cognitive development (Sinclair-de-Zwart, 1969; Bloom, 1970; Hayes, 1970; Huxley & Ingram, 1971; etc.) have focused almost exclusively on the reflection of cognitive development in semantic structures (which are in turn linked with underlying structures of syntax). It seems evident, on consideration, that language should reflect the cognitive nature of the speech act itself, as well as merely the cognition of what is spoken about.

An emphasis on the influence of developing pragmatic structures finds a basis in Piaget's early work (1926; 1928); in fact, *Language and Thought of the Child* begins by inquiring into the nature of language *functions*. This line of investigation was not brought to fruition, one suspects, because of the lack of a sufficiently structural notion of pragmatics. It should now be possible to reopen this area, with profit to our understanding of the interactive basis of both language acquisition and cognition. Thus, in dealing with the role of notions of, for instance, causality, time, rules, and reciprocal relations, one should consider not only the statements the child is able to make about causes, temporal relations, the nature of regulation, and reciprocal structures, but also the ways in which such notions are reflected in his functional linguistic interchange. Both in everyday life and in investigative setups, the child is acting in terms of an understanding of what is involved in communication (the way it is "caused," its temporal organization, the rules that bind it, and the relations of speaker and hearer). There is no need, for instance, to avoid questioning as an impure way of getting at what the child really thinks about something, if one tries to ascertain how his answers themselves may *show* (as well as describe) his orientation.

Such investigation would enlighten us about the many forms of communicative "decentration." Studies of communicative competence (Flavell, 1968; Krauss & Glucksberg, 1969; etc.) have tended to utilize tasks in which the function of the language centers in adequacy of reference. The speaker's problem is to convey what he is talking about; that of the listener is to determine what was talked about. This is one pragmatic feature of language (just as labeling is one way of "learning vocabulary"), and one that shows developmental variation, in terms of ability to "take the other's point of view." Also it is a feature that is limited by its close reliance on semantics. People do so much more in talking and listening than just getting across and identifying the referents. It is to be expected that children's dominant concern lies in "making their point" in what they say, and in "getting the point of what is said to them," both of which depend on dealing with a whole range of interlocutor characteristics.

When we know more about the growth of pragmatic structures, it is likely that we shall be able to cast aside the simple, linear model of communicative development which figures so prominently in Wernerian discussion of language, in which pragmatics is described in terms of "distance" between speaker and hearer as well as between speaker and referent. This spatial model is adequate if we have in mind the analogy of bodies in motion, not the one of structures in transformation.

Conclusion: Pragmatics of the Future

A model of pragmatics and pragmatic development must also be relevant to cross-cultural variation (as mentioned in Hymes, 1961, and exemplified in Gumperz & Hymes, 1972) and to the diachronic changes of culture. This essay cannot begin to sort out these phenomena in structural, orthogenetic terms. Observation of the current scene (contrasted with my own upbringing in what seem now to have been primitive surroundings) leads me to believe that we are dealing with rapid social changes in pragmatics. Youth of today, with greater leisure for socializing, pressure for open interpersonal exchange, and exposure to mass media, typically approach communication with a great deal of sophistication. They can detect and play with pragmatic factors in ways which, in my youth, were reserved for syntactic and semantic aspects. Psycholinguistics has the chore of catching up with their behavior, on a theoretical level, so that we can enlighten ourselves and them about what they face in an age of "other direction" and the "global village," one in which language has "ceased to be (if it ever has been) simply a tool or means the writer uses to communicate intentions given independently of language" (Merleau-Ponty, 1964, p. 233).

Epilogue:
Reflections on the Universalism of Structure

GEORGE C. ROSENWALD

The essays presented in this book demonstrate that structuralism figures at times as method, at times as theory, and at times as philosophy. To Piaget it portends the unity of science. Yet the uncertainty of its definition contrasts strangely with the peremptoriness of its *logos*. Structuralism appears to us less as a scientific movement than as a phase in our epistemological restlessness—the oscillation of scientific attention between the subjects and objects of knowledge.

Analytic philosophies have relativized the "facts" by subordinating their interpretation to an agenda of models, games, and paradigms. The conventionalism, psychologism, and logicism of the nineteenth-century positivists, with their emphasis on the knower's condition, founded the priority of thought and language. Psychology was the basic science into which all else had to be commuted (Riegel). This installation of the final epistemic authority dispensed with any questions as to the immanent structuring of the object-world. The door was open to the gathering of facts, and minds would surely fit them together in theoretical relations (Collingwood, 1946).

It has been said disparagingly that French structuralism filled its ranks from among those leftist intellectuals who had abandoned existentialism after the bourgeoisie no longer took offense and adopted it as a cosmetic. However that may be, structuralism, like existentialism and Marxist psychology, forced our gaze back to the gravity of things themselves, to the material world (Wozniak). Not only in the physical domain, but in that of human activity, autonomous structures came to be discerned—structures without need of a structuring mind, indeed structures that themselves structured the mind. According to Lévi-Strauss the subject moves as an unconscious particle, enacting his role in rituals and myths that are opaque to him. Foucault, too, impatiently awaits the disappearance of man, that self-conscious knower, and blesses his imminent reabsorption into the relations of Discourse, dispersed at the end of the eighteenth century and about to be reconstituted at any moment (Foucault, 1970). For these structuralists it is man himself who is a fugitive convention, a mere geometric point in which life, labor, and language, the enduring structures, intersect.

By this movement of scientific attention, we have been granted ''God's truth'' linguistics and formalisms which tell us little about speaker and listener (Blumstein), and cognitive development anchored in a timeless biology, but torn loose from its cultural and historical conditions (Wilden). Some have tried, in all abstractionist consistency, to raise structuralism to the status of a metaphysic (Overton). The drift of emphasis from man, the sovereign subject of all knowledge, to the eternal verities in whose midst he hovers precariously, has undercut the dialectic intention. The new abstract realism posits an objective world, stripped of history, innocent of conflict (Sartre, 1966). Man no longer disturbs the harmony.

But the movement does not stop; the subject shakes off his coma with the help of those hyphenated disciplines that pump life back into him. Some psycholinguists confound *langue* and *parole,* competence and performance. They forget that concrete utterance is an interaction between language and a psychological condition (Blumenthal). The encapsulation of interactional processes inside the individual, whether by segmentation in the laboratory or by the conceptual grounding of mind in biology, results in a lopsided interactionism at best (Wilden).

The Gestalt psychologists gave us structures that consisted of invariant relations among object-elements. Piaget, likening the elements of intelligence to those of natural objects, artificially bounded against the shaping social realities, urged us to recognize that such structures are themselves subject to transformations, that is, *genetic* structures. New ground was broken when subjects were seen in constitutive interaction with object-structures. That is, interaction came to be thought of as more than a ping-pong of cause and effect: Interaction constitutes the elements comprised within it. The cognitive (and linguistic) processes taking place between the subject and his world do not merely define their commerce; the subject's very constitution is at stake in them (Lewis & Lee-Painter).

Concern for man as a social being elevates interactionism to a still higher place. It goes beyond structuralism in that it is not content with awarding priority to the relations over the parts and over the wholes. Its ultimate concern is for the fate of those human elements whose autonomy can no longer be taken for granted. In the study of human affairs, we are not prepared to subordinate the interests of the elements to any set of invariant relations. We seek, instead, to revive the unconscious particles playing their roles within the opaque organized structures. The reawakened elements are thus empowered to reformulate their relations. Interactions transform elements and relations reciprocally, for they are mutually constitutive. The diachronic aspect of this commitment is that human *development* cannot occur without a development of the interrelations. These interrelations are judged to be developing, rather than merely changing, insofar as they support the development of the subsumed elements.

Before the claims of this humane task, the study of cognitive and linguistic development will no longer be bleached into formalisms. Language becomes the vehicle for insight effortfully obtained and persuasively conveyed (Riegel, Hass). Since language and knowledge are objective cultural attainments, differentially concentrated and dispensed to the individuals and groups within the culture, what each subject knows and each speaker says is not simply a greater or lesser slice of the common stock, depending on his individual constitution and capacity. Rather, his capacity is itself a function of the common stock, a determinate aspect of the structure.

For example, the self-regulating forces in what is considered the system of generally accepted public truth or standards of rationality in a community are reflected in corresponding characteristics of the cognitive structures of the individuals who live in that community. A survey of what passes for evident truth in *public* discourse (as against mere propaganda) and the inference of evident utility (as against mere advertised desirability) in *private* discourse indicates the reciprocal and transformative nature of interaction. Interaction is here, as it were, vertical and not, as in Piaget's view, confined to levels of discourse.

Several points are important in this connection. First, the structures of private and public intelligence need not in every case stand in a one-to-one structural isomorphism: Other complementarities occur as well. For example, it is possible to transform *private* standards of *desirability* by confronting subjects with new *public* standards of *evidentiality*. Secondly, whereas Piaget's notion suggests that structures discovered on inferior levels of analysis are nested in the structures pertinent to the superior level, the interactionist view suggests not nesting but vertical reciprocity of structural transformation. Third, and related to the previous point, even the double-headed arrow which links the two structural levels to one another does not portray the processes as well as would a spiral. This is true because the subjects of a community or a society constitute that society, but are then no longer in a sovereign relationship to it. Rather, the society is governed by transformative and self-preservative processes proper to itself. Because the subjects of a society then become that society's objects, and because they yet sustain and renovate it (within limits) out of their spontaneous (and often faltering) initiative, the individuals are at the same time unified, each as a person, and divided in regard to the levels. They are the subjects of their individual intellection and the objectified unconscious elements of the system of society in which they figure; putting it differently, they mediate as unified persons between the intellectual acumen characteristic of themselves and the social forces under which they are subsumed as reference points. Because any community is in part influenced by forces beyond it (political, macrohistorical, economic, sociostructural, etc.), it must equilibrate, that is, transform and self-regulate itself continually with consequences for the inner consistency of its constituent subjects. The cyclic relation between the individual subjects and communal or collective objectivity results in a spiral, instead of a mere mutuality of structural transformations. Whether that spiral leads, in the main, toward greater or lesser competence is, to be sure, a matter of great controversy.

Finally, it should be observed that this analysis implies a vertical communication between levels that are separated from each other by more than discourse, and that require other means of reconciliation than those possible in discourse. They are set off against each other not by a neutral natural boundary, but by a tension. An analytic structuralism that recognizes only one of the individual's engagements in structure, namely in the superordinate structure, takes the boundary between the level of element and the level of structural network for granted as an established fixity and ignores precisely the system of tension that suspends the individual between his interior structure and his social-exterior structure. The result is the subordination of man to his organized relations. What has been called the unity of science involves a deliberate disunity of discourse, rationalized as autonomous levels of analysis specialized within themselves. The main victim of this conception is the interaction of all objects of discourse across levels.

That is why we regard the transactional, illocutionary function of language as the paradigmatic one among those interactions that restore consciousness to the subject by means of his action on the object-world. The fullness of language and the concreteness of knowledge enrich subject and objectivity simultaneously; that is why we "need the pragmatic force to capture the syntactic features of language" (Hass).

The diachronic analysis of interaction attains legitimacy because the development of human relations and of their constituent elements occurs along a historical trajectory. Whereas Wundt spoke of the exfoliation of a finished *Gesamtvorstellung* in a communicative process, we speak today of the "sequential blending of synchronic structures" in a process whereby the person acquires reality with his energy (Riegel). Similarly, we expand the thesis of Tynianov and Jakobson (1928) that "the history of a system is in turn also a system . . . each synchronic system contains its past and future as inseparable elements of the system''. To us, the terms ''history'' and ''system'' do not refer to semantics and syntactics alone, but to their interlacing with the pragmatic interactions of speaker, listener, and the world which is their common object.

This theory has found its implementation in the recent hermeneutic conception of discourse (e.g., in psychoanalysis) as dissecting the layered, shaded, contradictory, and benighted (''fictitious capital'') synchrony, reassigning its elements to their respective sources, and reconstructing a store of language and knowledge that reflects the interactions more adequately (Lorenzer, 1970). Only in this way, can the relations attain a quality worthy of the elements.

References

Afanasyev, V. *Marxist philosophy.* Moscow: Progress Publishers, 1968.

Allport, F. *Social psychology.* Boston: Houghton Mifflin, 1924.

Allport, G. W. The open system in personality theory. *Journal of Abnormal and Social Psychology,* 1960, **61,** 301–311.

Anderson, T. R. A model of language use. Unpublished manuscript, Department of Linguistics, University of California, Los Angeles, 1966.

Andrade, E. N. *An approach to modern physics.* Garden City, N. Y.: Doubleday/Anchor, 1957.

Apostel, L. Further remarks on the pragmatics of natural languages. In Y. Bar-Hillel (Ed.), *Pragmatics of natural languages.* Dordrecht: Reidel, 1971. Pp. 1–34.

Aqvist, L. A new approach to the logical theory of interrogatives. Unpublished manuscript, University of Uppsala, Uppsala, Sweden, 1965.

Ardener, E. Introductory essay. In E. Ardener (Ed.), *Social anthropology and language.* London: Tavistock, 1971. Pp. ix–cii. (a)

Ardener, E. (Ed.) *Social anthropology and language.* (A.S.A. Monographs, No. 10) London: Tavistock, 1971. (b)

Ashby, W. R. *Design for a brain.* New York: Wiley, 1952.

Ashby, W. R. *An introduction to cybernetics.* New York: Wiley, 1963.

Austin, J. L. Performative utterances. In J. L. Austin, *Philosophical papers.* London: Oxford University Press, 1961. Pp. 233–252.

Austin, J. L. *How to do things with words.* London: Oxford University Press, 1962.

Austin, J. L. Performative-constative. In C. E. Caton (Ed.), *Philosophy and ordinary language.* Urbana, Ill.: University of Illinois Press, 1963. Pp. 22–54.

Avenarius, R. *Kritik der reinen Erfahrung.* Vols. I & II. Leipzig: Fues' Verlag, 1888, 1890.

Avenarius, R. Bemerkungen zum Begriff des Gegenstandes der Psychologie. *Vierteljahresschrift für wissenschaftliche Philosophie und Soziologie,* 1894, **18,** 137–161, 400–420; 1895, **19,** 1–18.

Baltes, P. B. Longitudinal and cross-sectional sequences in the study of age and generation effects. *Human Development,* 1968, **11,** 145–171.

Barthes, R. The structuralist activity. *Partisan Review,* 1967, **34,** 82–88.

Bartlett, F. C. *Remembering.* Cambridge: Cambridge University Press, 1932.

Bateson, G. *Steps to an ecology of mind.* New York: Ballantine, 1972.

Beilin, H. The development of physical concepts. In T. Mischel (Ed.), *Cognitive development and epistemology.* New York: Academic Press, 1971. Pp. 85–119.

Bernstein, B. *Class, codes and control.* London: Routledge & Kegan, Paul, 1971.

Bertalanffy, L. von. General system theory and psychiatry. In S. Arieti (Ed.), *American handbook of psychiatry.* Vol. 3. New York: Basic Books, 1959. Pp. 705–721.

Bertalanffy, L. von. *Problems of life.* New York: Harper Torchbook, 1960. (a)

Bertalanffy, L. von. In J. M. Tanner & B. Inhelder (Eds.), *Discussions on child development.* London: Tavistock, 1960. Pp. 69–76. (b)

Bertalanffy, L. von. General system theory—a critical review. *General Systems,* 1962, **7,** 1–20. (a)

Bertalanffy, L. von. *Modern theories of development.* New York: Harper Torchbook, 1962. (b)

Bertalanffy, L. von. *Robots, men and minds.* New York: George Braziller, Inc., 1967. (a)

Bertalanffy, L. von. General theory of systems: applications to psychology. *Social Science Information,* 1967, **6,** 125–136. (b)

Bertalanffy, L. von. *General system theory.* New York: George Braziller, Inc. 1968. (a)

Bertalanffy, L. von. *Organismic psychology and systems theory.* Barre, Mass.: Barre Publishing Co., 1968. (b)

Bever, T. The cognitive basis for linguistic structures. In J. R. Hayes (Ed.), *Cognition and the development of language.* New York: Wiley, 1970. Pp. 279–352:

Binet, A. *The mind and the brain.* London: Paul, Trench, Trübner, 1907.

Blakeley, T. J. *Soviet theory of knowledge.* Dordrecht-Holland: Reidel, 1964.

Bloch, B. Phonemic overlapping. *American Speech,* 1941, **16,** 278–284.

Bloch, B. English verb inflection. *Language,* 1947, **23,** 399–418.

Bloch, O. La phrase dans le langage de l'enfant. *Journal de Psychologie,* 1924, **21,** 18–43.

Blondel, C. *Introduction à la psychologie collective.* Paris: Colin, 1928.

Bloom, L. *Language development.* Cambridge, Mass.: M.I.T. Press, 1970.

Bloom, L. *One word at a time: The use of single word utterances before syntax.* The Hague: Mouton, 1973.

Bloomfield, L. *Introduction to the study of language.* New York: Holt, 1914.

Bloomfield, L. *Language.* New York: Holt, 1933.

Blumenthal, A. L. *Language and psychology: Historical aspects of psycholinguistics.* New York: Wiley, 1970.

Blumenthal, A. L. *The process of cognition.* New York: Prentice-Hall, 1974. (In press).

Boileau, D. A. The new French movement: Structuralism. *Perspectives of Nazareth College,* 1970 (Winter).

Boring, E. G. *History of experimental psychology* (2nd ed.). New York: Appleton-Century-Crofts, 1957.

Borkin, A. Polarity items in questions. *Proceedings, Regional Meeting, Chicago Linguistic Society,* 1971, **7,** 53–62.

Boulding, K. *The image*. Ann Arbor: University of Michigan Press, 1956.

Bowers, K. S. Situationism in psychology: An analysis and a critique. *Psychological Review*, 1973, **80,** 307–336.

Brainerd, C. J. The role of structures in explaining cognitive development. In K. F. Riegel & J. A. Meacham (Eds.), *The developing individual in a changing world: general and historical issues*, Vol. I. The Hague: Mouton, 1975, Pp. 204–216.

Brentano, F. von. *Psychologie vom empirischen Standpunkt*. Leipzig: Meiner, 1874.

Bridgman, P. W. *The logic of modern physic*. New York: Macmillan, 1928.

Brown, G. S. *Laws of form*. London: Allen & Unwin, 1969.

Brown, R. *Words and things*. Glencoe, Ill.: Free Press, 1958.

Brown, R. *A first language*. Cambridge, Mass.: Harvard University Press, 1973.

Brown, R. & Fraser, C. The acquisition of syntax. In C. N. Cofer & B. S. Musgrave (Eds.), *Verbal behavior and learning*. New York: McGraw-Hill, 1963. Pp. 158–197.

Bruner, J. S. Course of cognitive growth. *American Psychologist*, 1964, **19,** 1–15.

Bruner, J. S. Nature and uses of immaturity. *American Psychologist*, 1972, **27,** 687–708.

Bruner, J. S., Goodnow, S. S., & Austin, G. A. *A study of thinking*. New York: Wiley, 1956.

Buckley, W. *Sociology and modern systems theory*. Englewood Cliffs, N. J.: Prentice-Hall, 1967.

Buckley, W. (ED.) *Modern systems research for the behavioral scientist*. Chicago: Aldine, 1968.

Bühler, K. *Sprachtheorie*. Jena: Fischer, 1934.

Carnap, R. Foundations of logic and mathematics. In *International Encyclopedia of Unified Science*, 1939, **1,** 143–171.

Carnap, R. *Introduction to semantics*. Cambridge, Mass.: Harvard University Press, 1942.

Carnap, R. *Meaning and necessity*. Chicago: University of Chicago Press, 1956.

Carnap, R. Replies and systematic expositions. In P. A. Schilpp (Ed.), *Philosophy of Rudolf Carnap*. LaSalle, Ill.: Open Court Publishing Co., 1963. Pp. 859–1013.

Carnap, R. *Der logische Aufbau der Welt*. Hamburg: Meiner, 1928. (*Logical structure of the world*. Berkeley, Calif.: University of California Press, 1967.)

Cassirer, E. *Substanzbegriff und Funktionsbegriff*. Berlin: B. Cassirer, 1910. (Substance and function and Einstein's theory of relativity. Chicago: Open Court Publishing Co., 1923.)

Cassirer, E. *An essay on man: An introduction to a philosophy of human culture*. New Haven, Conn.: Yale University Press, 1944.

Cellérier, G. Modèles cybernétiques et adaptation. *Études d'Épistémologie Génétique*. Paris: Presses Universitaires de France, 1967.

Cerf, W. Critical review of *How to do things with words*. In K. T. Fann (Ed.), *Symposium on J. L. Austin*. New York: Humanities Press, 1969. Pp. 351–379.

Chao, Y. R. The non-uniqueness of phonemic solutions of phonetic systems. *Bulletin of the Institute of History and Philology, Academia Sinica,* 1934, **4,** 363–397.

Chao, Y. R. Review of Jakobson, Halle, Fant, preliminaries to speech analysis. *Romance Philology,* 1954, **8,** 40–46.

Chardin, T. de. *The phenomenon of man.* New York: Harper & Row, 1959.

Chelstowski, B. The constructivistic structuralism of J. Piaget. *Science & Society,* 1971, **35,** 481–489.

Cherry, C. *On human communication.* New York: Science Editions, 1961.

Chomsky, N. *Syntactic structures.* The Hague: Mouton, 1957.

Chomsky, N. Review of B. F. Skinner's verbal behavior. *Language,* 1959, **35,** 26–58.

Chomsky, N. *Aspects of the theory of syntax.* Cambridge, Mass.: M.I.T. Press, 1965.

Chomsky, N. *Cartesian linguistics.* New York: Harper & Row, 1966.

Chomsky, N. *Language and mind.* New York: Harcourt, Brace & World, 1968.

Cipolla, C. M. *Money, prices, and civilization in the Mediterranean world.* Princeton, N. J.: Princeton University Press, 1956.

Clark, H. H. Comprehending comparatives. In G. Flores d'Arcais & W. S. M. Levelt (Eds.), *Advances in psycholinguistics.* Amsterdam: North-Holland Press, 1970. Pp. 294–306.

Cohen, D. & Riegel, K. F. Time as energy: On the application of modern concepts of time to developmental sciences. Unpublished manuscript, Gerontological Center, University of Southern California, Los Angeles, 1972.

Cohen, M. Sur les langages successifs de l'enfant. *Mélanges linguistiques offerts à M. J. Vendryes.* Paris: Champion, 1925. Pp. 109–127.

Cole, M., Gay, J., Glick, J. A., & Sharp, D. W. *The cultural context of learning and thinking.* New York: Basic Books, 1971.

Collingwood, R. G. *The idea of history.* Oxford: Clarendon Press, 1946.

Coombs, C. H. *Theory of data.* New York: Wiley, 1964.

Cooper, W. E., Edens, T., Koenig, H. E., & Wilden, A., *Toward an economics of environmental compatibility,* Unpublished manuscript, East Lansing, Mich.: Michigan State University, 1973.

Davidson, D. Truth and meaning. *Synthese,* 1967, **17,** 304–323.

Dedekind, R. Continuity and irrational numbers. Excerpt in J. R. Newman, (Ed.), *The world of mathematics.* Vol. I. New York: Simon and Shuster, 1956, Pp. 528–536.

Dedekind, R. *Was sind und was sollen Zahlen?* (II. Aufl). Braunschweig: Vieweg, 1893.

Delbrück, B. *Grundfragen der Sprachforschung mit Rücksicht auf W. Wundt's Sprachpsychologie.* Strassburg: Trübner, 1901.

Derrida, J. Structure, sign, and play in the discourse of the human sciences. In R. Macksey and E. Donato (Eds.), *The languages of criticism and the sciences of man.* Baltimore: Johns Hopkins Press, 1970. Pp. 247–265.

Descartes, R. *Method, meditations and selections from the principles.* London: J. Veith, 1890.

Dewey, J. The reflex-arc concept in psychology. *Psychological Review*, 1896, **3**, 357–370.

Dreyfus, H. L. *Alchemy and artificial intelligence.* Santa Monica, Calif.: Rand Corporation (Pub. No. P-3244), 1965.

Durkheim, E. *Les formes élémentaires de la vie religieuse.* Paris: Alcan, 1912. (The elementary forms of religious life, a study in religious sociology. New York: Macmillan, 1915.)

Durkheim, E., & Mauss, M. De quelques formes primitives de classification. *L'Année Sociologique*, 1903, **6**, 1–72.

Ehrenfels, C. von. Über Gestaltqualitäten. *Vierteljahresschrift für wissenschaftliche Philosophie*, 1890, **14**, 249–292.

El'konin, D. B. Toward the problem of stages in the mental development of the child. *Soviet Psychology*, 1972, **10**, 225–251.

Engels, F. *Karl Marx and Friedrich Engels: Selected works.* Vol. II. Moscow: Foreign Languages Publishing House, 1958.

Feagan, J. M. The phenomenology of human development and self-fulfillment. Unpublished master's thesis, University of Wisconsin, 1972.

Fillmore, C. J. The case for case. In E. Bach & R. T. Harms (Eds.), *Universals in linguistic theory.* New York: Holt, Rinehart and Winston, 1968. Pp. 1–88. (a)

Fillmore, C. J. Verbs of judging. *Papers in Linguistics*, 1968, **1**, 91–117. (b)

Flavell, J. H. *The developmental psychology of Jean Piaget.* New York: Van Nostrand & Reinhold, 1963.

Flavell, J. H. *Development of role-taking and communication skills in children.* New York: Wiley, 1968.

Flavell, J. H. Cognitive changes in adulthood. In L. R. Goulet & P. B. Baltes (Eds.), *Life-span developmental psychology: Research and theory.* New York: Academic Press, 1970. Pp. 247–253.

Flavell, J. H. Stage-related properties of cognitive development. *Cognitive Psychology*, 1971, **2**, 421–453.

Flavell, J. H. An analysis of cognitive-developmental sequences. *Genetic Psychology Monographs*, 1972, **86**, 279–350.

Flavell, J. H., & Wohlwill, J. F. Formal and functional aspects of cognitive development. In D. Elkind & J. H. Flavell (Eds.), *Studies in cognitive development: Essays in honor of Jean Piaget.* New York: Oxford University Press, 1969. Pp. 67–120.

Fodor, J. A. Could meaning be an r_m? *Journal of Verbal Learning and Verbal Behavior*, 1965, **4**, 73–81.

Fodor, J. A. Ontogenesis of the problem of reference. In C. E. Reed (Ed.), *Learning of language.* New York: Appleton-Century-Crofts, 1971. Pp. 333–362.

Fodor, J. A. Towards a semantic theory of natural languages. (Chapter 8 of a book, in preparation.)

Foucault, M. *Les mots et les choses.* Paris: Gallimard, 1966.

Foucault, M. *The order of things: An archaeology of the human sciences.* New York: Random House, 1970.

Fraassen, B. C. *Formal semantics and logic.* New York: Macmillan, 1971.

Franke, C. Sprachentwicklung der Kinder und der Menschheit. In W. Rein (Ed.) *Encyclopädisches Handbuch der Pädagogik.* Langensalza: Beyer, 1899.

Fraser, B. An examination of the performative analysis. Unpublished manuscript, Linguistics Club, Indiana University, 1971.

Freedle, R., & Lewis, M. Application of Markov processes to the concept of state. Research Bulletin 71–34. Princeton, N. J.: Educational Testing Service, 1971.

Frege, B. *Grundgesetze der Arithmetik.* Jena: H. Pohle, 1903. (*The basic laws of arithmetic.* Berkeley, Calif.: University of California Press, 1964.)

Frege, G. *Foundations of arithmetic.* Oxford: Blackwell, 1959.

Freud, S. *General introduction to psychoanalysis.* Garden City, N. Y.: Garden City Publishing Co., 1943.

Furberg, M. *Saying and meaning.* Oxford: Blackwell, 1971.

Gaettens, R. *Inflationen.* Munich: Pflaum, 1955.

Gagné, R. M. Contributions of learning to human development. *Psychological Review,* 1968, **75,** 177–191.

Gandillac, M. de, Goldmann, L., & Piaget, J. *Entretiens sur les notions de genèse et de structure.* The Hague: Mouton, 1965.

Gardner, H. *Piaget and Lévi-Strauss:* The quest for mind. *Social Research,* 1970, **37,** 348–365.

Gardner, H. *Quest for mind: Piaget, Lévi-Strauss, and the structuralist movement.* New York: Random House, 1973.

Geber, M. L'enfant africain occidentalisé et de niveau social supérier en Uganda. *Courrier,* 1958, **8,** 517–523.

Geber, M., & Dean, R. F. A. Gesell tests on African children. *Pediatrics,* 1957, **6,** 1055–1065. (a)

Geber, M., & Dean, R. F. A. The state of development of newborn African children. *Lancet,* 1957, **1,** 1216–1219. (b)

Gewirtz, J. The roles of overt responding and extrinsic reinforcement in ''self''—and ''vicarious reinforcement'' phenomena and ''observational learning'' and imitation. In R. Glaser (Ed.), *The nature of reinforcement.* New York: Academic Press, 1971. Pp. 279–309.

Gibson, E. J. *Principles of perceptual learning and development.* New York: Meredith Corp., 1969.

Gingerich, O. Copernicus and Tycho. *Scientific American,* 1973, **226,** 86–101.

Goddard, D. Lévi-Strauss and the anthropologists. *Social Research,* 1970, **37,** 366–378.

Goss, A. E. Early behaviorism and verbal mediating responses. *American Psychologist,* 1961, **16,** 285–298.

Greene, J. *Psycholinguistics: Chomsky and psycholinguistics.* Harmondsworth, England: Penguin Books, 1972.

Guilford, J. P. *The nature of human intelligence.* New York: McGraw-Hill, 1967.

Guillaume, P. *L'imitation chez l'enfant.* Doctoral dissertation, University of Paris, 1925.

Guillaume, P. Les débuts de la phrase dans le langage de l'enfant. *Journal de Psychologie,* 1927, **24**, 1–25. (a)

Guillaume, P. Les développements des éléments formels dans le langage de l'enfant. *Journal de Psychologie,* 1927, **24**, 203–229. (b)

Guillemin, V. *The story of quantum mechanics.* New York: Charles Scribner's, 1968.

Gumperz, J. J., & Hymes, D. (Eds.) *Directions in sociolinguistics.* New York: Holt, Rinehart and Winston, 1972.

Halbwachs, M. *Les cadres sociaux de la mémoire.* Paris: Alcan, 1925.

Halbwachs, M. La psychologie collective d'après C. Blondel. *Revue philosophique de la France et de l'étranger,* 1929, **54**, 444–456.

Halbwachs, M. *La mémoire collective.* Paris: Presses Universitaires de France, 1950.

Hall, G. S. *Senescence: The last half of life.* New York: Appleton, 1922.

Harary, F., Norman, R. Z., & Cartwright, D. *Structural models.* New York: Wiley, 1965.

Hardin, G. The cybernetics of competition. In P. Shepard & D. McKinley (Eds.), *The subversive science: Essays toward an ecology of man.* Boston: Houghton Mifflin, 1969. Pp. 257–296.

Harrah, D. *Communication: A logical model.* Cambridge, Mass.: M.I.T. Press, 1963.

Harrah, D. Erotetic logistics. In K. Lambert (Ed.), *Logical way of doing things.* New Haven, Conn.: Yale University Press, 1969. Pp. 3–21.

Harrah, D. Formal message theory. In Y. Bar-Hillel (Ed.), *Pragmatics of natural languages.* Dordrecht: Reidel, 1971. Pp. 69–83.

Harris, Z. *Structural Linguistics.* Chicago: University of Chicago Press, 1951.

Hass, W. A. Why we can't say what we mean in transformational theory. *Proceedings, Regional Meeting, Chicago Linguistic Society,* 1970, **6**, 282–286.

Hass, W. A. On the heterogeneity of psychological processes in syntactic development. In C. S. Lavatelli (Ed.), *Language training in early childhood education.* Urbana, Ill.: University of Illinois Press, 1971. Pp. 49–59. (a)

Hass, W. A. Truth-functional and communicational bases for prescriptive discourse. *Proceedings, Regional Meeting, Chicago Linguistic Society,* 1971, **7**, 112–119. (b)

Hass, W. A. Syntactic reflections of hyperbole in polarity items and emotive predicates. Unpublished manuscript, Shimer College, Mount Carroll, Ill., 1972.

Hass, W. A., & Hass, S. K. Syntactic structure and language development in retardates. In R. Schiefelbusch (Ed.), *Language of the mentally retarded.* Baltimore: University Park Press, 1972. Pp. 35–51.

Hass, W. A., & Wepman, J. M. Surface structure, deep structure and transformations: A model for syntactic development. *Journal of Speech and Hearing Disorder,* 1969, **34**, 303–311.

Hayek, F. A. The primacy of the abstract. In A. Koestler & J. R. Smythies (Eds.), *Beyond reductionism.* Boston: Beacon Press, 1969. Pp. 309–333.

Hayes, J. R. (Ed.) *Cognition and the development of language.* New York: Wiley, 1970.

Heisenberg, W. *Physics and philosophy.* New York: Harper & Row, 1958.

Henle, M. (Ed.) *The selected papers of Wolfgang Köhler.* New York: Liveright, 1972.

Hilpinen, R. (Ed.) *Deontic logic: Introductory and systematic readings.* Dordrecht: Reidel, 1971.

Hockett, C. Two models of grammatical description. *Word,* 1954, **10,** 210–231.

Hölder, O. Die Axiome der Quantität und die Lehre vom Mass. *Berichte der Sächsischen Gesellschaft der Wissenschaften, Leipzig, Mathematische—Physikalische Klasse,* 1901, **53,** 1–64.

Holzkamp, K. *Kritische Psychologie.* Frankfurt/M.: Fischer, 1972.

Hooper, F. H., Fitzgerald, J., & Papalia, D. E. Piagetian theory and the aging process: Extensions and speculations. *Aging and Human Development,* 1971, **2,** 3–20.

Hornby, P. A. Surface structure and the topic-comment distinction: A developmental study. *Child Development.* 1971, **42,** 1975–1988.

Huttenlocher, J., & Higgins, E. T. Adjectives, comparatives, and syllogisms. *Psychological Review,* 1971, **78,** 487–504.

Huxley, R., & Ingram, E. (Eds.) *Language acquisition: Models and methods.* New York: Academic Press, 1971.

Hymes, D. H. Functions of speech: An evolutionary approach. In F. C. Gruber (Ed.), *Anthropology and education.* Philadelphia: University of Pennsylvania Press, 1961. Pp. 315–338.

Hymes, D. H. Competence and performance in linguistic theory. In R. Huxley & E. Ingram (Eds), *Language acquisition: Models and methods.* New York: Academic Press, 1971. Pp. 3–28.

Ianni, L. A three-person game model for the general language game. In R. H. Oehmke & R. S. Wachal (Eds.), *Proceedings of the Conference on Linguistics.* Unpublished manuscript, Department of Linguistics, University of Iowa, 1970.

Inhelder, B., & Piaget, J. *The growth of logical thinking from childhood to adolescence.* New York: Basic Books, 1958.

Jakobson, R. *Kindersprache, Aphasie, und allgemeine Lautgesetze.* Uppsala: Almqvist and Wiksell, 1941. (Child language, aphasia, and general sound laws. The Hague: Mouton, 1968.)

Jakobson, R. Observations sur le classement phonologique des consonnes. In *Roman Jakobson: Selected writings.* Vol. I. The Hague: Mouton, 1971. Pp. 272–279. (a)

Jakobson, R. The concept of the sound law and the teleological criterion. In *Roman Jakobson: Selected writings.* Vol. I. The Hague: Mouton, 1971. Pp. 1–2. (b)

Jakobson, R., & Halle, M. *Fundamentals of language.* The Hague: Mouton, 1956.

James, W. *Pragmatism.* New York: Reynolds, 1907.

James, W. *The principles of psychology.* New York: Holt, 1890.

Jameson, F. *Marxism and form.* Princeton, N. J.: Princeton University Press, 1971.

Jenkins, J. J., & Palermo, D. S. Mediation processes and the acquisition of linguistic structures. *Monographs of the Society for Research in Child Development,* 1964, **29**, 141–169.

Jensen, A. R. How much can we boost IQ and scholastic achievement? *Harvard Educational Review,* 1969, **39**, 1–123.

Jesperson, O. *Analytic syntax.* London: Allen and Unwin, 1937.

Johnson, H. M. *Sociology: A systematic introduction.* Chicago: Harcourt, Brace, & World, 1960.

Jones, E. *The life and work of Sigmund Freud.* London: Hogarth, 1956–58. (3 vols.)

Joos, M. *Readings in linguistics* (2nd ed.). New York: American Counsel of Learned Societies, 1963.

Kagen, J., Henker, B., Hen-Tov, A., Levine, J., & Lewis, M. Infants' differential reactions to familiar and distorted faces. *Child Development,* 1966, **37**, 519–532.

Kantor, J. R. *An objective psychology of grammar.* Bloomington, Ind.: Indiana University Press, 1936.

Kaplan, B. The study of language in psychiatry. In S. Arieti (Ed.), *American handbook of psychiatry.* Vol. 3. New York: Basic Books, 1966.

Kaplan, B. Strife of systems: The tension between organismic and developmental points of view. Unpublished manuscript. Clark University, 1967.

Kilmister, C. W. *The environment in modern physics.* London: English Universities Press, 1965.

Kiparsky, P., & Kiparsky, C. Fact. In M. Bierwisch & K. E. Heidolph (Eds.), *Progress in linguistics.* The Hague: Mouton, 1970. Pp. 143–173.

Klima, E. S. Negation in English. In J. A. Fodor & J. J. Katz (Eds.), *Structure of language.* Englewood Cliffs, N. J.: Prentice-Hall, 1964. Pp. 246–323.

Klir, G. J. *Trends in general systems theory.* New York: Wiley-Interscience, 1972.

Kohlberg, L. Stage and sequence: The cognitive-developmental approach to socialization. In D. A. Goslin (Ed.), *Handbook of socialization theory and research.* Chicago: Rand McNally, 1969. Pp. 347–480.

Kohlberg, L. Continuities in childhood and adult moral development revisited. In P. B. Baltes & K. W. Schaie (Eds.), *Life-span developmental psychology: Personality and socialization.* New York: Academic Press, 1973. Pp. 179–204.

Köhler, W. *Die physischen Gestalten in Ruhe und im stationären Zustand.* Braunschweig: Vieweg, 1920.

Koshland, D. E., Jr. Protein shape and biological control. *Scientific American,* 1973, **229**, 52–64.

Krauss, R. M., & Glucksberg, S. Development of communication: Competence as a function of age. *Child Development,* 1969, **40**, 255–266.

Kripke, S. A. Semantical considerations in modal logic. *Acta philosophica Fennica,* 1963, **16**, 83–94.

Krüger, F. E. *Über Entwicklungspsychologie, ihre sachliche und geschichtliche Notwendigkeit.* Leipzig: Engelmann, 1915.

Kuhn, T. S. *The structure of scientific revolutions.* Chicago: University of Chicago Press, 1962.

Labov, W. The study of language in its social context. *Studium Generale*, 1970, **23**, 30–87.

Lacan, J. *Écrits*. Paris: Le Seuil, 1966.

Lacan, J. The mirror-phase. *New Left Review*, 1968, **51**, 71–77. (a)

Lacan, J. The function of speech and language in psychoanalysis. In A. Wilden, *The language of the self*. Baltimore: Johns Hopkins University Press., 1968. Pp. 1–87. (b)

Lakoff, G. On generative semantics. In D. Steinberg & L. Jakobovits (Eds.), *Semantics: An interdisciplinary reader*. Cambridge, Engl.: Cambridge University Press, 1971. Pp. 232–296.

Lakoff, R. Some reasons why there can't be any some-any rule. *Language*, 1969, **45**, 608–615.

Lakoff, R. Language in context. Unpublished manuscript, Department of Linguistics, University of Michigan, 1971.

Lane, M. *Introduction to structuralism*. New York: Basic Books, 1970.

Langer, J. *Theories of development*. New York: Holt, Rinehart and Winston, 1969.

Leach, E. *Claude Lévi-Strauss*. New York: Viking Press, 1970.

Lenin, V. I. *Materialism and empirio-criticism*. New York: International Publishers, 1927.

Lenin, V. I. *Philosophical notebook* (Collected Works, Vol. 29). New York: International Publishers, 1929.

Lenneberg, E. *Biological foundations of language*. New York: Wiley, 1967.

Leonard, G. *Education and ecstasy*. New York: Delacorte, 1968.

Leontiev, A. N., & Luria, A. R. The psychological ideas of L. S. Vygotsky. In B. B. Wolman (Ed.), *Historical roots of contemporary psychology*. New York: Harper & Row, 1968. Pp. 338–367.

Lepschy, G. C. *A Survey of structural linguistics*. London: Faber, 1970.

Lévi-Strauss, C. (Comments). In S. Tax et al. (Eds.), *An appraisal of anthropology today*. Chicago: University of Chicago Press, 1953.

Lévi-Strauss, C. *Anthropologie structurale*. Paris: Plon, 1958. (Structural anthropology. New York: Basic Books, 1963.)

Lévi-Strauss, C. *La pensée sauvage*. Paris: Plon, 1962. (a)

Lévi-Strauss, C. *Le totémisme aujourd'hui*. Paris: Presses Universitaires de France, 1962. (b)

Lévi-Strauss, C. *The savage mind*. Chicago: Phoenix, 1966.

Lévi-Strauss, C. *Conversations*. (G. Charbonnier, Ed.). London: Cape, 1969. (a)

Lévi-Strauss, C. *The elementary structures of kinship* (2nd ed.) Boston: Beacon, 1969. (b)

Lévi-Strauss, C. *L'homme nu*. Paris: Plon, 1971.

Lévi-Strauss, C. A conversation with Claude Lévi-Strauss. *Psychology Today* (May 1972).

Lévy-Bruhl, L. *La mentalité primitive*. Paris: Presses Universitaires de France, 1922. (Primitive mentality. New York: Macmillan, 1923.)

Lewis, I. M. (Ed.) *History and social anthropology.* London: Tavistock, 1968.

Lewis, M. Infants' responses to facial stimuli during the first year of life. *Developmental Psychology,* 1969, **1**, 75–86.

Lewis, M., & Freedle, R. Mother-infant dyad: The cradle of meaning. In P. Pliner, L. Krames, & T. Alloway (Eds), *Communication and affect: Language and thought.* New York: Academic Press, 1973. Pp. 127–155.

Lewis, M., & Lee-Painter, S. An interactional approach to the mother-infant dyad. In M. Lewis & L. Rosenblum (Eds.), *The effect of the infant on its caregiver.* New York: Wiley, 1974. Pp. 21–48.

Lewis, M., Weinraub, M., & Ban, P. Mothers and fathers, girls and boys: Attachment behavior in the first two years of life. Paper presented at the meeting of the Society for Research in Child Development, Philadelphia, March 1973.

Lewis, M., & Wilson, C. D. Infant development in lower class American families. *Human Development,* 1972, **15**, 112–127.

Lewis, M., Wilson, C. D., & Harwitz, M. H. Attention distribution in the 24-month-old child: Variations in complexity and incongruity of the human form. *Child Development,* 1971, **42**, 429–438.

Lieb, H. H. On subdividing semiotic. In Y. Bar-Hillel (Ed.), *Pragmatics of natural languages.* Dordrecht: Reidel, 1971. Pp. 94–119.

Looft, W. R. The psychology of more. *American Psychologist,* 1971, **26**, 561–565.

Looft, W. R. Egocentrism and social interaction across the life span. *Psychological Bulletin,* 1972, **78**, 73–92.

Looft, W. R. Socialization and personality throughout the life span: An examination of contemporary psychological approaches. In P. B. Baltes & K. W. Schaie (Eds.), *Life-span developmental psychology: Personality and socialization.* New York: Academic Press, 1973. Pp. 25–52.

Lorenzer, A. *Sprachzerstörung und Rekonstruktion,* Frankfurt: Suhrkamp, 1970.

Lovejoy, A. O. *The great chain of being.* London: Oxford University Press, 1936.

Lunzer, E. Problems of formal reasoning in test situations. *Monographs of the Society for Research in Child Development,* 1965, **30**, 19–46.

Lusk, D., & Lewis, M. Mother-infant interaction and infant development among the Wolof of Senegal. *Human Development,* 1972, **15**, 58–69.

Lyons, J. *Introduction to theoretical linguistics.* London: Cambridge University Press, 1968.

Lyons, J. & Wales, R. J. *Psycholinguistic papers.* Edinburgh: Edinburgh University Press, 1966.

Mach, E. *Analyse der Empfindungen und das Verhältnis des Psychischen zum Physischen.* Jena: Fischer, 1886. (The analysis of sensations, and the relation of the physical to the psychical. New York:Dover, 1959.)

Mach, E. *Erkenntnis und Irrtum.* Leipzig: Barth, 1905.

MacKay, D. M. *Information, mechanism and meaning.* Cambridge, Mass. M.I.T. Press, 1969.

Malinowski, B. The problem of meaning in primitive languages. Supplement I. In C.

K. Ogden & I. A. Richards (Eds.), *The meaning of meaning*. New York: Harcourt & Brace, 1923. Pp. 296–336.

Malinowski, B. *Myth in primitive society*. London: Kegan, 1926.

Martinet, A. *Éléments de linguistique générale*. Paris: Colin, 1966.

Martinet, A. Structure and language. In J. Ehrmann (Ed.), *Structuralism*. New York: Anchor Books, 1970. Pp. 1–9.

Marty, A. *Untersuchungen zur Grundlegung der allgemeinen Grammatik und Sprach-philosophie*. Halle: Niemeyer, 1908.

Maruyama, M. The second cybernetics: Deviation-amplifying mutual casual processes, 1963. In W. Buckley (Ed.), *Modern systems research for the behavioral scientist*. Chicago: Aldine, 1968. Pp. 304–313.

Marx, K. *Lohnarbeit und Kapital*. Berlin: Vorwärts Verlag, 1891.

Marx, K. *Capital*. Chicago: Charles Kerr, 1912.

Marx, K. *Grundrisse*. Harmondsworth: Allen Lane, 1973.

McCawley, J. The Role of semantics in a grammar. In E. Bach & R. Harms (Eds.), *Universals of linguistic theory*. New York: Holt, Rinehart, & Winston Inc., 1968. Pp. 125–169.

McCawley, J. D. Semantic representation. In P. Garvin (Ed.), *Cognition: A multiple view*. New York: Spartan Books, 1970. Pp. 227–247.

McNeill, D. On theories of language acquisition. In T. R. Dixon & D. L. Horton (Eds.), *Verbal behavior and general behavior theory*. New York: Prentice Hall, 1968. Pp. 406–420.

McNeill, D. *The acquisition of language*. New York: Harper & Row, 1970. (a)

McNeill, D. The development of language. In P. H. Mussen (Ed.), *Carmichael's manual of child psychology*. New York: Wiley, 1970. Pp. 1061–1161. (b)

Merleau-Ponty, M. *The structure of behavior*. Boston: Beacon Press, 1963.

Merleau-Ponty, M. *Signs*. Evanston, Ill.: Northwestern University Press, 1964.

Miller, G. A. Some psychological studies of grammar. *American Psychologist, 1962,* **17,** 748–761.

Miller, G. A., & McNeill, D. Psycholinguistics. In G. Lindzey & E. Aronson (Eds.), *Handbook of social psychology*. Vol. 3. Reading, Mass.: Addison-Wesley, 1969. Pp. 666–794.

Mischel, W. Toward a cognitive social learning reconceptualization of personality. *Psychological Review, 1973,* **80,** 252–283.

Montague, R. Pragmatics. In R. Klibansky (Ed.), *Contemporary philosophy*. Firenze: La Nuova Italia, 1968. Pp. 102–122.

Montague, R. Pragmatics and intensional logic. In D. Davidson & G. Harman (Eds.), *Semantics of natural language*. Dordrecht: Reidel, 1972. Pp. 142–168.

Moore, K. The mental development of a child. *Psychological Monographs, 1896, No.* 3.

Morris, C. Foundations of the theory of signs. In *International Encyclopedia of Unified Science,* 1938, **1,** 77–137.

Morris, C. *Signs, language and behavior*. Englewood Cliffs, N.J.: Prentice-Hall, 1946.

Morris, C. Pragmatism and logical empiricism. In P. A. Schlipp (Ed.), *Philosophy of Rudolf Carnap*. LaSalle, Ill.: Open Court Publishing Co., 1963. Pp. 87–98.

Moscovici, S. (Ed.) *Psychosociology of language*. Chicago: Markham, 1972.

Moss, H. A., & Robson, K. S. Maternal influences in early social visual behavior. *Child Development*, 1968, **39**, 401–408.

Mostowski, A. *Thirty years of foundational studies*. New York: Barnes & Noble, 1966.

Newman, J. R. (ED.), *The world of mathematics*. New York: Simon and Shuster, 1956.

Nicolaus, M. The unknown Marx. In C. Ogelsby (Ed.), *The new left reader*. New York: Grove. 1969. Pp. 84–110.

Nida, E. The identification of morphemes. *Language*, 1948, **24**, 414 441.

Nida, E. *Morphology*. Ann Arbor: University of Michigan Press, 1965.

Olson, F. A. Language and thought: Aspects of a cognitive theory of semantics. *Psychological Review*, 1970, **77**, 257–273.

Osgood, C., & Sebeok, T. *Psycholinguistics: A survey of theory and research problems*. Bloomington, Ind.: Indiana University publications in anthropology and linguistics, Memoir 10, 1954. (Also *Journal of Abnormal and Social Psychology*, Supplement, 1954.)

Osgood, C., Suci, J., & Tannenbaum, P. *The measurement of meaning*. Urbana, Ill.: University of Illinois Press, 1957.

Overton, W. F. Piaget's theory of intellectual development and progressive education. In J. R. Squire (Ed.), *A new look at progressive education*. Washington: Association for supervision and curriculum development, 1972, Pp. 88–115.

Overton W. F. On the assumptive base of the nature—nurture controversy: additive vs. interactive conceptions. *Human Development* 1973, **16**, 74–89

Overton, W. F. The active organism in structuralism. Paper presented at the annual meetings of the Eastern Psychological Association, Philadelphia, Pa., 1974.

Overton, W. F., & Reese, H. W. Models of development: methodological implications. In J. R. Nesselroade & H. W. Reese (Eds.), *Lifespan developmental psychology: Methodological issues*. New York: Academic Press, 1973. Pp. 65–86.

Parret, H. *Language and discourse*. The Hague: Mouton, 1971.

Paul, H. *Prinzipien der Sprachgeschichte*. Halle: Niemeyer, 1886.

Payne, T. R. *S. L. Rubinstejn and the philosophical foundations of Soviet psychology*. New York: Humanities Press, 1968.

Peirce, C. S. How to make our ideas clear. *Popular Science Monthly*, 1878, **12**, 286–302.

Peirce, C. S. What pragmatism is. *Monist*, 1905, **15**, 161–181.

Peirce, C. S. *Philosophy of Peirce: Selected writings*. London: Routledge & Kegan Paul, 1940.

Perelman, C. New rhetoric, a theory of practical reasoning. In *Great ideas today, 1970*. Chicago: Encyclopedia Britannica, 1970. Pp. 273–312.

Peters, R. S. *Brett's history of psychology.* Cambridge, Mass.: M.I.T. Press, 1965.

Piaget, J. *Language and thought of the child.* London: Routledge & Kegan Paul, 1926.

Piaget, J. *Judgment and reasoning in the child.* New York: Harcourt Brace, 1928.

Piaget, J. *The psychology of intelligence.* New York: Harcourt, 1950.

Piaget, J. *The origins of intelligence in children.* New York: International Universities Press, 1952.

Piaget, J. *Six études de psychologie.* Paris: Gonthier, 1964.

Piaget, J. *Six psychological studies.* New York: Random House, 1967.

Piaget, J. The problem of common mechanisms in the human sciences. *The Human Context,* 1968, **1,** 163–185. (a)

Piaget, J. *Le structuralisme.* Paris: Presses Universitaires de France, 1968. (b)

Piaget, J. *Psychologie et épistémologie.* Paris: Gonthier, 1970. (a)

Piaget, J. *Structuralism.* New York: Basic Books, 1970. (b)

Piaget, J. *Genetic epistemology.* New York: Norton. 1971. (a)

Piaget, J. *Biology and knowledge.* Chicago: University of Chicago Press, 1971. (b)

Piaget, J. *Problèmes de psychologie génétique.* Paris: Gonthier, 1972. (a)

Piaget, J. Intellectual evolution from adolescence to adulthood. *Human Development,* 1972, **15,** 1–12. (b)

Piaget, J., & Inhelder, B. *The psychology of the child.* New York: Basic Books, 1969.

Pike, K. *Phonemics.* Ann Arbor: University of Michigan Press, 1947.

Preyer, W. *Die Seele des Kindes.* Stuttgart: Union, 1881.

Pylyshyn, Z. Competence and psychological reality. *American Psychologist,* 1972, **27,** 546–552.

Quarterman, C. J., & Riegel, K. F. Age differences in the identification of concepts of the natural language. *Journal of Experimental Child Psychology, 1968,* **6,** 501–509.

Quillian, M. R. Word concepts: A theory and simulation of some basic semantic capabilities. *Behavioral Science,* 1967, **12,** 410–430.

Radcliffe-Brown, A. R. The mother's brother in South Africa. *South African Journal of Science,* 1924, **21,** 542–555.

Radcliffe-Brown, A. R. The study of kinship systems. In A. R. Radcliffe-Brown, (Ed.), *Structure and function in primitive society.* London: Cohen and West, 1952. Pp. 49–89.

Rapoport, A. The use and misuse of game theory. *Scientific American,* 1962, **207,** 108–118.

Rapoport, A. Mathematical aspects of general systems theory. *General Systems,* 1966, **11,** 3–11.

Rapoport, A. Foreword. In W. Buckley (Ed.), *Modern systems research for the behavioral scientist.* Chicago: Aldine, 1968. Pp. xiii-xxii. (a)

Rapoport, A. Critiques of game theory. In W. Buckley, (Ed.), *Modern systems research for the behavioral scientist.* Chicago: Aldine, 1968. Pp. 474–489. (b)

Rapoport, A. The uses of mathematical isomorphism in general systems theory. In G. J. Klir (Ed.), *Trends in general systems theory*. New York: Wiley-Interscience, 1972. Pp. 42–77.

Reese, H. W. & Overton, W. F. Models of development and theories of development. In L. R. Goulet & P. B. Baltes (Eds.), *Life-span developmental psychology: Research and theory*. New York: Academic Press, 1970. Pp. 115–145.

Reichenbach, H. *Experience and prediction*. Chicago: University of Chicago Press, 1938.

Reichenbach, H. *The rise of scientific philosophy*. Berkeley, Calif.: University of California Press, 1951.

Riegel, K. F. Untersuchung über intellektuelle Fähigkeiten älterer Menschen. Doctoral dissertation, University of Hamburg, 1957.

Riegel, K. F. Untersuchungen sprachlicher Leistungen und ihrer Veränderungen. *Zeitschrift für allgemeine und angewandte Psychologie*, 1968, **15**, 649–692.

Riegel, K. F. The language acquisition process: A reinterpretation of selected research findings. In L. R. Goulet & P. B. Baltes (Eds.), *Life-span developmental psychology: Research and Theory*. New York: Academic Press, 1970, Pp. 357–399.

Riegel, K. F. Influence of economic and political ideology upon the development of developmental psychology. *Psychological Bulletin*, 1972, **78**, 129–141.

Riegel, K. F. Developmental psychology and society: Some historical and ethical considerations. In J. R. Nesselroade & H. W. Reese (Eds.), *Life-span developmental psychology: Methodological issues*. New York: Academic Press, 1973. Pp. 1–23. (a)

Riegel, K. F. Dialectic operations: The final period of cognitive development. *Human Development*, 1973, **16**, 346–370. (b)

Riegel, K. F. All the trouble with linguistics: A psycholinguistic critique. *International Journal of Psycholinguistics*, 1975. (In press)

Riegel, K. F., & Riegel, R. M. An investigation into denotative aspects of word meaning. *Language and Speech*, 1963, **6**, 5–21.

Roberton, M. A. Uni-directionality in life-span development: A necessary or unnecessary corollary of organismic theory? Unpublished manuscript, University of Wisconsin, 1972.

Robinson, W. P. *Language and social behavior*. Baltimore: Penguin Books, 1972.

Rommetveit, R. *Words, meanings, and messages*. New York: Academic Press, 1968.

Rubinstejn, S. L. *Grundlagen der allgemeinen Psychologie*. Berlin: Volk und Wissen, 1958.

Rubinstejn, S. L. *O Myslenij i Putjax ego Isslodovanija.* [*On thinking and the paths of its investigation.*] Moscow, 1959.

Rubinstejn, S. L. *Prinzipien und Wege der Entwicklung der Psychologie*. Berlin: Akademie Verlag, 1963.

Ruckmick, C. A. The use of the term *function* in English textbooks of psychology. *American Journal of Psychology*, 1911, **24**, 99–123.

Ruesch, J. & Bateson, G. *Communication*. New York: Norton, 1968.

Sartre, J.-P. Jean-Paul Sartre répond. *L'Arc*, 1966, **30**, 87–96.

Saussure, F. de. *Cours de linguistique générale*. Paris: Payot, 1916. *(Course in general linguistics*. New York: McGraw-Hill, 1966.)

Schaie, K. W. A general model for the study of developmental problems. *Psychological Bulletin*, 1965, **64**, 92–108.

Schon, D. A. *Invention and the evolution of ideas*. London: Tavistock, 1969.

Searle, J. R. *Speech acts*. London: Cambridge University Press, 1969.

Shands, H. C. Semiotic approaches to psychology. In T. A. Sebeok (ed.), *Approaches to semiotics*, Vol. 2. The Hague: Mouton, 1970.

Shubik, M. (Ed.) *Game theory and related approaches to social behavior*. New York: Wiley, 1964.

Sigel, I. The distancing hypothesis: A causal hypothesis for the acquisition of representational thought. Paper presented at the *Symposium on the Effects of Early Experience*, University of Miami, December 1968.

Simon, H. A. The architecture of complexity. *General Systems*, 1965, **10**, 63–76.

Simonis, Y. *Claude Lévi-Strauss on la "passion de l'inceste."* Paris: Plon, 1968.

Sinclair-de-Zwart, H. Developmental psycholinguistics. In D. Elkind & J. H. Flavell (Eds.), *Studies in cognitive development*. New York: Oxford University Press, 1969. Pp. 315–336.

Skinner, B. F. *Verbal behavior*. New York: Appleton Century Crofts, 1957.,

Skinner, B. F. *About behaviorism*. New York: Knopf, 1974.

Slobin, D. I. (Ed.) A field manual for cross-cultural study of the acquisition of communicative competence. Unpublished report, Department of Psychology, University of California, Berkeley, 1967.

Slobin, D. *Psycholinguistics*. Glenview, Ill.: Scott, Foresman & Co. 1971. (a)

Slobin, D. *The ontogenesis of grammar*. New York: Academic Press, 1971. (b)

Sokal, R. R., & Sneath, P. H. A. *Principles of numerical taxonomy*. San Francisco: Freeman, 1963.

Stalnaker, R. C. Pragmatics. *Synthese*, 1970, **22**, 272–289.

Steiner, G. *Language and silence*. New York: Atheneum, 1967.

Stern, C., & Stern, W. *Die Kindersprache*. Leipzig: Barth, 1907.

Stevens, S. S. Mathematics, measurement, and psychophysics. In S. S. Stevens (Ed.), *Handbook of experimental psychology*. New York: Wiley, 1951. Pp. 1–49.

Svoboda, C. P. The mind-body problem: An obsolete paradox. Unpublished manuscript, University of Wisconsin, 1971.

Tanner, J. M. & Inhelder, B. *Discussions on child development*. London: Tavistock, 1960.

Tarski, A. The semantic conception of truth and the foundations of semantics. *Philosophy and Phenomenological Research*, 1944, **4**, 341–376.

Tolman, E. *Purposive behavior in animals and men*. New York: Appleton-Century-Crofts, 1932.

Trabasso, T. Reasoning and the processing of negative information. Paper presented at the 78th Annual Convention of the American Psychological Association, Washington, D. C., September 1970.

Travis, C. A generative theory of illocutions. In J. F. Rosenberg & C. Travis (Eds.), *Readings in the philosophy of language.* Englewood Cliffs, N. J.: Prentice-Hall, 1971. Pp. 629–644.

Tribus, M., & McIrvine, E. C. Energy and information. *Scientific American,* 1971, **225,** 179 88.

Trier, J. *Der deutsche Wortschatz im Sinnbezirk des Verstandes.* Heidelberg: Winter, 1931.

Tucker, R. C. (Ed.) *The Marx-Engels reader.* New York: Norton, 1972.

Tulkin, S., & Kagan, J. Mother-child interaction: Social class differences in the first year of life. *Child Development,* 1972, **43,** 31–42.

Turiel, E. Developmental processes in the child's moral thinking. In P. H. Mussen, J. Langer, & M. Covington (Eds.), *Trends and issues in developmental psychology.* New York: Holt, Rinehart and Winston, 1969. Pp. 92–133.

Tyler, S. A. (Ed.) *Cognitive anthropology.* New York: Holt, Rinehart and Winston, 1969.

Tynianov, J., & Jakobson, R. Problems in the study of language and literature. In R. deGeorge & F. deGeorge (Eds.), *The structuralists from Marx to Lévi-Strauss.* New York: Doubleday, 1972.

Uexküll, J. von. *Mondes animaux et monde humain.* Paris: Gonthier, 1965.

Vachek, J. *The linguistic school of Prague.* Bloomington, Ind.: Indiana University Press, 1966.

Van den Daele, L. D. Infrastructure and transition in developmental analysis. *Human Development,* 1974, **17,** 1–23.

Varene, D. P. *Man and culture.* New York: Dell, 1970.

Volosinov, V. N. *Marxism and the philosophy of language.* New York: Seminar Press, 1973.

Vygotsky, L. S. The socio-cultural development of the child, I. *Journal of Genetic Psychology,* 1929, **27,** 415–434.

Vygotsky, L. S. *Thought and language.* Cambridge, Mass.: M.I.T. Press, 1962.

Waddington, C. H. (Ed.) *Towards a theoretical biology,* Vol. I. Chicago: Aldine, 1968.

Waddington, C. H. The theory of evolution today. In A. Koestler & J. R. Symthies (Eds.), *Beyond reductionism.* Boston: Beacon Press, 1971. Pp. 357–374.

Wartofsky, M. W. *Conceptual foundations of scientific thought.* Toronto: Macmillan, 1968.

Wartofsky, M. W. From praxis to logos: Genetic epistemology and physics. In T. Mischel (Ed.), *Cognitive development and epistemology.* New York: Academic Press, 1971. Pp. 129–147.

Wason, P. C. The processing of positive and negative information. *Quarterly Journal of Experimental Psychology,* 1959, **11**, 92–107.

Wason, P. C. & Johnson-Laird, P. N. *Psychology of reasoning.* Cambridge, Mass.: Harvard University Press, 1972.

Waterman, J. T. *Perspectives in linguistics.* Chicago: Chicago University Press, 1963.

Watson, J. B. *Psychology from the standpoint of a behaviorist.* Philadelphia: Lippincott, 1919.

Watt, W. C. On two hypotheses concerning psycholinguistics. In J. R. Hayes (Ed.) *Cognition and the Development of Language.* New York: Wiley, 1970. Pp. 137–220.

Watzlawick, P., Beavin, J. H., & Jackson, D. D. *Pragmatics of human communication.* New York: Norton, 1967.

Weimer, W. B. Psycholinguistics and Plato's paradoxes of the Meno. *American Psychologist,* 1973, **28**, 15–33.

Weir, R. H. *Language in the crib.* The Hague: Mouton, 1962.

Weiss, P. A. *Hierarchically organized systems in theory and practice.* New York: Hafner, 1971.

Werner, H. *Einführung in die Entwicklungspsychologie.* Leipzig: Barth, 1926.

Werner, H. *Comparative psychology of mental development.* New York: International Universities Press, 1948.

Werner, H., & Kaplan, B. *Symbol formation.* New York: Wiley, 1963.

White, L. The locus of mathematical reality. In J. R. Newman (Ed.) *The world of mathematics.* Vol. 4. New York: Simon and Shuster, 1956. Pp. 2348–2364.

Whyte, L. L. *The unconscious before Freud.* New York: Anchor, 1962.

Whyte, L. L., Wilson, A. G. & Wilson, D. *Hierarchical structures.* New York: American Elsevier Publishing Co., 1969.

Wilden, A. *The language of the self: 'The function of speech and language in psychoanalysis', by J. Lacan* (translated with notes and commentary). Baltimore: Johns Hopkins University Press, 1968.

Wilden, A. Analog and digital communication: On negation, signification and the emergence of the discrete element. *Semiotica,* 1972, **6**, 50–82. (a)

Wilden, A. Libido as language: The structuralism of Jacques Lacan. *Psychology Today* (May), 1972. (b)

Wilden, A. Marcuse and the Freudian model: Energy, information and Phantasie. In R. Boyers, (Ed.) *The legacy of the German refugee intellectuals.* New York: Schocken, 1972. Pp. 196–245 (c)

Wilden, A. Structuralism, communication, and evolution. *Semiotica,* 1972, **6**, 244–256. (d)

Wilden, A. *System and structure: Essays in communication and exchange.* London: Tavistock, 1972. (e)

Wilden, A. Ecosystems and economic systems. In A. Harkins & M. Maruyama, (Eds.) *Cultures of the future.* The Hague: Mouton, 1973 (In Press). (a)

Wilden, A. On Lacan. *Contemporary psychoanalysis,* 1973, **9**, 445–470. (b)

Wilden, A. Ecology, ideology, and political economy. In A. Idris-Soven & E. Idris-Soven (Eds.) *The world as a company town: Multinational corporations and social change.* The Hague: Mouton, 1974, (In Press). (a)

Wills, G. *Nixon agonistes.* New York: Signet, 1969.

Witte, W. Transposition als Schlüsselprinzip. In F. Weinhand (Ed.) *Gestalthaftes Sehen.* Darmstadt: Wissenschaftliche Buchgesellschaft, 1960. Pp. 406–412.

Wittgenstein, L. *Philosophical investigations.* (2nd ed). Oxford: Blackwell, 1958.

Wohlwill, J. The age variables in psychological research. *Psychological Review,* 1970, **77**, 49–65.

Wozniak, R. H. Verbal regulation of motor behavior: Soviet research and non-Soviet replication. *Human Development,* 1972, **15**, 13–57.

Wozniak, R. H. Structuralism, dialectical materialism, and cognitive developmental theory. Paper presented at the meetings of the Society for Research in Child Development, Philadelphia, PA., 1973.

Wundt, W. *Logik.* Stuttgart: Enke, 1880.

Wundt, W. *Die Sprache,* 2 vols. Leipzig: Engelmann, 1900.

Wundt, W. *Völkerpsychologie: Eine Untersuchung der Entwicklungsgesetze von Sprache, Mythus und Sitte.* 10 vols. Leipzig: Engelmann, 1900-1920.

Zivian, M. T., & Riegel, K. F. Word identification as a function of semantic clues and association frequency. *Journal of Experimental Psychology,* 1969, **9**, 336–341.

Author Index

Afanesyev, 29–33, 36, 37
Allport, 78, 135
Alston, 201
Anderson, 208
Andrade, 50
Andreev, 36
Apostel, 202
Aqvist, 202
Ardener, 90
Aristotle, 51, 73
Ashby, 26, 45, 93, 94, 98
Austin, 189, 200, 201, 205
Avenarius, 3, 12, 13, 22, 24, 38

Baltos, xiii
Ban, 131
Dandura, 63
Barthes, 25
Bartlett, 147, 148
Bateson, 49, 91, 109, 110, 112, 115, 116
Deavin, 193
Beilin, 121
Bekhterev, 19
Bergson, 196
Berkeley, 21
Bernard, 90
Bernstein, 97
Bertalanffy, xi, 61, 74–81, 98
Bever, 147
Binet, 145
Blakeley, 35, 36
Bloch, B., 159
Bloch, O., 144, 146
Blondel, 3, 17, 18
Bloom, 184, 212
Bloomfield, 7, 149
Blumenthal, 135, 148, 216
Blumstein, 67, 216
Boileau, 49
Boring, 4
Borkin, 209
Boulding, 110
Bourne, 189
Bowers, 71
Brainerd, 67
Brentano, 5, 22, 53
Bridgman, 52
Brown, G. S., 111
Brown, R., 184, 188, 210

Bruner, 188, 189
Buckley, 61, 78, 91, 114, 116
Buhler, 135, 141, 142, 171

Carnap, 3, 11–15, 22, 24, 184, 193
Cartwright, 182
Cassirer, 9–13, 24, 49, 65, 196
Cellérier, 27
Cerf, 201
Chao, 159
Chardin, 50
Charles XII, 175
Chelstowsk, 36
Cherry, 193
Chomsky, 3, 7, 25, 45, 64, 68, 69, 135, 140,
    141, 146–151, 159 163, 177, 178, 187,
    188, 199, 207
Cipolla, 172
Clark, 185
Cohen, D., 10
Cohen, M., 144, 145
Cole, 121
Collingwood, 215
Comte, 3, 16, 24, 99
Coombs, 7, 189
Cooper, 107
Cournot, 90, 100
Croce, 196

Darwin, 144, 154, 180
Davidson, 203
Dean, 131
Dedekind, 3, 10, 24, 111, 184
Delbrück, 141, 148
Democritus, 68
Derrida, 25
Descartes, 9, 26, 52, 105, 136
Dewey, 19
Dobzhansky, 110
Driesch, 13
Durkheim, 3, 17, 18, 24, 99

Ehrenfels, 5
El'konin, 59
Engels, 19, 31, 38–49, 86, 178

Feagan, 59
Fechner, 85, 98
Feldman, 203, 208

Subject Index

Abstraction, reflective, 20, 32, 55
Accommodation, 16, 20, 21, 23, 64, 69, 122
Activity, 191, 215
Act psychology, 5, 22
Adaptation, 33, 41, 69, 113n
Affect, 17, 147
Analog, 88, 89, 97, 100, 103, 111
Analysis, 130, 138
  componential, 205
  levels of, 217, 218
  sequential, 129, 130
Analysis-by-synthesis, 151
Analytic ideal, 65, 66, 76
Anamorphous, 80
Anti historical, 86, 87
Anthropology, 3, 16, 18, 24, 62, 74, 153
  cultural, 18
  dialectical, 19
  structural, 92, 93, 116, 117
Aphasia, 155, 157, 158
Assimilation, 20, 27, 33–35, 40, 41, 43,45,
  64, 69, 107, 108, 113n, 122, 143
Association, 16, 199
Associativity, 54
Asymmetry, 124
Atomism, 68, 99, 100, 104, 105, 108
  mathematical, 68
  physical, 68, 95
Attachment, 131
Attention, 136, 138, 139, 147
Attribute, 189
Autonomy, 216

Becoming, 65, 70, 78
Behavior, 7, 19, 128, 131, 135, 142
  animal, 146, 198
  infant, 127
  maternal, 127
  verbal, 146, 149
Being, 65, 70, 78
Biochemical, 178
Bioenergetics, 94, 95, 117
Biology, 4, 18–21, 23, 124, 179, 216
Boundaries, 86, 98–100, 102, 110–112
  and gaps, 100
  natural, 218

Cathexis, 106
Causality, 128, 216

dialectical, 64, 72
formal, 73
linear, 65, 77, 86, 91–94, 106, 110
reciprocal, 77, 79
Cause, final, 73
Chain, 129, 181
  initiator of, 129, 130
  length of, 129
  terminator of, 129, 130
Change, 64, 65, 97, 98, 107, 113–115
  individual, xii
  linear, 64
  societal, xii
Class, 169, 177, 181–187, 190
  middle, 127
  social, 123, 127
  working, 127
Closure, 96–98, 101, 102, 116, 117
Cognition, xv, 24, 100, 122, 136, 139, 167,
  212, 216, 217
Cohort, xii
Collective mind, 17, 18
Commodity, 95, 97, 108, 171–175, 190
Communication, 15, 16, 88, 89, 100, 101,
  103–112, 127, 131, 135, 141, 151,
  174, 192–194, 213, 218
Community, 217, 218
Compensation, 98n
Competence, 23, 27, 28, 146, 147, 149, 193,
  212, 216, 218
  linguistic, 160
Complexity, 103, 107
  derivational, 151, 163
  simple, 61, 76
  organized, 61, 78, 79, 92
Comprehension, 151, 165
Conflict, 216
Conjunction, 169, 187
Conservation, 171
Constituent, 138, 140
Constraint, 86, 87, 94, 107, 116
Construct, primitive, 64, 66, 73
Constructivism, 12–14, 22, 24, 54, 64
Content, 35, 36n, 38–40, 42–44, 131
  psychology of, 5
Context, 91–93
  social, 84, 97, 100, 114–116
Contingency, 113–115, 130
Contract, social, 99

245